'The historian (a mantle Watson wears so lightly it is near invisible) supplies the context that makes the questions so pointed. But it is the ironist who makes them rasp in the reader's mind. Culture warriors very quickly divide the world into those who love and those who hate America. *American Journeys* is a detailed and articulate general response to such lazy dichotomies. Watson understands exactly how much the experiment of America matters.'
MORAG FRASER, *THE AGE*

'In prose so perfect it makes you gasp, Watson captures what it feels like to live in contemporary America: the smells, the sounds, the shared beliefs and points of contention, and the everyday barriers to the good life.'
BIG ISSUE AUSTRALIA

'*American Journeys* is a beautiful work. Not so much a woodworm in the bark of the republic as a probe deep into the American mindset.'
THE COURIER-MAIL

'Criss-crossing the greatest nation by car and train, Watson proves the perfect traveling companion: funny, well versed, generous, uncomplaining. And observant. Watson is sublimely attuned to the subtleties of language, self-delusion and bastardry, his observations ranging from gentle to wry to cut yourself sharp. He allows himself, and the reader, to be pleasantly surprised by and even faintly – very faintly – hopeful about the America he encounters in his travels. But it is Americans' treasured notions of freedom, forcing itself constantly under Watson's gaze, that shapes his journey's destination.'
ROBYN ANNEAR AND BRENDA NIALL – JUDGES *AGE* BOOK OF THE YEAR AWARD

'The strength of *American Journeys* is Watson's resistance to the ecstatic pleasures of disapproval with which this country has long dazzled, even beguiled its visitors. He is as prepared to observe the extraordinary kindnesses of fellow passengers as he is to note their less attractive qualities. Alert to America's physical beauty, he often evokes it with poetic deftness.'
DELIA FALCONER, *THE MONTHLY*

AMERICAN JOURNEYS

DON WATSON

VINTAGE BOOKS

Australia

A Vintage book
Published by Random House Australia Pty Ltd
Level 3, 100 Pacific Highway, North Sydney, NSW 2060
www.randomhouse.com.au

First published by Knopf in 2008
This edition published by Vintage in 2009

Addresses for companies within the Random House Group can be found at
www.randomhouse.com.au/offices

National Library of Australia
Cataloguing-in-Publication Entry

Watson, Don, 1949–.
American journeys.

ISBN 978 1 74166 621 2 (pbk).

Watson, Don, 1949– – Travel – United States.
United States – Politics and government – Philosophy.

973

Cover design by Christabella Designs
Map design by Caroline Bowie
Illustrations by Craig McGill/www.realnasty.com.au
Typeset in Janson by Midland Typesetters, Australia
Printed and bound by The SOS Print + Media Group

10 9 8 7 6 5 4 3 2

To E.M.W.

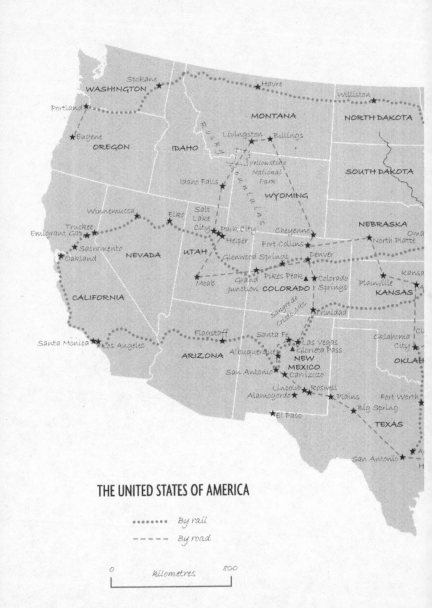

THE UNITED STATES OF AMERICA

.... By rail

----- By road

0   kilometres   800

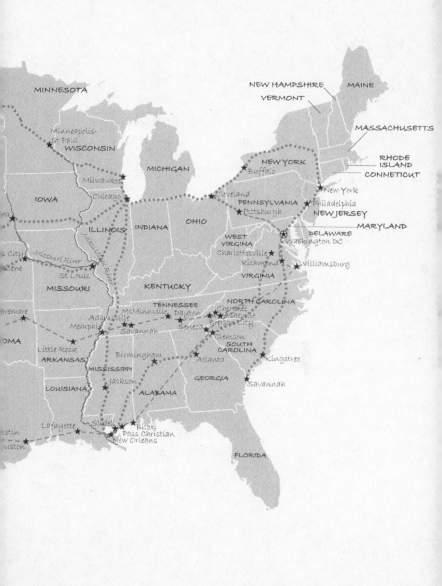

CONTENTS

America, you have it better.

Goethe

INTRODUCTION

O beautiful, for spacious skies,
For amber waves of grain,
For purple mountain majesties
Above the fruited plain!

Katherine Lee Bates, America the Beautiful

IT WAS THE EVE OF MEMORIAL DAY, MAY 2005. ON A RISE OUTSIDE the old Kansas City Union Station, 25,000 people had gathered under the darkening sky to remember the fallen, to honour those who had served and to thank all those still serving in the United States armed forces.

The air was soft and cool and scented with the kettle corn that vendors sold in bags big enough for the weekend shopping. The Kansas City Symphony and a good tenor were there to play and sing America's rousing songs. The people carried little flags which they waved whenever something stirred them, and they washed their corn down with cola. The tenor sang *America the Beautiful*. The words were written in 1893 by Katherine Lee Bates, who said they had come to her one day while standing on Pikes Peak, Colorado. The tune was borrowed from a seventeenth-century hymn, and a hymn it remains with the new words, and it has a hymn's fortifying effect, even on ambivalent hearts.

The tenor also sang *God Bless America*, a song composed by a young Jewish immigrant named Irving Berlin who knew how to make hard men bawl their eyes out. Then came *Nessun Dorma*, which means 'None shall sleep' and is by Puccini and has nothing to do with the United States; but the people loved it and waved their flags as if it were their own. And finally the tenor said he would go out on a song 'made famous by the late, great Frank Sinatra'. He began to sing *The House I Live In* ('What is America to me? A name, a map or a flag I see . . .') and a little wave of applause rippled up the rise.

Kansas City is, for all practical purposes, segregated. Earlier that day in the beautiful Plaza, built in the 1930s on the model of Seville, there were dozens of musicians playing in the streets. It took me a moment to realise what was missing: the city derives much of its fame from black music and black musicians – including Charlie Parker – yet in the Plaza there wasn't a black American to be seen. A third of Kansas City's population is black, but the only black people I'd seen that day were two men I stumbled on under the freeway when I went looking for the Missouri River, and a couple of attendants at the Nelson-Atkins Museum of Art. Now, here at the Union Station, this also was an all-white audience. But they seemed as happy to hum along with 'All races and religions, that's America to me' as they had been with 'the fruited plain'.

Next the orchestra played the songs of the various services, and the conductor asked veterans of each to rise as their song came round. And so they did. Standing, some of them teetering, these old men who had fought in France and the Pacific and Korea and Vietnam turned their stiff and craggy necks to acknowledge the clapping and cheering that wafted over the music. The marines got the most applause and, as the orchestra played *The Halls of Montezuma*, there was not a dry eye under the stars.

The MC called upon the audience to thank the veterans – for 'protecting us', he said. It seemed an odd way of putting it: as if all wars Americans have fought had that purpose. Where was 'manifest destiny' and the fire in the belly? Where was the meaning of a soldier's sacrifice and the evidence of imperishable good that Lincoln extracted for American posterity? The words that night were all mash and no fibre. In truth, for all the flag-waving sentiment, the mood was much less triumphant than reverent and wistful. But 'protecting us' spoke of an amorphous fear – or an amorphous threat. It was a phrase that owed less to Washington and Lincoln than to George Orwell.

The evening ended with the *1812 Overture*. It's hard to know why music commemorating Napoleon's failed assault on Moscow should make it into the Kansas City Memorial Day program, but it gave the Missouri Civil War Re-enactment Society an opportunity to fire their cannon and let the people have a taste of what war is like. From up the back, near the Doric column with the eternal flame, there was the most tremendous bang and the crowd got a terrible fright. The men of the society reloaded and fired again. Smoke billowed down the rise towards the orchestra and saltpetre mingled with the smell of kettle corn, and everyone turned their chairs around and watched a fireworks display.

The MC exulted in the splendour of the evening – and it *was* splendid – and he said 'Safe home' and 'God bless America'. Everyone applauded and then packed up their deckchairs and put their trash in bins wheeled around by black people employed for the occasion. The people of Kansas City made their way home, and I made my way to the train. The working station – a dismal mass of concrete and iron at the back of the grand old Union Station – was as if designed to say trains were marginal and doomed; that this thing I was boarding belonged in the museum which, like so much of the American rail system, Kansas City's station had become. But, drawn by three mighty diesel locomotives, the *Southwest Chief* set out south-westward, creaking over the points and through the suburbs and, when it hit their fringes, gathering pace and cantering out onto the dark prairie.

—

I'm not obsessive about trains, but I do like the way they ease you in and out of towns and cities; the way they deliver you, like Spencer Tracy at the start of *Bad Day at Black Rock*, into the heart of things. I like being able to get off and stretch my legs on station platforms and breathe a local sample of the earth's air. I like the sound and sway of them. I like the way they commune with the countryside. I like the fact that the rails on which trains run – or at least the paths they follow – were in the main surveyed a century or more ago and, much more than modern roads, follow the contours of the land. I like the way trains change speed according to those contours, and how you hear the variation in the rhythmic clatter of the wheels.

I like the intimacy of trains, the close connection with other passengers and the opportunities they afford for voyeurism: the angle on the people and their backyards and porches, their clothes lines, pets and vegetable patches, their dogs and barbecues. I like not having to drive. I like not having to go to airports and stand in queues and empty my pockets and remove my boots. I like trains at night, when there is nothing on the dark plain and you hear that whistle and, on a bend, a light peers deep into the blackness – the train's light, your light.

I had caught the *Southwest Chief* in Chicago, where I found myself at the end of a book tour. I'd a notion that the train might be a way of peering into the United States, like a woodworm boring a tiny groove in the bark of the republic. Three days and nights getting to Los Angeles, with the

American landscape and American towns and American history unfolding on the outside, while inside a tiny particle of the American people talked among themselves.

On a train, or pretty well anywhere in America, you can hear two or three conversations at a time and get them down on paper and people think you are writing postcards. It is not that Americans have louder voices than the people of other countries, but rather that they use them as essential instruments of commerce and belief. 'Let freedom ring,' Martin Luther King said, and Americans do. The habits of their speech seem to have come down from the great political, religious and economic contests of American life, for all of which the primary skill is persuasion. Speech is a free-for-all, a primal force animating the whole society. The whole humdrum world is like a stage or film set, and the people are actors who at any moment might break into song, or make a speech, or passionately kiss and ride off to fight some Spaniards. To journey in America is to journey in the language.

I sat down next to a young woman who was reading C. S. Lewis's *Mere Christianity*. She told me that it was a book she felt she *should* read rather than one that she wanted to, and that this was her third attempt. After fifteen minutes she put it down and picked up a copy of *Style*. Across the aisle a little woman of sixty or so unzipped the embroidered jacket of a family Bible. She opened it at the Book of Revelation and then she opened a study guide and she didn't look up for 300 miles, not even when we stopped at Bloomington, Lincoln or Springfield. I wondered if she was seeking confirmation that the doom of Babylon 'within a single hour' referred to the attacks on the World Trade Center. A large woman in front of me told her two young nephews to recite the story of Daniel in the lion's den. They did, each in turn. Somewhere else along the way, she asked one of them where Grandpa was, and the other chimed in before him: 'He's with the

Lord Jesus.' The young woman beside me trashed her food wrappers, phoned her husband, put on a miniskirt and started on *Mere Christianity* again.

As we slid along the banks of the wide Missouri, a young man changed seats to sit beside the wiry, pale, unshaven youth who had been sleeping most of the way. The youth revealed he was a reservist returning from Iraq.

'K-9 squad,' he explained. 'Dogs. Sniffing out bombs.'

'Where were you?' asked the young man.

'Mosul. It's a town there.'

'Did you drink much?'

'Sure,' said the soldier, 'we did a lot of drinking.'

'Did you see much shooting?'

'Got mortared most days,' the soldier said.

Outside, families in flat-bottomed powerboats surged up and down the Missouri River. We clattered past miles of trailer parks and, where the train's course diverged from the river, the gleaming barbed wire and floodlights of a new suite of penitentiaries. Before he left the train the young man went to the cafeteria and returned with a beer for the soldier. But the soldier said he didn't want it.

'Go on. I want you to. You protected us,' said the young man. He didn't mention freedom, only security. 'Most people want security in their world, not freedom,' H. L. Mencken said with his usual derision.

'I said I'm not drinking,' said the soldier.

'I'm leaving it with you,' the other said, and he put the beer on the seat beside him. 'You protected us.'

On Memorial Day morning we sailed through Colorado. It had rained in the night. Amid sheets of water, trailers loomed in the mist, gathered in groups of three or four at dams and streams like cattle come to drink. The backyards of the poor towns were sodden. Shacks, mobile homes and car bodies co-mingled in long domestic scenes populated mainly by hens and curs. Everywhere the flag flew. It always flies. But this was Memorial Day and it flew with added purpose.

—

That was the eve of summer 2005, and I left soon after. President Bush, though slipping gently, was still polling in the forties. The consensus 9/11 had granted him was fracturing, and yet anyone who tuned in to the mainstream media knew the national mood was jumpy and that a modest fright would give him back unrivalled sway. By October, when I returned, the hurricanes on the Gulf Coast had exposed the cracks in American society, and deep inadequacy in the government and the president. Katrina blew a hole in the philosophy of the modern Republican Party and gave its opponents some encouragement and spine. New scandals had spilled into the news. Iraq looked more and more like the sort of quagmire that Donald Rumsfeld had assured the world he didn't 'do'. The president had dipped into the thirties. It seemed quite possible that the political tide was turning. But the culture wars were no less intense. The divides between neocon and liberal, Christian fundamentalist and humanist, red state and blue were just as wide. America was still America.

I came back intending to travel on every Amtrak route I could. For the Americans I told, I might as well have been off to see the country on a mule. The railway has faded from their consciousness. Amtrak is the shadow that remains, a nether world of obsolescence inhabited only by the poor, who have no choice, or by purposeless eccentrics with nothing better to do than ride the dinosaur to extinction. Yet Amtrak trains still run almost the length of the coasts, and they traverse the vast distances between them in the north, the south and the centre. They run to most of the biggest cities and through some of the remotest towns. They run on routes that total 22,000 miles. You miss a lot, of course, but not as much as you miss when you fly. You miss things when you drive the highways, and many of the things you miss driving you can see from the train. You miss a lot floating down the Mississippi on a raft: but, as we know, you can learn a lot as well.

The truth, however, is that in the United States a car is just about compulsory. American trains run to only a fraction of the places that they used to and not half as often. They don't even run to Chattanooga. So, when I had seen nearly everything I could by train, I hired a car. Much as I like trains, I also like driving open highways and back roads. It's one of the seductive New World pleasures; in America it has a mythic dimension that has been there since the settlers ventured west in their wagons.

It was while driving through Colorado in January 2006 that I read of a survey which found more than half of all Americans are frightened of 'monsters'. The tennis player Serena Williams is afraid of them, the newspaper report said. She is also afraid of the dark. Twenty-five million Americans are frightened of Friday the thirteenth. It just shows you what a traveller can miss. I had travelled 8000 miles by car and at least twice that many by train, and in the whole five months my journeys took I met not a soul who expressed or in any other way betrayed a fear of monsters. Terrorists, yes. Mexicans, Europeans, liberals, China, environmentalists, Darwinists, climate change, wolves, Fidel Castro, Hugo Chavez, Edward Kennedy; and, in other parts of the country, neocons, rednecks, gun lobbyists, creationists, Dick Cheney – there are no limits to fear and loathing on the radio – but, unless you count Osama bin Laden and the Beast of Revelation, no monsters in the way that, in general, we understand them.

The fear must lie too deep for the ordinary traveller to see, and of course it never occurred to me to ask. The wealthiest, most ingenious, mightiest nation on earth, forged in the fires of the never-ending frontier, land of the free, home of the . . .

monsters. Sometimes it is better to be confounded, to live with paradoxes without question or complaint.

In any event, the result of the survey might be less significant than the fact that it was taken. If the French or the Brazilians are ever asked about monsters, we don't seem to read about it. Yet everything eccentric, brutal or dimwitted among Americans seems always on show to the world. We know about their obesity, their fetishes, the variety of their religions, their fundamentalist streak, their addictions, that what they spend on botox or breast implants exceeds the combined gross domestic product of the world's fifty poorest nations – or something like that. We know that most of them don't believe in evolution and do believe in heaven, hell, handguns and capital punishment. We know everything that is old-fashioned and newfangled about them: that half the country seems dedicated to the Biblical proposition that there is nothing new under the sun, and the other half is no less determined to prove that there is – or that there can be, if you believe in yourself.

We expect the bizarre from America and a lot of Americans expect it too. A lot depend for their living on it. But what seems bizarre to one person, to another is but an expression of the multitudes of the human soul. On some days and from some angles the United States does present as a freak show, but seen from another angle on another day it is a mighty social laboratory, the bravest human enterprise in the history of the world; and from yet another it is, in the main, a realm of suburban or small-town tranquillity, a regular heaven on earth for ordinary people. Of course, it is all those things.

From the laboratory has come a civilisation of incomparable genius, sophistication and riches, a nation of unprecedented variety and invention, an empire of unrivalled might. From it also have come violence, desecration, injustice and militarism. As the tribune of human freedom and opportunity, the United States is the most altruistic of nations, but the great altruist is as well a solipsist, a bully, a hypocrite, an epic vulgarian – which is to say, it shows all the characteristics of humanity. America retains a raw, unformed element that brings with it the chaos as well as the religiosity of its origins and unfolding. It is a land of heroes, but demons also attend its progress, and between the two extremes – legendary good and omnipresent evil – there exist doubt and anxiety. Here is a country that for most of its life has believed in a manifest destiny, an at least semi-divine right of conquest and occupation; a country whose secretary of state declared, more than a century ago, that it was 'master of the situation and practically invulnerable as against any and all other powers'; and a country that is now determined to have what it calls 'full-spectrum dominance'. It is curious and probably no accident that these defining ideas of American power and identity – sometimes known as 'American exceptionalism' – are also characteristic of the unweaned infant. They may also help explain why the dominant power has long been prone to nervous obsessions about national security; why it quakes at shadows cast from within and without; and why, as in the recent case, it often projects its power in ways that betray as much ignorance and fear as reasoned self-assurance.

And herein, maybe, is the source of America's perpetual internal combustion. Soon after reading about the monsters I saw the novelist Rick Moody writing that the 'great spiritual benefit of the Krispy Kreme original glazed doughnut is the sensation of nothingness. The satori that is Krispy Kreme is the obliteration of self, the silencing of the voices that are attached to the oppressions of life.' Only an American could come up with such a thing as Krispy Kreme; but just as remarkable and just as typical is that another American could establish its philosophical place in the realms of American functionalism.

On the United States of America my senses swing like a door with no latch. They are moved by fierce gusts and imperceptible zephyrs. Love and loathing come and go in about the same proportion. Rage is common. But then, one rages about one's siblings from time to time, and one's own country: it is not rational, in the main. Yet there had been a time when anti-Americanism took on the gleam of reason. As earnest student radicals in the late 1960s, we saw the thread that joined the vicious white mobs of the South to the very foundations of the republic – because we learned that such founders of American democracy as Washington and Jefferson owned slaves. We learned what we took to be the real truth about the Indian Wars, the Mexican Wars and the Monroe Doctrine, and it persuaded us that Vietnam was part of a pattern which, when you looked at it hard, revealed IMPERIALISM.

But just as we were thinking it was in the 'nature' of America to be brutal, racist and imperialistic, a paradox appeared. The Freedom Marchers had been Americans. Martin Luther King was American. Sidney Perelman was American. Mark Twain was American. Portnoy was American. Louis Armstrong, Bob Dylan, William Appleman Williams, Herbert Marcuse and Robert Crumb were all American. Our jeans were American. The most articulate critics of America – the most articulate people on earth, and the most liberal – were American. The America of my most avid anti-American phase was the America of my first rational adult heroes. That paradox, greatly modified though it is, animates me still.

It was the same in my childhood. As much as I grew up with Australian landscapes, Australian voices and Australian stories, I also grew up with American ones. We children did not play beneath the gum trees at being Ned Kelly; we were Davy Crockett and Daniel Boone and our adversaries were bears and Indians. We did not hum *Waltzing Matilda* on the way to school, but the songs from *Oklahoma!* or the hits of Elvis Presley, Harry Belafonte, Peggy Lee and Perry Como. The heroic faces of my childhood were not those of

Australians, but Gary Cooper's and Gregory Peck's; beauty belonged to Marilyn Monroe and Audrey Hepburn. The good was Spencer Tracy and Sidney Poitier; the bad was Lee Marvin, who threw boiling coffee in Gloria Grahame's face in *The Big Heat*. The mystery was in Gloria Grahame. For all their Anglophilia, most Australians were raised part-American, and these days it is a much bigger part. It follows that to be anti-American is a form of self-loathing.

The Iraq War accentuates the paradox. In Melbourne, before the invasion, a Somalian who had lived with tyranny told me how much he hoped the Americans would drive out Saddam. It was hard to argue with his case. For him, America was still the last best hope of the oppressed, and the war was exactly as President Bush said: a war for freedom. 'For what avail the plough or sail, or land or life, if freedom fail.' And then came 'Shock and Awe' and all the military hardware, and the brutal, swaggering, insane rhetoric, and the images of American troops dressed like creatures from another planet – and the door slammed shut. And it slammed the harder for my own country's cynical support.

—

At the southern tip of the Sangre de Cristo Mountains, on the old Santa Fe Trail just west of the Glorieta Pass – where 400 Confederates with their eyes on New Mexico were routed in 1862 and all their horses and mules were killed with bayonets – the conductor announced that we would thank all those who were serving or had served the United States.

'We thank them for protecting us,' he said. 'It is because of them that my family and your family are safe today.' He told us that there were two soldiers on board, Annabelle Lopez and Troy Thomas, and he thanked them on our behalf. 'In a little while the train will blow its whistle to honour those who served,' he said.

Climbing to Raton Pass, at about 8000 feet, the train slowed, creaked, stopped. The conductor announced that the third loco had given up, but they would charge its batteries and we would soon be on our way again. On the side of a hill a coyote – 'a living, breathing allegory of want', as Mark Twain called him – was looking for a feed. Ten minutes later we cleared the pass and, as we glided downhill, the *Southwest Chief*, along with every other train across the country, blew its whistle for Memorial Day – three long, yearning, echoing calls from deep in the heart and imagination, mine as much as theirs.

CHAPTER 1

We finally cleaned up public housing in
New Orleans. We couldn't do it, but God did.

Republican Congressman Richard Baker

ON 29 AUGUST 2005, HURRICANE KATRINA ROARED THROUGH
New Orleans and other cities on the Gulf Coast. Nearly two
thousand people died. Hundreds of thousands were made
homeless. Katrina was the sixth-most-powerful storm ever to
strike the United States, and it did more damage than any
other – $80 billion worth. A few weeks later, an even stronger
hurricane called Rita ripped along the coast to the west of New
Orleans. Though it caused only a fraction of the destruction
and cost far fewer lives, the chaotic evacuations before Rita
seemed to confirm the impression left by Katrina: how could it
be that four years into the War on Terror, American governments were not competent to deal with something as familiar
as a hurricane?

There were people for whom the scenes in New Orleans
were proof that the famous city was really nothing better than
a sink of crime and dissolution. Other people – a majority,
surely – saw in these same scenes the devastation of a place

they cherished. Louis Armstrong was born, raised and began playing in New Orleans. King Oliver, Jelly Roll Morton, Sidney Bechet, Professor Longhair, the Marsalises, Fats Domino: if you count only the music, scarcely half a dozen cities in the world can claim more than New Orleans can. But New Orleans also meant a way of life, a culture, a history unlike that of any other city in the United States. 'Free and unembarrassed' were the words Mark Twain used in *Life on the Mississippi*. New Orleans is the last stop before the Mississippi reaches the sea, a unique and inescapable geographical fact matched by the place it occupies in American affections. For the millions of Americans who loved New Orleans despite the crime and violence, Hurricane Katrina was a personal calamity. The novelist Richard Ford grew up on the Gulf Coast and lived for years in New Orleans. 'Empathy is what we long for,' he wrote as the place lay ruined.

Empathy there was, and not only among Americans. Empathy was one of the reasons I decided to go there: my own empathy, in part, but also to witness that of others – empathy made manifest. At the very least, it seemed a good place to see what Americans meant to other Americans.

The train left from Chicago at night. The man who drove me to the station used to drive a bus between Chicago and New Orleans. When I told him where I was going he said: 'You go on down South, but don't expect any sympathy from me.' In the morning we were in Mississippi, heading for Jackson.

───

There was just one taxi outside the station in Jackson, and the driver was asleep. His legs were hanging out the passenger side door and his massive body was tipped back on the front seat. The car radio played and a woman sang a sort of blues:

Each drop of blood bought me a million years;
A soul was born each time he shed a tear.
He loosed the chains that fettered you and me;
He bought my soul through death at Calvary.

'You should have that song in your house, in your automobile and in your place of business,' came the voice of the radio host.

The driver said nothing when I woke him and asked to be taken to the Microtel. He pulled himself upright, loaded my suitcase and squeezed and panted until he got himself behind the steering wheel. We travelled in silence for a few minutes and then, when a Toyota sedan crossed in front of him at an intersection, he accelerated and missed its back fender by inches. The driver of the Toyota appeared to be Asian.

'Don't see why any American should drive a Japanese car!' he gasped. 'Even one like her.'

He'd had Ford and GM cars for forty years, and anyone telling him that Japanese make better cars than Americans . . . well, he didn't know why they'd say that. It was the same with the Chinese.

'We buy every damn thing off the Chinese and they's the most ungodly nation there is. They's the biggest threat to peace. Got no respect for human rights or the laws of the ocean. No respect for the life that lives *under* the ocean. They kill all the animals that lives there, all the whales for a few body parts and throw the rest back in the sea. All that technical equipment. Plasma TVs. You tellin' me Americans can't make them just as good?'

'Of course not,' I said. 'But they might cost more, I suppose.'

'I'd pay more for American,' he said, and we bumped into the motel's car park.

I had taken him for a man barely alive to his environment

and – being black, hugely overweight and driving a cab in Jackson – very likely sunk in existential despair. And yet he was a super-patriot and, I had no doubt, prepared to kill for his country.

'This here's the Microtel Inn,' he said.

'Where's downtown?' I asked, looking around at the highway and the rodeo ring, the fast-food franchises and the chain motels.

'This here's downtown,' he panted. And without turning he swept back his arm and proffered a bent and battered card. 'Call this number if you wantin' to go somewhere.'

Something at the centre of the American spirit cannot tolerate human insignificance. There can be no defeat, spiritual or temporal. Americans are geared to believe in themselves: and if that is not possible, they must believe in Jesus risen, or Elvis risen, or the president, or sports stars, or movie stars, or a brand of motor vehicle or soft drink, or the United States itself, or any other surrogate for the imperfect self. No other culture is so disinclined to believe in the futility of existence. The cross, the high-five and the facelift all express the same conviction that life is winnable. For the outsider, at first this feels unnaturally positive: but in time the same radical notion takes hold, and he finds himself wondering if the really unnatural thing is to think life lacks meaning and death always wins. He thus regains his innocence and becomes an American in spirit.

—

Two days later the train crawled across the barren lake towards New Orleans; across the swamps with the blasted cypresses and shards of gleaming plastic hanging in their bare branches; across the channels nestled by the elevated highway. On the channel banks new sheds had been tacked together from pieces of the old ones retrieved after the storm. Men sat by their flat-bottom boats, smoking. There were herons, cranes and darters. Hours before Katrina hit, birds from the sea and the bayous had appeared hundreds of miles away in the car parks of Tennessee supermarkets. They went home the next day. Now, two months later, people were also going back. They were poor people, white and black, and most of them were young. Passing poor houses with tarpaulins for roofs and a trailer park with a sign saying JESUS IS LORD, a teenager rang his mother: 'Watcha doin'? Watchin' TV? Are you watchin' TV? Gonna send you some money as soon as I get there. I said, soon I'm going to send you some money. I will. Soon. All right. I love you.'

As the train gathered a little speed crossing the lake and created a faint rhythm in its wheels, the passengers began to talk. The closer we came to New Orleans, the louder grew their voices and the more bitter their sentiments. The conversation spread until it extended from one end of the carriage to the other. Black and white alike, on everything there was agreement. George W. Bush was unfit to lead the country. For Mayor Ray Nagin they had some sympathy, but Louisiana's Governor Kathleen Blanco was an asshole. Black and white alike had heard that fences had been built to separate the people – black from white, rich from poor.

In the last seat in the carriage, in a cheap but exotic ensemble with a wide red and yellow hat, sat a middle-aged woman who, back at the station in Jackson, had talked without pause to anyone who'd listen. In particular, she'd talked about her sister, who had written from Texas to say that daily she encountered more Mexicans who could not speak English than Texans who could. No-one, the lady had said, Mexicans or anyone else, should be allowed into the country if they could not speak English. She had talked all the way onto the train, but once it started rolling she'd fallen silent; now, as we creaked towards New Orleans, she was staring out the window at the desolation.

Row upon row of gutted houses. Thousands of rusting, abandoned, useless cars. Mountains of rubbish. Mangled hoardings. Uprooted trees. Empty streets. Only from some angles and in some lights did it look like a hurricane had been through here: from others it looked more like the man-made catastrophe of the modern imagination. Nearly half a million people had lived in New Orleans before Hurricane Katrina; now there were only 70,000.

We passed the gaol and saw, scrawled in fresh paint on the wall: THE LORD'S TEMPLE MUST BE REBUILT. Then the Superdome. One man said New Orleans was 'trashed before Katrina. The place was geared up for tourism and the real town couldn't breathe.' A young white man said he'd heard tourists were already going back. Someone said he'd heard that a tourist liner was in the port, and another of the young white men said that they should 'ram it. Open up on it like those people did to the liner off Madagascar. Board the fucking thing and throw 'em overboard.'

Someone said: 'Well, I'm here for five days, then I'm leavin' and I ain't never comin' back.' A black guy with a two-way radio said: 'I'm staying for two weeks and then I'm going for good.' It seemed that no-one intended to stay.

Then the woman in the hat came down the aisle towing her bag and saying she had lived in New Orleans all her life and she was never going to leave. A black woman who had slept most of the way stood up from her seat and said: 'Well, you can try, honey, but I'm going just as soon as I put my sister in the ground on Saturday. Good riddance to bad rubbish.'

Outside New Orleans Station a white band played *When the Saints Go Marching In* by way of welcome. No-one seemed moved by it. The mood was desultory and unforgiving.

I hired a car and set off for Biloxi, the devastated casino

capital of the Gulf Coast, where a friend knew a volunteer doctor who had agreed to show us the relief effort from the inside. Cutting through New Orleans on the freeway that runs above the tattered rooflines, the Superdome loomed out of the dusk, a monument less to Hurricane Katrina than to the bewildering paralysis that preceded and followed it. The press had arrived two days before the marines, the marines before the head of the Federal Emergency Management Agency (FEMA), and five days had passed before the president came over from his ranch in the neighbouring state of Texas. Because a large part of the city – the poorest part and the blackest part – had not been evacuated, many people had died. Even more died because help was so late to arrive.

The president, when he finally showed up, made a point of telling Mike Brown, the old buddy he had appointed to head up FEMA, that he was doing 'one heck of a job'. 'I don't think anybody anticipated the breach of the levees,' he said. But it was anticipated, and not by just anybody: experts on hurricanes had anticipated it and told the president in a video conference before the storm hit. Soon after the conference, Mike Brown had told him again. 'I really love this city,' the president said. Then he went to Jackson Square and, with civic authorities and the press all around, declared that the rebuilding of New Orleans would be 'one of the largest reconstruction efforts the world has ever seen'.

There was only one lane open on the hurricane-damaged bridge out of New Orleans across Lake Pontchartrain. The traffic crawled along in the dark. An orange moon climbed into the night sky and dropped a dozen shimmering replicas in the water. As it rose, so did a smell: of something like sewage but less organic and fouler. By the time I had crossed the lake to Slidell, the moon was pale – 'soft and copious', as Walt Whitman called it.

Another forty minutes down the highway is Pass Christian,

population (pre-Katrina) 7000. For 150 years the New Orleans gentry kept substantial houses in Pass Christian. One of those houses was now jammed under the awnings of a Shell gas station. Something about the moonlight gave the whole scene the look of an avant-garde opera set. Pass Christian is ten feet above sea level. On the night of Katrina it was several feet below, and houses roamed the streets and scuttled other houses. The sea came ashore and moved concrete slabs, washed away asphalt roads, flattened buildings made of brick and flooded every building. There were houses without roofs and roofs from which the houses had gone; houses spreadeagled on the ground. Katrina ripped large trees from their trunks three feet from the ground, leaving torn and jagged stumps as proof of its brutality. It made houses disappear. Yet clusters of smaller trees were standing and for every half a dozen houses in pieces, as if by an arbitrary exercise of will – or the grace of God – a flimsier structure had survived the wind. But nothing survived the sea surge.

Refrigerators lined the streets, taped up because the stink of them, which was intolerable inside the houses, polluted the air outside as well. Rubbish mucked out of the houses and stuffed in plastic bags lay in the pearly moonlight like heaps of innards. Signs were painted on the walls, circles with quadrants indicating the day of inspection, the organisation that inspected it, the number of human corpses, if any, and the number of cats, dogs or other pets found dead.

Somewhere along the road a light glowed under awnings stretched across makeshift kitchens and trestles loaded with groceries. In the tents and vans around the awning, volunteers and refugees were sleeping. The vans wore the badge of churches from Florida to Minnesota. One said: PASTOR AND PEOPLE, ONE IN THE SPIRIT SEEKING A MORE EXCELLENT WAY. The light was on for security, but it was also the light of American Christianity.

Despite the casino towers, it's easy to miss Biloxi on the highway strip of fast-food franchises, Wal-Marts, Walgreens, real estate outfits, drive-in banks, mortgage houses, credit agencies and churches, all in much the same architectural style and all set on profligate amounts of land. The strip runs forever along the Gulf Coast, and it makes you wonder why, on the night of Katrina, the Holy Comforter didn't take the opportunity to make a more comprehensive town-planning statement. Some of the big signs were still bent at 160 degrees, but corporate America never lies down and the really big companies like Wal-Mart, Wendy's and McDonald's had replaced their tattered roofs and straightened up their signs within a fortnight.

A few miles east of Pass Christian, Biloxi had been famous for shrimp, oysters and canned fish until in 1968 Hurricane Camille – the strongest hurricane ever to hit the United States, stronger than both Rita and Katrina – wiped out the town. Gambling came in the 1990s and brought Biloxi spectacularly back to life. To show that they disapproved of gambling – but not so much of the revenue generated – the state of Mississippi made the operators build their towering casinos offshore, on barges abutting the waterfront. But Katrina did not respect the law: it pushed the monsters onto dry land. Recognising necessity, or perhaps sensing divine will in this jaw-dropping phenomenon, the city fathers made the casinos' new onshore location legal.

Naturally, the sea that drove Biloxi's casinos onto land also surged into the residences of the 17,000 people who worked in them. It first knocked down the more opulent houses along the beachfront. Everything went, except the swimming pools and crazy-paving. Massive oaks lay hundreds of yards from where they once grew. Down by the casinos, an area still cordoned off by the army, a green fishing boat was hard up against one of the walls from the old part of town. The skipper, apparently, had been on board. Looking back towards the water, you could see the path he steered when the surge picked him up and hurtled him towards the shore: through a two-lane driveway under the casino, past the five-storey-high guitar of the Hard Rock Cafe and a quarter of a mile inland, till his boat hit what might have been the post office. In the rubble between the boat and the Hard Rock Cafe a waitress from the nearby Waffle House found a Fender guitar signed by Johnny Cash. Hard Rock headquarters in Florida promised to pay the shipping costs if she sent it back.

Once past the brick houses the water surged unimpeded into the weatherboard bungalows of the black and Vietnamese communities behind them. Every house was inundated. Of those that survived, most had been mucked out and piles of plasterboard, floor linings and furniture were heaped beside them. The air was full of mould, and when the temperature rose in the mornings the other, incomparably worse smell rose with it. For every three houses there were two ruined and abandoned cars, grey-brown with salt and dirt – some of the tens of thousands of useless cars on the Gulf Coast. The houses had circles on the front walls. An odd one indicated a corpse had been found. That story was not over – in the previous week eight more bodies had been discovered, including two children. No-one knew how many more they would find, or how many had been sucked out to sea when the surge retreated.

The people of Biloxi had no homes to go to. More than a million had left the coast, many more than left the Dust Bowl in the 1930s. They were living in hotels and motels, temporary shelters, trailers, state parks, with relatives and friends. Birmingham had organised accommodation for 3000. The schools took in the children. The local chamber of commerce found 3000 jobs. In total, Alabama registered 22,600 evacuees, but authorities thought the real number was closer to 60,000; they also thought there were more in Baton Rouge than the 26,000 registered, and the 150,000 in Houston.

———

Loaded with bottled water, nurses and supplies, we crawled around the streets like the ice-cream van of the apocalypse, looking for survivors. We were the Red Cross. Our leader and driver was a gracious grey-haired Vietnam vet from New York whose father had been in the 1942 landing at Guadalcanal. When a spectrally thin woman appeared on a porch – and I thought at once of heroin – he stopped the van and, with brittle military courtesy, said through the window: 'American Red Cross, ma'am. Is there anything you need, anything we can help you with, ma'am?'

'Batteries,' she said.

'We've got batteries, ma'am,' he said.

And his assistants got out of the van and filled a box with Kix breakfast cereal, apples, bananas, crackers, chocolate, a mop, vacuum packs of Alaskan salmon, toilet paper, diarrhoea formula and batteries.

Whole blocks were deserted. Millions of tons of debris waited to be cleared – tens of millions. But the mounds were just mounds. A bulldozer could have pushed them away from the houses in an afternoon. One sensed paralysis. Another woman appeared, and a young man. 'Y'all need anything?' asked the New Yorker, adopting the local style.

Over the next couple of hours our Red Cross van found about twenty people living strangely dignified lives in what remained of this black suburb. It was a great coming together. A volunteer nurse who had driven down from Connecticut replaced the dressing on a young man's wounded foot, and a nurse from South Dakota watched on. While a young man from Phoenix who was serving ten months in a remnant of one of Bill Clinton's national youth programs ferried groceries into her trailer, a black woman caring for a diabetic multiple amputee told us about her devotion to the Lord.

A soft-spoken, immaculately groomed woman who looked about thirty-five took what she was offered reluctantly. She said yes when she was asked if she had children, but no when she was offered an armful of soft toys: one of her children was thirty and the other twenty-five. Her sister-in-law bounded into the Red Cross van to kiss us. There were smiles and hugs and blessings all round until the groceries ran out and the van went back to the church on the highway.

It was odd to be dispensing medicine for diarrhoea and not portable lavatories; Honey Smacks when doctors were concerned about scurvy; crackers when a generator and a barbecue and fresh meat might have done for several blocks. It seemed just as odd that the same nation whose army took Baghdad in a fortnight, and which, forty years earlier, had landed two men on the soft and copious moon, could not find a bulldozer to push the rubbish away from the houses. But we had been made welcome, just the same, and as our leader said, it was a good day – 'We emptied the van.' It would have been churlish not to share his sense of satisfaction, or to allow any doubt about whose souls – ours or theirs – had been ministered to that afternoon.

Evangelical America is as indomitable as American business – and seeks opportunity no less enthusiastically. As Adam Smith saw a beneficent 'hidden hand' in the operation of a competitive economy, and Joseph Schumpeter saw what he called 'creative destruction' as the unseen dynamo of American capitalism, American evangelicals saw the hand of God in the hurricanes and inferred that He had visited them upon the Gulf Coast to create converts. Katrina had hardly blown out to sea and the birds returned to the coast than a wave of volunteers of all denominations from all parts of the country descended on the wreckage.

At eleven pm in the Lutheran Church only a half-dozen of sixty-five volunteers were awake. The rest were sleeping on camp stretchers and inflatable mattresses on every bit of floor that was not taken up with doctors' equipment or donated groceries: breakfast cereal, toilet paper, batteries, canned fruit, mops. 'Where did all this come from?' I whispered to a volunteer, and I expected her to say it had been donated by Wal-Mart or Dixie but instead she whispered back: 'God. God our guide.' I crawled between a pastor and a snoring layperson sleeping on the stage at the front of the hall and slept very badly.

In the morning God made the pancakes. 'He works through our hands,' the lady said as she mixed them. Beside her the polystyrene cooler was marked: THE LORD IS LIFE. At breakfast the pastor called on everyone to stand and he led us in prayer.

When God sent Katrina he sent miracles, the pastor's wife said. She also told me a saying popular in Louisiana and Mississippi: if you're a Lutheran, you must be from somewhere else. But Katrina had done more than a bit for the Lutheran profile; or, as she insisted, God had done it through Katrina. He brought together so many people from all over in a spirit of Christian love, and they had dispensed groceries and medicine and mucked out houses, but they had also seized the missionary opportunity. She wanted to stay and talk, but had to leave for the first meeting of Interfaith, a body representative of all the denominations working in the disaster areas which had been established to decide who got what from federal government funding.

A lady from New England, a retired doctor, offered me a bed in her Winnebago. She and her husband had planned to drive it all over the United States, but soon after he gave up work her husband died. She had not known what to do with the Winnebago, and then Katrina hit. Like everyone else in the world she watched it all on the news. Then she packed the Winnebago. I don't know how she parked it in the Biloxi trailer park, much less how she drove the huge thing 1500 miles with her car attached to the back of it. It was a comfortable suburban house on wheels, doubling as a chapel.

It surprises people from countries where religion long ago retreated to the background to find evangelical churches on the front line of disaster relief. But religion is on the front line of just about everything in the United States. The first people to be consulted about Supreme Court nominations are religious leaders, and the first question asked of nominees concerns the separation of church and state. It's a country where God is in the storm and the pancake batter. He is present at rodeos and in football stadiums, where national and college teams – in breach of their Lord's injunction to pray privately and without display – go down on their knees, hold hands and pray together. He's in the White House. And He's at congressional, gubernatorial and every other kind of election, where many of the candidates also go down on their knees.

—

Downtown New Orleans was functioning again, but with the hotels full of FEMA people and insurance assessors it wasn't easy to get a room. Eventually I found one in a place that still had damp parts and whose elevators brought up a stench from the basement. There were two or three police cars on every block. Army vehicles were lined up in Canal Street and soldiers stalked up and down in full battle dress. That night black men hung about in surly groups, going nowhere, while gangs of Mexican workers – who by day dragged the plaster and carpets out of the houses – surged past on their way to the bars, restaurants and strip clubs, and the raucous, pulsing music in Bourbon Street.

Doubtless there were good reasons for so quickly sending

in the troops. New Orleans was notorious for crime and violence, and the hurricane had hardly passed when scenes of looting appeared on TV screens. But the soldiers brought with them other meanings: signs of the old fear of a black uprising; signs of social failure. As evidence grew of government ineptitude and indifference to suffering, the troops became a symbol of that as well – as if sending in the army was *all* a government could do.

And the evidence came in ways and from places that could not be ignored. The way-out reporter Geraldo Rivera seized a black baby from its mother's arms and shouted at his Fox News anchors that government efforts in the six days since Katrina had been 'as bad, or worse' than the hurricane itself. Another reporter, Shepard Smith, for a moment seemed to lose patience with his employer for grasping neither the implication nor the dimensions of the crime – that people were still locked in the Superdome and the Convention Center without food or water or formula for babies, that the bridge was open but not a single bus had arrived to take these poor people away. Frenzied venting is Fox News's *modus operandi* and rage is the most popular emotion. Rage, but not insurrection. This was Fox News – the patriotic channel, the Bush–Cheney channel – and its employees appeared to be saying that the country and its government had failed.

One commentator said that in the government response one could see 'all the symptoms of a failed state'. Marty Bahamonde, the FEMA man in New Orleans, called it 'systematic failure at all levels of government'. Bahamonde knew better than most. On 31 August 2005, while sheltering in the Superdome, he read an email from the press secretary for Mike Brown, head of FEMA:

Also, it is very important that time is allowed for Mr. Brown to eat dinner. Given Baton Rouge is back to normal, restaurants are getting busy. He needs much more than 20 or 30 minutes. We now have traffic to encounter to get to and from a location of his choise (*sic*), followed by wait service from the restaurant staff, eating, etc. Thank you.

Bahamonde emailed his deputy director in response: 'Just tell her that I just ate an MRE and crapped in the hallway of the Superdome along with 30,000 other close friends so I understand her concern about busy restaurants.'

As people drowned or waited to be rescued from their roofs and attics, Bahamonde sent emails on his BlackBerry telling Brown they were running out of food and water, that many would not survive the night, that the situation was 'past critical'. Brown replied: 'Thanks for the update. Anything specific I need to do or tweak?'

Then there was Michael Chertoff, the friend the president had made his secretary of homeland security. Chertoff said the problem was that the hurricane came in the middle of a 'second stage review' of disaster planning. As a consequence, he said, FEMA lacked the 'skill set' for 'preparedness'. It sounded like the hurricane made landfall before they finished designing the PowerPoint presentation. Of course, that's how twenty-first-century public servants talk – like private-sector people.

I opened the *Times-Picayune* in the morning and among the obituaries read: 'Dance as if no one were watching . . . live every day as if it were your last.' Down at the river end of Canal Street, a black kid who looked about seventeen came out of one of the portable toilets that stood in a row there and waited for me to reach him. 'Do you think it will ever be the same again?' he asked. He walked with me up the ramp towards the wharf where the ferry docked. He came from Alabama and happened to be there when Katrina hit New Orleans. Now he'd returned to look for a job. After working the previous day the contractor told him he'd pick him up this morning, but he hadn't shown up. Most days, the kid said, he rode the ferry across the river and back, two or three times. That's where he was going now. He just liked being on the water, he said.

Some affluent white areas had been flooded out by Katrina and some poor black areas had escaped, but the odds of suffering serious damage were much greater if you were black, poor or a renter. Half the people whose homes were wrecked were renters and a third were below the poverty line. Those with the least resources, the least control over their lives and the least capacity for recovery were the most numerous among the victims. A house I visited in the Seventh Ward had been built four feet above the ground, but the water that reached the front door was four feet two inches deep. The two inches that swirled inside the house grew into two feet of mould and made it impossible to live there. An uprooted tree lay across the fence in the backyard. The owner of the house was still waiting for an insurance assessment and a contractor. No-one had moved back to the street and it was easy to see why.

The Seventh Ward was bad but the Ninth Ward was worse. The Ninth Ward was eighty-five per cent black, and fifty per cent lived below the poverty line. The area nearest to the levee, like the foreshore at Biloxi, had been completely demolished. Half a dozen people poked about in the rubble. Men with jackhammers tore at the old levee, trying to finish with machinery what nature began on the night of Katrina. How the water pushed through something so massive is beyond imagining, and it is not so hard to understand why some people were insisting the levee was breached with explosives. A barge, a monster about fifty yards long, had been washed onto the wall, and its front had tipped down onto the nose of a yellow school bus and crushed it. When Katrina hit, all the school buses that might have been used to evacuate people from New Orleans before the hurricane, or from the Superdome after it, were parked in a yard. They were flooded. Would this school bus still be under the barge in Chicago or New York? Would it still be there in a city that meant more to the national economy? New Orleans is the biggest port in the country, but it's a through-port. The city itself isn't so important. The corn, steel and chickens don't stop in New Orleans.

A congressional report had just declared 'that Katrina was a national failure, an abdication of the most solemn obligation to provide for the common welfare'. Yet it was now as good as official: what the president had billed as the one of the greatest recovery operations in the history of the world would be market-driven – it *had* to be market-driven. As for the church, so for the private sector: Katrina was an 'opportunity'. 'We have a clean sheet to start again,' said Joseph Canizaro, a developer. 'And with that clean sheet we have some very big opportunities.' As it happened, the last bit of substantial public infrastructure built in the city had been the 1970s Superdome, and it was the Superdome in which the masses huddled in their hour of peril. The corporate towers, the buildings most impervious to the wind and water, did not open their doors. No-one expected them to. And if anyone drew a lesson from that, they weren't saying.

There was Baghdad and there was New Orleans. Hundreds of billions of dollars had been poured into Iraq and still people complained that electricity had not been restored. In New Orleans, three or four blocks from the French Quarter, it was the same. In Iraq, a good part of the war and most of the reconstruction was carried out by private contractors. It was the same in New Orleans: and some of the contractors were the same as well. Likewise, some of the National Guard sent to New Orleans were not long back from Baghdad. As in Baghdad, there had been progress. But it was uneven. They were fixing up the places about which there could be no question. There could be no New Orleans without commerce, so the commercial centre had been restored. But in the problematic places – the low-lying, poorer, blacker places – they seemed paralysed by doubt and disagreement. And this is as one would expect, because these places posed questions of race and poverty for which America had never found satisfactory answers – and in recent times had all but stopped looking.

An artist whose family had lived in New Orleans for many generations, the diffident, soft-spoken grand-nephew of the legendary jazz musician Sidney Bechet, told me that he was a lifelong New Orleanean, and as that was all he could be, he would never leave.

What was a New Orleanean?

'A certain kind of spirituality is involved,' he said. 'They invent themselves. They improvise on themes.'

He said the conservative takeover of the Baptist Church had had a very bad affect on African Americans and worked counter to their ebullient spirit. He had no doubt that Washington's failures with Katrina had their origins in the deeper failures of social and economic policy. What we saw on our television screens after Katrina were signs of the dysfunction that had preceded it: the social consequences of low wages and the race divide. There was as well the shrinking of the public realm, the ineptness of managerialism and the greed of private interest. Katrina could not be contained as a disaster story or even as a human interest story: the bodies floating in the streets days after the hurricane had gone, the disproportionate losses of the black and poor communities, the military response arriving before the humanitarian aid, and the media preceding both spoke with inescapable eloquence of a modern *American* story.

33

I turned on the TV back in my downtown hotel room, and there was Mayor Nagin in a suit with a bright patterned shirt open at the neck saying: 'You know the rules, man. No cussin'.' It was one of his town hall meetings.

A woman was weeping and the mayor said: 'You take it easy, baby. We're gonna take care of you, right.' And another woman stepped up and put an arm around her and gave her a handkerchief to mop her eyes and led her from the lectern. The weeping woman was beautifully groomed and her Red Cross clothes were perfectly pressed and, as she went, she said she was sorry to talk like that. 'I'm happy. I really am. God has blessed me. I know that.' But she so wanted something by Christmas, somewhere to live, because she had three children. She had spent two days on a roof with those children after Katrina hit. She was sick of travelling, sick of being kicked out.

Then another woman came forward and said she had found somewhere to live for $450 a month, which left her nothing over – but then she got a light bill for a God-awful amount. So the energy company representative stepped up and said one of his customer service people would look after her; but before that happened someone said he'd pay her bill. We didn't see who it was but it might have been the next speaker, a loquacious, exquisitely dressed contractor. He said he was New Orleans born and raised: so what did it say about his city that he had the equipment and 400 local workers, but the work was going to outside contractors who used illegal foreigners? And if his local workers went to the outside contractors, 'they got treated like dogs'. The hall resounded to cheers.

And it resounded again when speakers began to name price-gouging landlords and insurance companies that wouldn't pay. And then a woman with a child sleeping on her shoulder told the meeting: 'You know what it's like living with people – people who don't want you. I sit in a corner. Just give me somewhere of my own, bare boards, a sink and something to cook on, and throw the piss out the window,' she said.

A Muslim called Omar said he had a masters from the University of Maryland but he came from the Ninth Ward and everyone there has 'PhDs in life and love and they shouldn't be ignored'. Then a man addressed the mayor: 'You push for us and I'll vote for you. But you don't and I'll do everything to stop you, and I've got a big mouth.' The people were silent. Nagin was unfazed: he knew they didn't like the man's tone.

And then another man said there should have been a national day of mourning. Mayor Nagin looked sad. 'We've still got bodies we can't identify and bodies are still being found,' he said. Melancholy seemed to descend on the hall, and it found its way into my hotel room.

—

It didn't help the mood in New Orleans when the president, who had stayed on his ranch for Katrina, turned up in his brother Jeb's state of Florida within hours of Hurricane Wilma going through a few weeks later. And yet the anger was tempered by the common belief – much older than the modern free-market concept – that sensible citizens should not expect very much of governments. In general, where there is more faith in God there is less faith in government, and less reliance on it: or, as Alexis de Tocqueville expressed the equation 170 years ago, 'if faith be wanting in him, he must be subject, and if he be free, he must believe'. Tocqueville said it and so did Walt Whitman: democracy is inseparable from religion. 'At the core of democracy is the religious element,' Whitman said, and he meant 'all the religions, old and new'.

That is the sense one had among the religions, old and new, on the Gulf Coast – and in the meeting of social justice and religious ecstasy at the Lutheran church in Biloxi. In experiencing Christian fellowship and purpose, they experienced America as a place that filled needs beyond the self. And in experiencing this, it seems likely that they felt they were enjoying democracy as God intended it in their country.

The churches carried so much of the responsibility in part because the expanded role of faith-based organisations is a defining element of the administration's strategy. But the faithful would likely have said that the responsibility was 'naturally' theirs, regardless of government strategies; that it was not something they could ever cede to anyone. It was as if Katrina re-created the original ground for Christianity: God rained on rich and poor alike, on the just and the unjust. When everyone's lost everything the words of the old spiritual apply to all God's people:

> *I got shoes, you got shoes, all o' God's children got shoes.*
> *When I get to heaven I'm gonna put on my shoes . . .*
> *And walk all over . . . heaven.*

There were people who said Katrina would have a more profound and lasting effect than 9/11; that it laid bare all the fault lines of American society: race, inequality, energy, the environment. This might explain the seeming paralysis in the place where decisions about such things are made: Washington DC. Everything after the dimwitted insouciance of the president in the first few days suggested that Katrina created problems beyond the government's reach and comprehension. Two months later no-one had decided what was to be done: about the broken levees, about the rubbish, about the evacuees, about what sort of rebuilding there should be, and – in some parts of New Orleans – if there should be any rebuilding at all.

There was no leader. People who knew about disasters and people who knew New Orleans and the environment of the

Gulf Coast could not understand why a 'czar' had not been appointed, as Herbert Hoover had been after the 1927 Mississippi floods. In the time it took Mike Brown to reach New Orleans, Hoover managed to evacuate 300,000 residents. Why hadn't one of the New York mayors, Bloomberg or Giuliani, been called in? Why had no-one asked the Academy of Science to work with such a czar and the Army Corps of Engineers? Why was the government not interested in the questions posed in the opinion pages and letters columns of newspapers every day?

Would they take the opportunity to rebuild the regional ecosystem from the ground up, or just rebuild the levees – but sink them deeper this time? There were people who said the whole of the Ninth Ward, at least, should be razed and returned to the cypress swamp which is its natural state. Would they make a Venice of New Orleans, or a Florida-style resort? Or, as someone wrote to a Birmingham paper, would it be 'a slum of the future . . . hastily and shabbily reconstructed on sinking earth . . . prepared for suffering souls to live out their lives, periodically casting their votes for morsels that promises entice'? The handful of people in the bar of the newly renovated boutique hotel where I stayed generally agreed that New Orleans should become a modern high-tech city. These were 'new' New Orleaneans, I suppose: the type my fellow Amtrak passengers wanted to throw in the river. They reckoned the old city could never be restored and that it was worse than pointless to try, because no sensible person wanted to restore a slum.

Yet perhaps there was a plan, after all. On the television I saw Newt Gingrich telling young people at a business school that wherever government went on the Gulf Coast there would be failure. Government, in his view, was constitutionally incapable of providing the services people need. He asked his audience to imagine New Orleans if FedEx were in charge. Or

McDonald's. Or Travelocity, an internet travel company – it was easy to see that Newt hadn't made his own bookings for a while. A lot of people on the Gulf Coast might have said that Gingrich was giving the game away: that right from the start the government and its corporate friends had seen Katrina as an opportunity to remake New Orleans along free-market lines.

Gingrich's student audience, it goes almost without saying, were all ears and among them not one could think of a single thing to say in favour of government at all. How could they see it any differently? It was governments that had failed to prepare for a disaster predicted by just about everyone for years, and governments that repeatedly cut the funds needed to repair the levees. But watching all their heads nodding in agreement with Newt Gingrich, one wondered if they would have believed someone who told them that governments rebuilt San Francisco after the 1906 earthquake and Galveston after the 1900 hurricane. How would they react if they heard a voice saying the citizenry 'must effectively control the mighty commercial forces which they themselves have called into being'? Or if, out of the blue, they heard the same voice call for 'far more active government interference with social and economic conditions in this country'? To what outrageous liberal would they attribute such notions? Susan Sarandon? In fact, the words are those of the old tiger of American individualism and imperial can-do, Theodore Roosevelt. Obsolete or not, it's hard to imagine the rubbish would still be lying in the streets, or the barge would still be resting on the school bus, if Teddy Roosevelt was in charge of the government. Or FDR or LBJ or Nixon, for that matter.

The country couldn't decide: was the government incompetent because it was a government, or because it was an incompetent government? Was it an incompetent government because it had put essential agencies into the hands of private-sector cronies, or because it hadn't put enough into private hands? Were the cronies incompetent because they were working for the government, or because they were working for other private interests? In a Gulf newspaper a local contractor complained that he could not get a tender for his fleet of bulldozers: but Halliburton could. Some people said the cronyism and incompetence reflected a general decline in the status and abilities of government over the past twenty-five years. Katrina was not a failure of government *per se*, they said, but a failure of a government in an era when government was out of fashion and consequently run-down. Decried every day as a feckless thing without initiative or ambition, a thing not to be mentioned in the same breath as private enterprise, government became that thing. First sequester its responsibilities, sell off its functions, grant it no respect; run it into the ground and then declare it incompetent.

This might have been the truth of it. Katrina excited religious and commercial feeling in equal proportion. Church and corporation both saw the disaster as creating opportunities, and in both cases they were opportunities to exercise their true natures: the church to do the Lord's work administering comfort and creating converts; the corporation to seek profit and, through that natural instinct, to create miracles from the destruction. As profit and efficiency were in the nature of business, and charity and salvation in the nature of churches, incompetence and bureaucracy were in the nature of governments.

But consider where this proposition leads: if it is true that private businesses are efficient because it is in their nature to seek and maximise profit – which is to say, their self-interest – then the pursuit of the public interest is *not* in their nature, and one may as well look to a rattlesnake for kindness as to corporations for the rebuilding of a city full of people. It is pointless; and it follows that it's just as pointless to imagine that a country governed by the principle of private interest is capable of fixing problems in the public interest – be they local, like New Orleans; national, like poverty; or global, like the environment or peace. If 'nature' is the rule, it is not in America's nature to solve anything unless there is a dollar or a soul in it.

The notion is, of course, absurd, but scarcely more absurd than arguments you can hear on the radio or television every day. Yet, while it is manifestly true that American churches and American corporations – and the American nation – do good and selfless works at home and abroad, it is also true that, in these days of culture wars, the idea of government being the principal agent of such works is faded. That is what New Orleans revealed about government: religion has a purpose and a principle; the private interest also has them. Both are granted the capacity to imagine something beyond and higher than the present reality and to make it possible for people to transcend themselves. But government is denied these things, or has voluntarily relinquished them. Government has no purpose or belief to guide or energise it. It is expected to fail and it lives up to the expectation.

———

Before I left New Orleans I went down to a big Chase Bank on the corner to get some cash. As I took the notes from the ATM I heard a blast on a horn. An old van had rolled at an odd angle into the kerb and the driver was slumped over the wheel. He had already opened the door when I reached him and he sat there grey-faced and gasping. I saw a puffer in his top pocket so I took it out and put it in his hand. The van smelt like the inside of his lungs.

As he took a puff I saw the plastic bands around his wrists: I asked him if he'd been in hospital. He nodded. He was on his way there, he said, but he needed to go to a bank, not an ATM. But it's Saturday, I said. The banks are closed.

There was a uniformed guard, a burly black man with a revolver on his hip, patrolling the building. I walked over and asked him if there was a bank open somewhere. Maybe Slidell, he said.

I went back to the man in the van and told him. I'm out of gas, he said. I gave him twenty dollars. He looked at me with his cloudy grey eyes and shook my hand.

Then the guard came over. With another puff of Ventolin the man managed to explain that FEMA had put a cheque into his account, but when he went to the bank last night it hadn't cleared. He needed to talk to someone in the bank. He needed the money. The guard took twenty dollars from his wallet, gave it to him and walked away without a word.

Intending to leave, I shook the man's hand again, but he eyeballed me and clung to my hand and begged me to listen to his story. On the night of Katrina he was in an old person's hostel. He was watching the storm through the window when a nurse came and gave them each a pill to make them sleep. When he woke up, he said, all the hostel workers had gone and water was lapping around the beds.

He gasped for air. 'Seven people drowned,' he said. 'Old people. They took the young and left the old people to die.'

He gripped my arm more tightly. Tears rolled through the stubble on his chin. His voice had come down to a whisper.

'The water rose and rose,' he said.

He had tried to swim to the window, but he went under. He held up three fingers.

'Three times,' he said.

And he went down a fourth time and knew it was the last, but – and he gripped me tighter still.

'I tell you, the Lord saved me. An angel came. I saw him. He got me to the rail by the window. I hung on. I could see the bodies. Floating. And the helicopters.'

And then, he said, the National Guard found him but the

helicopters wouldn't come. No-one would, he said, and shuddered.

When finally they rescued him, he was flown to a university hospital in San Antonio and kept there for three weeks until he felt like a new man. He bought the van with the money he got for a watch and a ring and he drove it back to New Orleans and had been living in it ever since. The hostel where he'd lived for three years was gone.

I told him he'd better go to the hospital. He was wheezing badly. We shook hands and he drove off. Two hours later I still had the smell of that van in my lungs, and the faintest suspicion that the guard and I were not the first people to give him twenty dollars for his story.

CHAPTER 2

*'. . . a lightless and gutted empty land where women
crouched with the huddled children behind locked doors
and men armed in sheets and masks rode the silent roads
and the bodies of white and black both, victims not so
much of hate as desperation and despair, swung from
lonely limbs: and men shot dead in polling-booths with the
still wet pen in one hand and the unblotted ballot in
the other . . .'*

William Faulkner, *The Bear*

OUR TRAIN WENT VERY SLOWLY ACROSS LAKE PONTCHARTRAIN, AND
slowly across the bayous, as if picking its way through the
ragged trees and hanging moss. A young black man was travelling with his five-year-old daughter. Her mother had left when
she was six months old. His house in Slidell had been washed
away and all he owned was on the rack above him in a duffle
bag he had kept from his days in the navy. He was going to
Maryland, where a couple of old friends had told him he might
be able to get a job. In the seats in front, a poor white family
of eight travelled as families do, babbling and laughing
and crooning, crying and admonishing, seeming to exist like

45

atoms, in a state of perpetual movement. Katrina had sent seven feet of water through their house in New Orleans. They were going to start again in New York, or maybe New Jersey – they weren't sure. An old black couple told them that New Jersey was better for bringing up kids.

A hundred years after emancipation, John Steinbeck drove through the South and visited New Orleans, a place he knew and loved. He went to see for himself the women known to the world as the Cheerleaders. Every morning and afternoon, the Cheerleaders gathered outside a desegregated school to shout abuse at the black children coming and going under police escort. Steinbeck heard them hurl 'bestial and filthy and degenerate' words, words so foul he chose not to repeat them in the book he wrote. Even more venomously than they abused the black children, they shouted at a white man who brought his child to the school. Crowds gathered to watch the Cheerleaders and urge them on.

Steinbeck called it 'demented cruelty'. He was shocked; he 'churned with weary nausea'. Worst of all, he knew the Cheerleaders and their acolytes would rush home 'to see themselves on television, and what they saw went out all over the world, unchallenged by the other things I know are there'. Nothing agitated him more than this: where were the *good* people of New Orleans? He left at once and headed home to New York.

Birmingham, Alabama, resonates in my baby boomer memory as Steinbeck's South. It brings to mind images of police dogs and water cannon, jeering white supremacists, the Klan, bombings. In the decade of our radicalism, the city was a byword for American racism – and, in the form of civil-rights marchers, for American heroism. In today's South – the Republican-voting, modernised South – the signs that used to segregate the public places have gone, the lynching has stopped, the Ku Klux Klan is mainly a joke and the Cheerleaders are no more. Steinbeck's absent friends, the better angels of the South, are reputed now to be in charge.

It was mid-afternoon on a Saturday and there were no taxis at the station, so I towed my suitcase to a broad street and ambled along in the sunshine to where there was a cinema and a man out the front sweeping. He looked up as I approached and went back inside. The names of Alabama's most famous were cut into the pavement. The first was Truman Capote: half a dozen later, Harper Lee. The film *Capote* was playing everywhere in the United States, but not at this cinema.

I waited an hour for a cab. Birmingham didn't look like a battleground. It didn't look like the South, for that matter. It looked orderly, prosperous and deserted.

When the cab came, I said to the driver that Birmingham seemed to be doing well. But the new biotechnology and medical research institutes, the new office blocks, the banks and all the newfangled jobs did not impress him. He said the prosperity was phoney. He remembered Birmingham when it was an industrial city, a steel city, 'the Pittsburgh of the South'. All the money for research institutes had come in, but 'real' industries were folding up; the 'real' economy was puffed up with this research and the public spending on black people – seventy per cent of Birmingham's 240,000 inhabitants are black – and now more was going to the folk from the Gulf Coast, who had only added to the twenty per cent already living below the poverty line. And then there was all the crime. Birmingham has the seventh-highest crime rate in the country.

Whatever it is that constitutes the modern South, this taxi driver wasn't buying it. It seemed possible that there were other memories and other reasons for his disgruntlement, and there was a time when he would have let me hear them. But not now.

When I woke on Sunday morning, two people in the room next to mine were shouting at each other. 'You mother-fuckin'' son of a bitch,' she shouted, and he shouted something like that back at her. Then she unleashed another torrent of curses, and he was silent. There was a thud and then, from her with a great intake of breath like a sob: 'You mother-fucker!' And another thud. They seemed to crash into the wall.

They thundered and thudded intermittently for a quarter of an hour, and I did think that any moment they might come right through the plaster. Then, it seemed to me, they started wrestling: they thumped about in the room adjacent to my lavatory and she shouted at him: 'You broke the goddam toilet, you mother-fucker! You always break the goddam toilet!'

There was another thud and I thought he'd killed her, and for the third time I reached for the phone. But then her voice came: 'This is the last fuckin' time! I'm going to the police!' And the door slammed and I saw her for a moment through the yellowing gauze curtains on my window. She yelled 'Mother-fucker!' one more time for good measure and disappeared.

Not a sound came from the room next door. Five minutes must have passed. And then I heard what sounded like the lid being ripped from the toilet and hitting the front door; and then another noise like the toilet seat being ripped from its moorings on the bowl, and then what could have been a cistern torn from a water pipe. And the man's voice boomed: 'Mother-fucker!'

The hotel's receptionist told me 'they' often check into motels on Friday and Saturday nights 'because they don't want to trash their own places'. I moved to a little hotel at Five Points, an old part of town built around four churches on hills of various sizes. The bells of one church were ringing and I watched a few white Presbyterians file in. The hotel had recommended the steakhouse but I chose the Japanese, where the sushi came with slabs of tuna for which the template must have been a schnitzel.

Martin Luther King was in Birmingham in 1963, when it was 'the most thoroughly segregated city in the United States'. It was, King said, notorious for the brutality its police inflicted on black people, the bias of its courts against black people, the frequency with which the houses and churches of black people were bombed, and the failure of the city authorities to solve such crimes. He said this in a letter from the Birmingham gaol, to which he'd been sent for civil disobedience. The letter was his definitive case for non-violent resistance. He made it searing and unanswerable; by turns a sulphurous expression of black Americans' suffering, humiliation and anger, and a measured Christian disquisition on St Augustine's maxim: 'An unjust law is no law at all.'

In 1992 Birmingham established a Civil Rights District and built a Civil Rights Institute next to the old Sixteenth Street Church, founded in 1871 and built in 1911 from a black architect's Romanesque design. White terrorists planted a bomb in the Sunday school in 1963 and killed four little black girls. Condoleezza Rice and the British foreign secretary, Jack Straw, had been photographed there the day before I got to Birmingham, and it was on the front page of the *Birmingham News*. They held the hands of four little girls; and Rice, a native of Birmingham, paid tribute to the girls who were killed and to the civil-rights movement: 'Because we were not denied, Birmingham was not denied, and because Birmingham was not denied, America finally came to terms with its birth defect . . . that when the Founding Fathers said "We the people" they didn't mean any of us.' The secretary of state may have come to terms with the birth defect, but not everyone would say the country has.

Outside the institute stands a statue of Rosa Parks, the little forty-two-year-old seamstress from Montgomery who in 1955 defied segregation laws by refusing to give up her seat on a bus to a white passenger. Her manner of doing this so blurred the distinctions between grace, courage and politics that it had the effect of a moment from the New Testament. The gesture inspired a year-long boycott of Montgomery's buses that only ended when the Supreme Court ruled the buses were to be desegregated. Rosa Parks and her husband were threatened with violence and lost their jobs, and it was to escape this persecution that they moved to Detroit in 1957. Before I saw her statue that day I'd forgotten Rosa Parks had lived. Back in the hotel that night I saw on the news that she had died.

The Civil Rights Institute tells the story of the pre-civil-rights South in words and images that shock in much the same way and to the same extent that Holocaust museums shock. It is not a matter of counting the dead, but of confronting depravity. It goes beyond the lynching and the casual killings (the swamps, they say, have hundreds of bodies in them) to the hatred of one human being for another, the contempt of the strong for the weak, of one putative Christian for another, the depths to which prejudice, once sanctioned, sinks us. Governments and the FBI are trying to make some form of restitution. They are investigating murders and convicting people of crimes committed more than half a century ago. But they have no power over words and glances. They have no power over the real estate agents and landlords who decide who lives where in cities and towns across the country.

—

Threatened and exhausted, sitting at a kitchen table in Montgomery, Alabama, in 1956, Martin Luther King found himself exclaiming: 'I've come to the point where I can't face it alone.' Having said it, his fears 'suddenly began to melt away' and an 'inner voice' at once began directing him. From Booker T. Washington around the end of the nineteenth century to King in the middle of the twentieth, all kinds of philosophical differences will be found, but among black Americans and their leaders, religion – *lived* religion – has always been at or near the core of things.

The black American novelist Richard Wright spent his youth in Jackson, Mississippi, much of it hungry and in a state of terror. He became convinced that 'the meaning of living came only when one was struggling to wring a meaning out of meaningless suffering'. This conviction, though it led Wright to give up religion, explains just as well why others cling to it. His terror came in part from the whites and was implanted in his mind 'as though I had been the victim of a thousand lynchings'. But it also came from his grandmother, whose own fear had found a form of resolution in the Seventh-day Adventist Church, and who instinctively terrorised the child to protect him from the devil – which was to say, from those instincts that might have given the whites a pretext to abuse him.

One night in a Jackson Shoney's restaurant, where folk stood by bain-maries and piled their plates high with eggs, fried chicken, bacon, sausages, ham, beans, mayonnaise, cheese, croutons and potatoes, I heard an old black man behind me tell his young male companion about 'the plan that the Lord has for us, as it is revealed in the story of David'. He told the story as other people might talk about their pension or a holiday. After a while a young waitress sat down with them and joined in the discussion.

The idea that a divine plan is at work is a powerful theme in America, and not just among preachers in the South or the people who regularly listen to them. You hear it from politicians, celebrities and sportspeople, and you hear it from people on the street. Even if you share their belief in a living God, and suppose that such a God must have a plan of sorts, you might still wonder why he would concern himself with the football results; or why he would provide a surfeit of bad food for poor people in a Shoney's and none at all for hundreds of millions of people in other parts of the world. What can't be questioned is the part religion plays in the lives of both those who overcome their circumstances and those for whom circumstances are too strong against them. Nor can you question what Americans of this persuasion sometimes achieve in their lives, or the love they inspire in others, the example they set or the rare grace their religion gives them.

Grace *and* forbearance – and passivity, some will say. There are 500 Muslims in Jackson, 200 of them African American. The one I met was an elegant woman who welcomed me to the modestly housed International Museum of Muslim Cultures with a warm, irresistible smile. The South is as racist as ever, she said, though no white Southerner welcomes the accusation these days. She knows they're racist from the way they recoil when she extends her hand: what she feels every day in their glances, the downward turn of their eyes, what she picks up in their conversations. Every black American feels it, she says, and Christianity teaches them to accept it. She might be describing what, a hundred years ago, the black American leader W. E. B. du Bois called 'double consciousness': 'this sense of always looking at oneself through the eyes of others, of measuring one's soul by the tape of a world that looks on in amused contempt and pity'.

At the museum, the lady thought Christianity was just about the worst thing that ever happened to African Americans: they could throw off slavery, but a God in the white man's image was much harder. Islam does not differentiate between races (she rejected the black Muslim leader Louis Farrakhan because he does): Islam treats everyone as the sons and daughters of Adam and Eve. She was one of seven children in a Baptist family, raised on a little cotton farm her father and his friends had made out of several small lots. Even as a young girl she could not accept Christianity with its white saviour and its graven images. She became a Muslim when she moved to Jackson thirty years ago, about the time her son was born. Her son and her two daughters were raised as Muslims – no easy thing, she says, when fashion dictates that 'you can't be beautiful without being half-naked' and when it is much more expensive to clothe your children in something that accords with the teaching of the Prophet.

Her grandfather was born a slave in Louisiana, and that was all she knew about her forebears; save that her father had been a meticulously clean man who washed with a kind of ritual that included the inside of his nose, and she could not help but think that his habit had been passed down from a Muslim ancestor.

Jackson is the Rome of the First Baptist Church: its buildings stand over two whole city blocks. Several hundred other churches serve the city, whose population is substantially fewer than 200,000, two-thirds of them black and a quarter of them below the poverty line. In addition to the churches, there are countless preachers on local radio and television. Bob Cornuke, the author of *Ark Fever*, is one of them. 'There's an agenda out there to tell us the Bible is not historically true' and the national media had 'gone crazy' for it, Bob said on the radio. But one of the astronauts who walked on the moon had told him: 'Bob, you go look for the Ark;' and he did and he reckoned he had found it. Not on Mount Ararat, as generally assumed, but in Iran. Some scientists were saying that it was just a rock, but Bob was pretty sure the stuff was petrified wood or 'gofer wood', as the Bible tells us; and, as Bob said, no scientist can say what kind of wood God was talking about when he told Noah to use 'gofer'.

Two hours north of Jackson is Greenwood and ten minutes beyond Greenwood is the little village of Money. Here, in August 1955, fourteen-year-old Emmett Till stepped off a train from Chicago. He had come to spend school holidays with his great-uncle, Moses Wright. A few days later, white men dragged him from the bed in which he slept with his cousins, pistol-whipped him, broke his arms and legs, shot him through the head and threw him in the Tallahatchie River with a seventy-five-pound fan from a cotton gin tied with barbed wire to his neck. One of the men was the husband of a woman whose dignity Emmett was alleged to have offended with a wolf-whistle.

From the witness box at the murder trial, Moses Wright pointed to one of the accused and said: 'Dar he.' It did not impress the all-white jury – in just over an hour they acquitted the husband of the outraged woman and his half-brother. The men knew they could not be tried again. Four months later they described in a magazine interview how they had killed Emmett Till.

It is perhaps in keeping with the provenance of such crimes that Greenwood, where the trial took place, has the largest Bible-binding business in the United States. This is a fact of some cultural significance in a country where ninety per cent of households have at least one Bible – the average is reckoned to be four – and twenty-five million new Bibles are sold each year. That you can read, cross-reference and download every version of the Bible in an instant on the internet makes the figure all the more astounding and may indicate that, just as there was for the early Puritans, there is power in the book itself.

Of those twenty-five million new Bibles, the old King James Version still accounts for a respectable proportion, though nowadays buying a Bible is a bit like choosing your coffee in Starbucks. Some Bibles have recipes in them. Some can tell you how to remove stains from clothing. One may also buy Personal Promise Bibles, in which the name of a loved one may be substituted for 'thy' or 'thou' or 'thee': thus, 'Whither Ted goest, I will go.' Parents can also buy CDs on which passages from the Bible have been 'personalised with their children's names': 'Whosoever believeth in me, Colin . . .' and so on. Under United States law all Bibles are exempt from sales tax – a ruling that the American Civil Liberties Union reckons should be extended to any publication that deals with the meaning of life. For some years the biggest seller has been the New International Version, and now there's Today's New International Version. Both versions and many others are published by Zondervan 'with the utmost respect for God's holy word and the conviction that we are called to spread that word'. The name Zondervan comes from the Dutch evangelical Lutherans who founded the company in the 1930s. Now it is owned by Rupert Murdoch's News Corporation.

Jackson seemed a sad place. It was even sadder in the motel I was at. It existed, it had a presence, but there was almost as much absence. It offered more shelter against the weather than a tarpaulin, but a tarpaulin would have been better against the spectres of the night. The hotel manager was conspiring with two gents I took to be hitmen when, at about nine o'clock, I went out into the rain and wind and trudged over the concrete and gravel – past Shoney's, Popeye's, a Taco Bell, a Waffle House and a Wendy's – to a Whataburger. Across the rainswept highway, next to the Texaco, next to the Shell that was also the liquor store, was a Homer's Barbecue – but it was closed. The road was a six-lane highway, and to provide rest for those who travelled it there was a Holiday Inn, a Days Inn, a Red Roof Inn, a Quality Inn, a Hampton Inn and a Best Western.

I went into Whataburger and ordered a chicken salad to go. I was the only customer. It came with vinaigrette in a plastic tub, crackers in a plastic bag, and six croutons, two napkins, and a plastic knife and fork in a cardboard box. Back at the hotel I ate three mouthfuls and tipped it all in the trash and allowed myself the thought that there is an impoverished strand in American life. It's the car, of course. These cities without people, the roads without pavements, the chicken without taste, the cardboard and plastic without end – blame the car. But what explains the prodigious general appetite?

It wasn't the motel, or the food. It was the place. It was the South. On the morning I arrived, the city presented as nine parts dead. Like so many other cities, some time ago it took the modern way and emptied itself of all humanity – except the part of it that works in offices. Out along the highway, no doubt there was a mall where life existed, but only a car could get you there. Civility, however, lived on. Three people I passed in the street said: 'How are you doin', sir?' and another said it while overtaking me. When William Tecumseh Sherman told the South that all he wanted was their obedience, he left them with their graces as well as their Negroes and lands and all, and in some quarters with a gelatinous sentimentality. Near the old Capitol, on the rise with the Confederate Monument, there's a memorial with these words:

How sweet must be the peace that heroes find when,
Crusade ended, death has borne them home,
Home to God who made their soldiers' hearts
Beat with selfless zeal to right Satanic wrong.

If it weren't so sanctimonious it might be treason. You wish for Sherman to return and set them straight about who seceded and started the bloody war. Jackson was one of the towns Sherman burned down in the Civil War. He did it so thoroughly that it was called 'Chimneyville' for a while – chimneys being the only things left standing.

As a general, Sherman has been ranked with Julius Caesar. At other times he has been called a harbinger of twentieth-century totalitarianism and Total War. Whatever one makes of him, when he defeated the Confederate army at Atlanta and put the city to the torch he very likely saved the Union: very likely, because the victory in Atlanta saved Abraham Lincoln from electoral defeat. In photos taken by Matthew Brady in that year of 1864 and after Lincoln's death in 1865, the general's frame is as gaunt and narrow as a greyhound's and the great head seems not to fit it properly. He has a massive brow, a raptor's eyes fixed on some helpless and contemptible prey in the corner, a mouth weighted down, a ravaged right cheek and hair that looks as if he combed it with his bayonet. There's violence in Sherman's face. More so than Grant's, and much more so than Pershing's, Patton's or Macarthur's, Sherman's is the face of the United States in its military aspect. 'Shock and Awe' might be traced to Sherman.

He got his military spurs in the 1840s, at the fag end of the Seminole Wars in Florida, rounding up the few remaining Indian families 'concealed in the most inaccessible hammocks and swamps' and – minus any warriors the soldiers thought it best to kill – shipping them west in irons. After the Civil War, while leading the campaign against the Plains Indians, he declared his intention to impose the 'final solution of the Indian problem'. 'War is war,' he said, as if by then there were any doubt.

The unflinching pragmatist was just one of the American archetypes Sherman's character contained: he was also the failed adventurer and habitual loser who, in the end, knew triumph and fame; the frontier tough guy with the PhD in life; the liberator; the Jeremiah; the great general. He was also the master of psychology. He terrorised the enemy with words as well as deeds. To defeat the Confederacy he declared his intention to 'reach them in their recesses' and in their 'very bowels'; and this he did, making generations of Southerners hate him for it, even though they shared his beliefs that Negroes were not worthy of the vote, nor of much else that civilisation offered.

He left Atlanta 'smouldering and in ruins, the black smoke rising high in the air, and hanging like a pall over the ruined city', and as his soldiers made their way towards the sea, they destroyed the plantations and railways and burned the crops that made the Confederate campaign possible. As they marched, the men sang *Glory, Glory, Hallelujah* and the bands played patriotic airs. Forty days later Sherman rode into Savannah, Georgia, with 65,000 Union soldiers 'in splendid flesh and condition'. He wrote at once to President Lincoln: 'I beg to present you as a Christmas gift, the city of Savannah with 150 heavy guns and plenty of ammunition, also about 25,000 bales of cotton.'

Sherman led an army of both conquest and liberation. 'The Negroes,' he wrote, 'were simply frantic with joy.' While the soldier in him worried that in the jubilation of deliverance they would follow him and 'load us down with useless mouths', he admitted he was not immune to the sentiment overflowing: 'Whenever they heard my name, they clustered about my horse, shouted and prayed in their peculiar style, which had a natural eloquence that would have moved a stone.' But Sherman, who could be more like a stone than most men, had little time for Negroes or their emancipation. If indeed he was moved at all by their gratitude, it was not so much as would delay or obscure his purpose.

'War is cruelty, and you cannot refine it,' the general said. 'But you cannot have peace and a division of our country.' On this unyielding assessment, and on the lives of a half-million soldiers, the Union was re-established. On it, also, the South re-established itself, like a tumour. The Negroes Sherman didn't want, Southerners wanted – for cheap labour and the pleasure afforded one category of people by the presence of another they have rendered subservient and inferior.

In 1870 a Fifteenth Amendment to the Constitution guaranteed that the right to vote was not 'denied or abridged . . .

on account of race, colour, or previous condition of servitude', but the era of 'Black Reconstruction' lasted not much more than a decade. The obedience to US laws Sherman had demanded, the Southern states sullenly gave: and then they wrote some of their own. There grew in the South a regime of segregation, discrimination and exploitation hardly less vicious and humiliating than slavery had been. No longer could white men and women own and sell black men and women, but they retained a licence to do with them pretty well what they liked. The Civil War delivered black Americans from slavery to a form of institutionalised terror and abuse known as Jim Crow. It was the 1960s before the next deliverance came.

—

Leaving Birmingham, the station attendant told me that they'd taken off the sleeping carriage, so those who had booked berths would have to sit up like everyone else. He looked glum, but not in the way people are glum when they have had training in hospitality. It was true glumness. He was sorry. It could be that Amtrak staff are civil because the people who are their customers tend to be drawn from much the same level of society as themselves. It could just as well be that civility is good policy and the best defence against neurosis when every train is late, the rolling stock is run-down, most of the stations are primitive and the politicians and media wiseacres never tire of saying that your company blights the economic landscape and should be closed down. Someone should tell them that while there is no saying when your journey will end on an Amtrak train, you don't always want it to.

I read in the paper that Dr Adrian Rogers, international evangelist, founder of Love Worth Finding Ministries and Pastor Emeritus of the Bellevue Baptist Church, had died in Memphis; or, as Dr Rogers put it in a fundraising letter as death approached: 'God has called me into His glorious presence and

I am now with our dear Lord Jesus.' A Calvinist might reckon that an outrageous presumption, but Dr Rogers did not hold with Calvinism any more than he held with homosexuality, abortion or the rights of Palestinians. He believed in 'biblical inerrancy', and the duty of Christians to involve themselves in politics, capital punishment and the invasion of Iraq. 'When I'm with you, I feel closer to the Lord,' James Dobson of Focus on the Family told him. It was Dr Rogers who led the fundamentalist takeover of the Southern Baptist Convention, which led the former president Jimmy Carter to leave it. While the old Calvinist churches are dropping away, Dr Rogers' church has 16.3 million members.

We arrived in Atlanta an hour and a half behind schedule, almost to the minute. Atlanta is the jewel of the modern South; a sprawling, spreading city of five million people, more than half of whom are African American. National Highways 20 and 75 meet in the centre of Atlanta. The airport is an international hub. Downtown sparkles. And the Amtrak station has two public phones, two Pepsi machines, parking for a dozen cars and no taxi rank.

Martin Luther King was born in Atlanta and is buried there, next to the King Center. You walk down a hill from the supermodern Atlanta CBD, down Auburn Avenue and under a freeway through 'Sweet Auburn', once 'the richest Negro street in the world'. There's a little museum housing various black American inventions (including the golf tee) and mementoes of black commercial enterprises. But Atlanta's considerable black middle class doesn't live here any more. On the way to the King Center you pass defunct and down-at-heel businesses, boarded-up shops and groups of lost and listless-looking youths. Across the street from the Ebenezer Baptist Church, where King and his father both preached and where both their funerals were held, a couple of voodoo shops were operating.

A blind attendant offered a cursory welcome to the

Ebenezer Church. His dog was asleep under the front pew. A recording of a speech King gave at Selma, Alabama, in 1965 came from a speaker next to the little pulpit, the organ and choir stalls behind it. In 1974 King's mother was shot dead while playing the Lord's Prayer on the organ. The church is plain: white walls and ceiling, red carpets and pew cushions, a stained-glass window with Jesus in the Garden of Gethsemane and below it a white illuminated cross. I took a seat next to the dog and listened to King.

At his funeral in 1968, 800 people somehow crammed into this church and 60,000 waited outside in Auburn Avenue. From here, the leaders of black America locked arms with famous white liberals and walked behind the coffin on a wagon drawn by mules to the graveside. Marlon Brando, Harry Belafonte, Vice President Hubert Humphrey and Edward, Ethel and Jackie Kennedy were there. Now there was not a soul in the church: just King's voice, which has the power to stir something in a human being the way a wolf's howl stirs something. And then a family of black English tourists came in, walked down the aisle talking in Cockney accents, crossed in front of the pulpit, walked up the other aisle and left, all in the space of a minute.

His words are inscribed on the crypt – 'Free at last, free at last. Thank God Almighty, I'm free at last' – but there's no sense of liberation at the King Center. Where one might have expected busloads of black pilgrims, there were just a few Japanese and the English family. The story of how the civil-rights movement delivered the South from Jim Crow and segregation is laid out, but there was no-one there to see it. There was not a single African American in the building except for the staff. On the TV screen in the souvenir shop they played the speech King gave in Memphis on 3 April 1968. By then the movement was fragmenting. Black power was rising as King's non-violent remedies lost ground. He had declared his opposition to the war in Vietnam. He had proposed widening the front to a campaign for all the poor of America. That was why he was in Memphis: to support the city's sanitation workers, part of the Poor People's Campaign he had launched in the last half of 1966. He expected to be killed, but it didn't matter. He just wanted to do God's will, and God had let him go up to the mountain top and look over into the Promised Land. 'I may not get there with you,' he said, but 'we as a people will get there'. He was happy. He was 'not fearing any man'. His eyes had seen the glory.

The following evening, in a room of the cheerless Lorraine Motel, Martin Luther King prepared himself for a speech at the Memphis Temple. He shaved with Magic Shave Powder and, while his friend the Reverend Ralph Abernathy went to get him some cologne, King walked onto the balcony. That was when James Earl Ray, hiding in a nearby rooming house, shot him through the right side of his face.

That it was all the work of one man, and a man without a history of violent crime, was not a story that satisfied everybody, of course – not then and not now. It was well known that J. Edgar Hoover, the FBI boss, loathed King and thought him, if not a communist, then a stooge of communists – a communist who wanted to stir up trouble in the South. From the nation's highest offices to the humblest white trash homes, there were people with reason to want him gone. Riots broke out all over the United States. Forty-six people died; 35,000 were injured; 20,000 were gaoled. Fifty-five thousand troops were stationed in 110 cities across the country.

There was not a soul outside the King Center: in the green park and the red brick and the marble, not a hint of feeling. The King family are reported to be arguing about handing over the Center to the National Parks Service; selling King's deteriorating papers for $20 million to private collectors; deciding which of the sons will have the lucrative job of running the Center. *The Atlanta Journal-Constitution* reported that $11 million is needed for repairs, and that since 2005 $4.2 million has been paid into a company owned by Dexter King, the son who at present controls the board. The article said that Dexter went to Graceland to learn how to turn his father's legacy to gold. A journalist, Leonard Pitts, wrote that an interview with King's widow, Coretta, cost him $5000. The family has licensed King's image and voice. They sued *USA Today* for publishing the text of the Lincoln Memorial speech. They demanded payment for the construction of a monument in Washington. When Coretta King died in 2006, while Americans from the president down honoured a woman of dignity, courage and principle, the message had already been posted on the King Center website: 'Make an online donation in living memory.'

It sounds like the grossest venality, but they are not the first people to take advantage of a father's or more distant forebear's fame or success. 'Venal' is one word for it. 'Entrepreneurial' is another.

To the extent that black Americans can rise from poverty and the 'hood', it is not always an unalloyed good to do so: it is admirable, just and necessary, but it also fractures. Moving to a better suburb and up the salary scale is no proof against prejudice, and the successful still have their battles to fight. In similar vein, the leaders of black America enjoy salaries, lifestyle and connections to political and corporate power that put them worlds away not only from the realities of life for most black Americans, but also from their forebears in the civil-rights movement. Thurgood Marshall never knew such luxuries. Martin Luther King never dreamed of them. While their successors can hardly be blamed because they do know them and do dream of them, they will never have the transforming power of those men.

———

Jeff rooted for the Dallas Cowboys.

'Why root for the Dallas Cowboys when you're from Virginia?' I asked him.

He spoke in a deep, perfectly elocuted drawl: 'You might ask that, sir, seeing how most people around here are Redskins people. I root for the Dallas Cowboys because they are America's team. They always have been seen as America's team.'

I asked him why that was so.

'Yes sir, good question,' he replied. 'It's because of the way they always play. Their arrogance. They've been in seven Super Bowls, and won four of them. You can't beat that. My roommate, he roots for the Redskins and we always argue about it, but I always say you can't beat that. And you can't. No sir.'

Jeff can't have been a pound less than thirty stone. A car passed with two banners flying from the windows and he said: 'Yes sir, the basketball season has begun.'

He didn't support a basketball team. His sports were professional football and Nascar. Dallas in football and, until his death in 2001, Dale Earnhardt Senior in Nascar.

'Why Dale Earnhardt Senior?' I asked.

Well, Jeff also supported his son, Dale Earnhardt Junior, but to a lesser extent. Overall, these days he roots for Chevrolet.

'Is that right?' I said.

'Yes sir,' he said. 'Dale Earnhardt Senior was the greatest Nascar driver ever.'

'And what made him so good?'

'His arrogance. He'd sooner spin you off the track than go past you.'

'Mean, was he?' I said.

'Yes sir. Mean. But gentle. He was gentle, sir.'

I asked if he drove Chevrolets.

'Yes sir, he did.'

As if I didn't know.

———

That night in Atlanta the train was three hours late, a minor matter in the great scheme of things. Amtrak and all who travel on her do not live in the same dimension as the rest of America: time exists, but not as consistently as it does elsewhere. For one of the missing hours I waited in the little station watching the Houston Astros play the Chicago Cubs. Period posters on the walls drew us out of ourselves and into an Arcadia of sunshine and locomotives and sophisticated others laughing gaily on the way to catch their trains. 'Magic,' they said. There were no lockers so I dragged my luggage across to the Borders bookshop. Borders had wireless internet and a café with an extensive menu. Nowhere in America does Amtrak have wireless internet and in very few places are there cafés.

The *Crescent* came in at 11.18 pm, which meant the dining car was closed, but the snack bar was open. I tried the bagel. Amtrak bagels come in a vacuum wrapping. The whole thing is heated in a microwave, along with the cream cheese which comes inside a sort of plastic ravioli. The heating turns the bagel into rubber and the cream cheese into sour milk. They put it in a cardboard box with a plastic knife and a serviette, and when you've eaten it you have to sit quite still for an hour, like a cormorant after swallowing a salmon, and let the thing dissolve inside you. I lay in my bunk, swaying in the dark, as the *Crescent* cantered towards Virginia – I imagined through deep woods.

The Charlottesville cab driver who took me in his old black Ford Galaxy from the station to the Days Inn spoke in a wise and compelling baritone. His name was Michael and he inclined to the Republican Party, which he conceded was not common among black Americans. No-one on either side of politics much appealed to him, but he thought Bill Frist the most impressive. He'd only have Hillary Clinton if she'd 'start believing in something of her own' and not whatever she thought convenient.

'The president of the United States needs to be strong,' he said. 'The president must believe in the United States and be willing to do whatever it takes to protect the country.' That's why Bush was right. 'Someone keeps breaking into your house, sooner or later you got to go get 'em.'

But it wasn't Iraq that was breaking in, I said. Maybe Bush should have gone after the Saudis.

'The Saudi thing is too political,' he said.

I asked him if the next day he'd take me out to Monticello, which, as every student of American history and Palladian architecture knows, was the home of Thomas Jefferson.

On the television in the Charlottesville Days Inn, Matt Austin gave thanks to the good Lord who had been 'watching over' him all year. 'He's been protecting me. So all credit to Him,' he says. Matt's from Texas. He wears thick, rimless glasses, and if he took off his big white Texan hat he'd look at home in a 1920s Berlin bar. He's in Oklahoma City and he's just got off a bull, so he's a bit dusty and short of breath. Those bulls are big and specially bred to buck like fiends and make rag dolls of any human being who gets on their backs. Most of the riders last three or four seconds, but Matt has hung on till the bell and won the event. He's high in the 'world rankings' and a real prospect for the upcoming 'world championship'. Tonight he has beaten, among others, Howdy Cloud and Tate Stratton; and of course the bulls: bulls that go by names as various as Manifest Destiny and Typhus. After barely surviving his bull – it might have been Whisker Burn – Tate dropped to his knees in the rodeo ring, looked up to the darkened sky and crossed himself.

At the Starbucks in the street where students from the University of Virginia promenade, *Autumn Leaves* was playing on a trumpet. Starbucks' founders married the name of the first mate on the *Pequod* in *Moby Dick* to what they called 'the romance of Italian coffee bars' and created a giant American mutant. The thing about first entering a Starbucks is not to be intimidated by all the varieties of Frappucino and Mocha Grande Latte, nor even the Quadruple Grande Americano. Remember, this company declares profits of more than $2 billion a quarter, so they know what they're doing. And the basic coffee is good, at least if you can stop them before they fill the cardboard cup with froth. It takes a long while to eat a cup full of froth with one of those ice-cream sticks they use for spoons, and then you have to get rid of the cup. They should use edible cups – and sticks.

But you can sit around for as long as you like in Starbucks, checking your email, surfing the net, preparing your balance sheet or PowerPoint slides. You can read *Moby Dick* from beginning to end and no waiter will bother you, because they don't have them. What they do have is a smell which, though unlike the smell in Italian cafés and not the same as a whaling ship's, is nevertheless 'the most powerful non-verbal signal' the company has. That's how the chief executive of Starbucks puts it, and with profits like that, who is going to argue with him? I became addicted to Starbucks in America. I searched for the sign everywhere. I developed brand loyalty.

The Jefferson Society takes the view, the Monticello tour guide told us, that Thomas and his black servant Sally Hemmings *were* in an intimate relationship and that Sally's children were Thomas's. Nevertheless, when it was suggested that a road be named Sally Hemmings Drive, Jefferson's descendants successfully opposed it. Hemmings's descendants were in favour.

A man in the tour party must have been seven feet tall in his prime; and being very thin and with a grey moustache turned up at the tips, he looked like Peter the Great. Though he was stooped with old age, his walking-stick was taller than his wife. He knew all the Jeffersonian fundamentals: the tour guide posed the questions in his silky Southern way, and the tall man answered them. He knew that a township was thirty-six square miles; that with his polygraph as an aide, Jefferson left for posterity 19,000 letters; and that he'd died on 4 July 1826, which was fifty years exactly after Independence and four hours before his friend John Adams – and he could bring all these things to his old mind before the rest of us could blink. He knew that Jefferson believed in 'a wall of separation' between church and state; that 'amalgamation' of the races was degrading to the human character yet he kept a black concubine; and that he opposed slavery yet kept slaves. So did James Madison, the fourth president and 'Father of the Constitution', who lived forty miles from Jefferson. Madison had a hundred or so of them.

It was a golden day. Golden leaves lay thick on Jefferson's grave. Monticello glowed. It is not hard to understand why Jefferson loved it; why all those Virginians loved it; why Madison said he lived 'a squirrel's jump from heaven'. It was, as well, not hard to imagine why Jefferson could write that all men are created equal, even as he looked out from his study in Monticello and saw men labouring in the fields who were his slaves; or that he could write 'When a long train of abuses and usurpations . . . evinces a design to reduce them under absolute despotism, it is their right, it is their duty, to throw off such government . . .' without drawing back for fear he was making his Declaration of Independence a manifesto for a slaves' rebellion. It was a reasonable inference from the beauty and the harmony of everything within the scene that the 'laws of nature and of nature's God' had thus intended it. It was self-evident.

On the way back, Michael said he couldn't help but have 'mixed feelings' about Jefferson. I asked him if he thought black America was making any progress.

'Creeping progress,' he said. 'The problem is psychological.' Martin Luther King was a great man, but it was going to take longer than anyone of King's generation had imagined, he said. It was like the years after emancipation: everyone thought things would get better straight away, but in some ways Jim Crow was worse than slavery. It was the same with desegregation: it made some things more difficult, created the psychological problems. 'We're still working through desegregation,' he said. He thought it was going to take a couple more generations. Michael believed too many black Americans had an inferiority complex. Too many blamed white Americans for everything. All they saw was their own disadvantage.

'They do bad at school, and never think they can do better in life.' Young black men had too much pride, too much ego. It gets wounded when they're young and doesn't heal. 'Ninety-one per cent of millionaires are self-made men,' Michael said. 'I tell 'em that they got to remember that. They got to recognise that to be successful you have to believe in yourself. Themselves is what's holding them back. God put everyone here for a purpose, and each and every one has some purpose to fulfil.'

The bus connecting Charlottesville to Richmond – and Amtrak's *Crescent* line to the *Palmetto* – couldn't leave until the train came in, and the train was five hours late. It took another hour to get to Richmond, which made six hours in all. General Lee would have reached it sooner on his grey horse. I travelled with a blonde woman on her way to Florida who was wearing a

T-shirt that said no-one would mock her generation or her God.

Lee's horse would have taken him directly to his quarters; I waited another hour and a half at Richmond's Amtrak station for a taxi. I waited with a woman whose train from Washington, where she worked, had been cancelled, and the one she took instead didn't stop at Fredericksburg, where she lived. There was no train back to Fredericksburg until the morning. Born and raised in New Orleans, she said she'd never been conscious of her colour until she joined the navy and was posted to Maine. She served for ten years, most of it in Guam; and, after 9/11, that experience had set her up for a job in the new Department of Homeland Security. It did seem a strange thing that in the superpower's hub, an employee of Homeland Security – believing in 'accountability and teamwork to achieve efficiencies, effectiveness and operational synergies' – had to spend a night sleeping on a bench in a railroad station.

I had learned that it is now almost unknown for passengers to step from trains into the Union Station and from the station into a Main Street hotel. One's arrival can no longer be conspicuous or charged with meaning, as it was in the old films. If the old Union Station is used at all, in most cases the city's heart has moved away from it. But rarely has it moved as far, or even in the same direction as the highway clusters of chain motels and chain fast-food outlets that gather on the fringes of every city and substantial town across the United States. These clusters are the Union Stations of the late twentieth century, but trains don't run there. Train travellers do not book hotels there. But I did. This Holiday Inn was called the Crossroads Holiday Inn – and it was a reasonable name, in the circumstances.

When I opened the curtains in the morning I saw the intersection of two six-lane highways. It was a comfortable, well-equipped, practical sort of place, as Holiday Inns tend to be. You can be happy at a place like this so long as you stay away from the coffee. And the restaurant, if you want to be sure. Perhaps not happy, but not unhappy. Or if unhappy, at least not threatened. A good motel creates a kind of stasis for the soul in transit. One should leave no worse than one arrived: that is the minimum requirement.

It being October, there were pumpkins in the foyer. There are pumpkins everywhere at this time of the year. Americans put pumpkins on the verandahs of their houses, or if they haven't a verandah, in the garden, or in a window. Many people put lights inside their pumpkins, and Amtrak travellers can see them glowing as they whip by in the night or linger in an anonymous siding. It is surprising that so few houses fail to observe the custom. Halloween is a ritual of signal importance in the associative life of the United States. The pumpkins appear to be all of the same (large) size, colour and variety: orange, and taller than they are wide.

It is another custom for farmers to allow people to pick their own pumpkin from their fields. So, as well as pumpkins on every porch, one sees pumpkins in unlikely profusion along roads and rail lines. The year before, there had been a scandal when the press revealed that in some fields the pumpkins were not the natural offspring of the vines by which they rested. A few cynical farmers had taken to adding pumpkins grown elsewhere. To be truthful, I thought as much the first time I saw about 500 pumpkins in a half-acre patch, evenly distributed and all sitting on their ends in the moonlight.

At the shopping centre on the other side of the freeway there were pumpkins everywhere, and all the kids were dressed as witches and wizards and the like as they went from store to store in search of free candy. They had so much candy they had to ask their parents to carry their broomsticks, which made it harder for the parents to film their children on video cameras. The scene was pretty happy, nonetheless, and good for the economy. It was only eleven in the morning, but a couple of families had already sidled over to the counter beneath a sign that said: SHOVE SUM CHICK'N DOWN YER CHIMNEY!

On television that evening the Fox people seemed ever so slightly rattled about Special Prosecutor Patrick Fitzgerald's judgement on the Lewis 'Scooter' Libby/Valerie Plame story, but President Bush's new nomination for the Supreme Court, Samuel Alito, was a bigger story for the time being. The Jack Abramoff corrupt Indian lobbying story was nosing its way into the picture, however, and threatened to be bigger than both of them. Senator Edward Kennedy, looking ever more like some benign forest-dwelling critter, came forth to question Alito's appointment. In *The New York Times*, David Brooks accused the Democrats of being too gleeful about Bush's recent failures, which seemed a little unfair given the gloating from the White House – and from an aircraft carrier and a golf course – not so long before. Fox News, along with its Murdoch syndicated print-news friends, thundered away as every day they do, feverishly emoting in the name of liberty and moral clarity – though the latter seemed to be less fashionable now that things had grown confused in Baghdad. But the wheels did seem to wobble in the conservative camp. The president maintained his smile – but so do many creatures when they're cornered – and his swagger. 'Nobody who had a serious end in view could walk like that,' Hermann Broch once said about one of his characters.

Politics aside, that night on television there was nothing but America for Americans to see. America contains multitudes, as we know, but TV is the great kitchen blender. It makes pap mainly, but more importantly, pap from which it is impossible to form even a remotely informed view of the rest of the world. There is America, and the nearest places after that are heaven and hell.

'Reason and free enquiry are the only effectual agents

against error,' Thomas Jefferson wrote in 1781. 'They are the only natural enemies of error, and of error only.' If you read it slowly, it has the cadence of early advertising. But Jefferson knew nothing of such things, or of brand loyalty, or of spin. His words are inscribed on the walls of the Virginia State Library, which stands among the other neoclassical buildings of the old Confederate capital. The Capitol would make a very respectable seat of government for any middle-ranking nation. It did for President Jefferson Davis during the four years of the Civil War that cost the Confederate states a quarter of a million lives, and now it does for the state of Virginia. The statue there of Robert E. Lee on his horse, Traveller, is everything a statue should be. No-one does equestrian statues better than the Americans: understandably so, because no country owes more to the horse.

Taken simply and as a whole, Richmond is beautiful and impressive to the eye, but to the mind it speaks mainly of error. Perhaps it was because it was a Saturday and the streets were all but empty – or because a person can have too much of the neoclassical, too many columns and domes, flags and even equestrian statues – but the city seemed like a museum of unreason, a temple of vanities. There was something bloated and corpse-like about it. The Museum of the Confederacy, the White House of the Confederacy, the pyramid with 18,000 soldiers of the Confederacy buried under it: it was too much of the Confederacy altogether.

Tocqueville saw reason when he wrote 'there is no intervening state that can last between excessive inequality created by slavery and complete equality naturally promoted by independence'. The Confederates didn't see it. They thought slavery could last forever. Richmond is the intervening state. The Confederate flag still flies there: a sign of life to distinguish this city from the ruins of those other slave states, ancient Greece and Rome.

Walk beyond the boundaries of the old city and look up from the James River and it *is* imposing. But walk a little further and you find yourself confronted by the massive freeway that rips through the heart of Richmond and cuts it off from the river. In this, it's like many American cities where roads have been built like parasites along the paths of great rivers and railways. You can lament their demotion and still find vertiginous, gut-churning pleasure in standing on a bridge and looking down on the mighty, roaring American road. Walk on and you will find yourself amid black poverty – and the instinct, felt first in your head and a moment later in your legs, is to retreat, find an exit, vanish, before that surly look on the faces of the young men turns in your direction.

———

In the Amtrak station in Richmond, while I waited for the train south to Savannah, CNN announced that six US soldiers had died in Iraq the day before. The total for October was ninety. CNN moved on to another story. The people in the waiting room went back to their newspapers, magazines and phones. Did their minds silently register some emotion? Did they think, at that moment, what the memorials would later declare – that these people died in the defence of their freedom and to make their families safe? To protect them? Did they think they died for democracy? Did they feel the bond with these dead soldiers that the president and the vice president would say they felt the next time they addressed some cheering element of the armed forces?

CNN moved on to the memorial service for Rosa Parks, whose body lay in honour in Washington DC. Forty thousand people came to the Capitol Rotunda to see her. Two thousand, five hundred crowded into the African Methodist Episcopal Church for a memorial service and many more joined in the singing outside. Then her body was flown to Detroit, where in the Greater Grace Temple, Aretha Franklin was singing to 4000 people. The funeral would go on for eight hours.

For grandeur it lacked little in comparison with Princess Diana's funeral, and it said as much as about the soul of the United States as Diana's did about her particular world. Both Clintons spoke, as did the young black 'presidential hopeful' Barack Obama. Every speaker referred to her grace, humility and courage. But it was also a very political funeral, a call to arms for black America. The Reverend Jesse Jackson said President Bush's nomination to the Supreme Court of an 'extreme right-wing judge', Samuel Alito, on the same day he purported to honour Rosa Parks was 'hypocrisy'. Congressman John Conyers, in whose office Parks worked for many years, told the congregation that America was engaged in a race between its 'imperial destiny' and its 'democratic destiny'. He said Rosa taught him that 'you can't maintain a democracy and an empire simultaneously'.

An hour behind schedule, the train positively streaked through the woods of North Carolina: shadowy green-gold woods, shadows million upon million, blown about by the breezes. No shadow in nature is ever still, John Constable said. Among my father's very few books was one called *Nick in the Woods*, by Robert Montgomery Bird. As I recall, what Nick did in the woods was hunt Indians and wild creatures. And sometimes he was hunted. It was man against savage or varmint. And man against shadow.

'They recognised at once their Old Testament foe in the New World wilderness,' the Kiowa poet and artist N. Scott Momaday wrote. 'The Fiend was everywhere present in the painted faces which peered from behind the trees and in the suspicious forms which strode noiselessly over the brittle leaves.' That view of the Indians was the moral foundation for slaughtering them, taking their land without compensation, denying them natural and legal rights. 'On this day we have sent six hundred heathen souls to hell,' said the Reverend Cotton Mather after English settlers wiped out the Pequods in 1637.

The woods of the United States are beautiful beyond words, and they are as well a battleground of the imagination. Fear and temptation and the 'salutary dogma of original sin' (to use Momaday's words) stalk those who walk in them; so it is wise to carry a gun, or at least a Bowie knife and a Bible.

Wherever the woods ended, a brown cotton field began, or a patch of houses gathered for no purpose that I could identify: simple, unfenced bungalows with mown grass all round, a shrub sometimes, but not a vegetable or flower. The sun set over swamps, cotton fields and trailer parks. The farmers' houses were two-storey, white and finely proportioned, with verandahs looking over manicured grass. There is an aesthetic to American rural housing: they do not nestle into nature, but stand apart from it assertively, perhaps also to see enemies coming. With a flag – Confederate, state or the Stars and Stripes – every family home is a patriotic statement, a miniature White House, America personified.

The train stopped in Kingstree, South Carolina. It stretched through the town and cars lined up on either side of the crossing. The conductor stepped down with his little yellow step and, in this quaint Victorian way, half a dozen new passengers got on. A decrepit little used-car lot had a big sign out the front, roughly made as if by a citizen who had a sudden thought upon waking: TRUST JESUS.

Unlike Atlanta and Jackson – and Columbia, South Carolina – Sherman did not burn Savannah down when he took it in 1864. For this reason, today's Savannah is very like the one he described in his memoirs. The trees made it then and they make it now. The Regency houses in the elegant squares, 'though comfortable', said Sherman – who had seen inside a few good houses in the previous year or two – 'would hardly make a display on Fifth Avenue or the Boulevard Haussmann'. But the 'majestic live-oak trees . . . covered with grey and funereal moss' he found 'sublime'. The trees and the moss are still there and still sublime – and still, one imagines, 'gloomy after a few days camping under them'.

I chose the Thunderbird Inn, which was billed on the internet as a classic renovated retro masterpiece of the 1950s. It did look the part, with the neon sign and the girl in the office paring her nails, a Coke machine her only friend. In the manner of classic motels, you could spit on the road from the door of your room. But there was a smell inside that penetrated the sinuses like a bamboo skewer and went deeper by the minute. The girl gave me a key to another room where the smell was less venomous but, it turned out, insidious. Was it a smell of the 1950s that I had forgotten? Or the cockroaches? Stepping out of the shower, I was confronted by a roach as big as a small mouse, sitting back on its hind legs like a kangaroo defending its territory. It took three blows with my suitcase to finish him. It was an American cockroach – a species that came from Africa with the slave ships – and I wondered if his ancestors had seen Sherman march in. With such a story behind him, I might have felt guilty about taking his life; but as Sherman said to the mayor of Atlanta, my actions 'were not designed to meet the humanities of the case'.

The taxi driver had left her home in Michigan fifteen years ago. She had just packed up and put the children in the car and drove away, leaving behind her husband who used to get drunk and beat her black and blue. The Gulf War was on at the time and she had a sister in the services in Savannah, so that was where she headed, hoping to see her before she wound up in Iraq. The husband she left was now in gaol and he'd be there 'for a long time', she said. She'd divorced him and married another man, but at the age of thirty-nine he ran off with an eighteen-year-old.

She asked about the Thunderbird Motel and was not surprised when I told her about the smell. For years it was the place where all the hookers took their johns, she said. Then it was renovated on the cheap: they just got the roaches out and gave it a coat of paint. She wondered if it 'smelt of pee'.

'Worse than pee,' I said.

She gave me some Tylenol for my sinuses. It's a bad town for sinuses, she said. Later I read in the *The Best Guide to Allergy*: 'When they die or are exterminated, cockroaches slowly dry out and are pulverized, eventually creating a strong airborne allergen. Their faeces are also allergenic. This explains the special advantages of the cockroach mould. As the ad. says, "They check in but they don't check out."'

I was panhandled within minutes of leaving the motel. He even looked like a panhandler: comically spruced up to hide the fact that he'd slept under a bridge, but with enough Southern graciousness to suggest he'd been raised in a good home. I thought at once that he might be living in the shadow of an overbearing father, but that was not the line he used on me. He said his house in Florida had been all but demolished by Hurricane Wilma; that the mission in Savannah had refused to take him in because he was not a local; and that now he was trying to find his sister who, last he heard, was living somewhere in Georgia. I gave him five dollars. He took it with the merest nod of his head and went straight across the road to pitch his story to a man in a suit. I was standing somewhere between the grave of the seventeenth-century Creek Indian leader Tomo Chi-Chi and the Lutheran Church of the Ascension, while a black man with a long beard played *The Star-Spangled Banner* on a saxophone. He didn't play it well but the effect was poignant. He then played *Mona Lisa*. I gave him a couple of dollars. He asked me where I was from, and when I told him he extended his hand to me and said: 'Welcome to America.'

Savannah is a very musical city, the young attendant at the art museum told me. He liked all music, including Bach, Dvořák and Chopin, and composed gospel music for his church. Like Bach, he said. His family has 'always' lived in Savannah, which probably meant that they were among those delivered on that day in 1864 'by an angel of the Lord'. We were in a room full of Maxfield Parrish paintings of implausibly gorgeous women in Grecian gowns playing lutes or dancing in untrammelled nature. The attendant, whose name was Anthony, liked one in which they played on the edge of a mighty canyon. 'I ain't ever been half so relaxed in my life,' he said.

Savannah, as the signs say, has 'given freely of its sons' and not only in the Civil War. In the War of Independence it was besieged by the French. It gave freely again in the First and Second World Wars. A memorial among the live-oaks had the names of 130 men who made the 'ultimate sacrifice' in Vietnam. Savannah's population is 130,000. To match Savannah's sacrifice in Vietnam, Australia – America's most avid ally – would have lost not 500 men but at least 15,000. There are memorials to sons freely given in thousands of towns across the United States. The numbers of dead are shocking. Reading of them under the oaks and the grey moss of Savannah inspires a kind of horror.

—

The train was not very late leaving Savannah, but there was time to read *The New York Times* while a couple of freight trains passed. Condoleezza Rice was in Canada, telling people up there that their relationship with the United States was 'broad and deep and strong'. Canadians were not inclined to agree: a poll showed more than half of them thought their neighbour was 'rude and greedy and violent'.

General Sherman got what he demanded of the South. The

nation was made one and undivided. But the South was in many things a law unto itself and with allegiances, prejudices and symbols entirely its own. 'Better to die a thousand deaths than submit to live under you or your Government and your negro allies,' General John Hood of the Confederate army wrote to Sherman in 1863, and the same sentiment could still be heard in the South a century later. One of the men who murdered Emmett Till expressed it in 1956: '"Chicago boy," I said, "I'm tired of 'em sending your kind down here to stir up trouble. Goddam you, I'm going to make an example of you – just so everybody can know how me and my folks stand."' And mayors and governors and policemen and civilians said it again and again as the civil-rights movement grew. The South was a 'sickness', as the Washington publicist I. F. Stone wrote in the 1950s; but, as he also wrote, the rest of the country was not immune. Generations of politicians, journalists and teachers gloried in America's freedom while millions of their fellow citizens lived in a police state.

I was one of three white people in the carriage. The black women, as usual, manifested all the self-possession, calm and happiness. All the talk came from them, too. The older black men evinced a faded spirit of survival. The young men, in every case, seemed downcast and suffocating in resentment and self-loathing. It's in the way they walk, their eyes, the tension in their faces, their absurdly oversized clothes. Black male teenagers are the most consistently sad sight in America.

The new investment and the new demographics have done much to change the culture of the South in the years since John Steinbeck drove through. What remains of the sickness is more shadow than substance. But shadows are not without effect. One in three black American males in their twenties is in prison, on bail or under some legal order or supervision. Only one-eighth of the general population, black American men fill half the prison cells.

A hundred and eighty years since its invention, the train still has the power to exhilarate and make us feel like conquerors. We went north towards Washington DC with its shuddering heartbeat, crackling along the plains, wending through the dark woods. On every habitation the flags flew. Across the aisle, a young woman woke and looked out at the setting sun. She put on a pair of sunglasses and pulled her sweater down over her back. Her waking seemed to ignite some sweet perfume in the carriage. Blowing its horn at every half-made track across the line and every forlorn dwelling, the train coursed fearlessly into the dark.

CHAPTER 3

There are lots of folk in Washington
who need vilifying.

Mark Twain

THE ORIGINAL STAR-SPANGLED BANNER, THE FLAG THE AMERICANS
flew when the British were bombing them at Fort McHenry in
1814, is stretched out in an air-conditioned, glass-walled room
in the National Museum of American History in Washington
DC. It was the sight of the original Stars and Stripes flying in
the dawn's early light that inspired the poet Francis Scott Key to
write the anthem now known to the whole world, and which
many cell phones play instead of ringing. Over several years
a team of women and men, playing the country's collective
mother, repaired the vast cloth while visitors observed their
devotions through the glass. One million, seven hundred
thousand stitches held the flag to its original backing: the team
unstitched each one. Through the glass one day they saw a man
with tears in his eyes saluting. Another time they saw schoolgirls
singing the *The Star-Spangled Banner*.

Outside the Museum of Natural History, Japanese with
video cameras captured close-ups of the squirrels. Inside, I

looked at a stuffed passenger pigeon. The earliest Europeans, including the Reverend Cotton Mather, reported seeing them in flocks miles wide that took days to pass, flying at sixty miles an hour. At the beginning of the nineteenth century there were upwards of four billion of them. Someone calculated that 850 square miles of a Wisconsin forest housed 136 million nesting pigeons. They were to the air and the forests what bison were to the plains, but while a few bison survived no passenger pigeons did. The last one, Martha – named after George Washington's wife – died in a Cincinnati museum in 1914. The forests had been reduced, and the birds were hunted in their millions and sold on the streets of eastern cities for fifty cents a dozen, salted.

Washington's soft autumn light was streaked with vapour trails. The planes come in three minutes apart; low over the Lincoln Memorial, down the Potomac until they veer right to Ronald Reagan Airport. They fly low enough to see the rivets in the wings, and the wings reflected in the water. Out the window of the Channel Inn, I watched them landing and taking off. Every half an hour or so, an army helicopter cut its way up the river. The Channel Inn is in a black neighbourhood: it has a black bar and down the road a hundred yards there's a black nightclub called Zanzibar. You can hear jazz from the rooms and from the balconies as the lights go on in the boathouses and cruisers tied up on the river. But then another helicopter goes past, and it's that chopper sound which reminds you that this is United States imperial headquarters.

Hotels do not reveal their character on the first day. Not a lot *have* character, but the ones that do hide for a while behind the standard rituals of civility. The Channel Inn has character. It is an inscrutable place, and the more I stayed the more inscrutable it became. The staff let their moods show. The elderly maître d' in the restaurant greeted me with a smile one night, and the next as if I were his most ardent enemy; the third night he ignored me altogether and on the fourth I might as well have been an old comrade just back from the wars. He must have been seventy-five but he was as moody as a teenager.

The front desk was manned – there were never any women – by someone different every time I passed; he was always white, about twice as old as modern hotel staff and of sallow and mysterious appearance. They were all polite in a cool and distracted way that gave the impression something more important than their guests was going on in their lives: as if, perhaps, a big card game was being played out the back, or Castro was being overthrown in the morning. As with many worthwhile establishments, there was a whiff of something illicit about the place; and a sense that Sydney Greenstreet might appear in the foyer and clip some underling on the ear and tell him to help the lady with her bags. It is certain that nothing short of that could make anyone help a lady at the Channel Inn.

Yet the hotel had many graces. The food in the restaurant was old-fashioned, French- and Southern-influenced, authentic, generous and tasty. The wine list was good. One or two very old white people with white hair and white moustaches dined alone. Younger middle-class black Americans dined in couples and groups. In the mornings in the breakfast room a breezy black cook did eggs to order and served them with crisp bacon and passable coffee. It was another, somehow older world. If you spend a few days at the Channel Inn you can find yourself wondering if this was how Martin Luther King imagined a future America.

Abraham Lincoln – prophet, priest, pharaoh, saviour, idol – looks down from his marble throne in the memorial, the words of his Gettysburg and Second Inaugural addresses inscribed on the walls adjacent. On the television in the tiny bookroom a very young Dan Rather and two other reporters talk to Martin Luther King on *Face the Nation*. These days King's name is uttered with reverence, but in his lifetime he was widely loathed and feared. The reporters ask if J. Edgar Hoover is right to say he is 'under the influence of communists'. King does not blink: communism, he says, practises 'ethical relativism', which he cannot abide. He refers to a few other 'isms', including totalitarianism. He fires out the syllables like balls from a pinball machine. He says it's time Mr Hoover acknowledged the patriotism and loyalty of 'the Negro', even in the long dark night of their experience. More film shows him standing by Lyndon Johnson as the president signed the Civil Rights Bill, which ended segregation – and lost the South for the Democrats – in 1964. King's name is everywhere in the United States: a boulevard or building bears his name in every half-substantial town. Not that anybody was watching him on that television in the Lincoln Memorial: he might as well have been singing *Rambling Rose*.

At the Vietnam Memorial, people attach little American (and Canadian) flags to the names of the 60,000 dead. There are letters from children: Elkred Christian Academy's fifth-graders – with a little help from their teachers, one imagines – thanked the soldiers 'for fighting the evil of communism'. The shining black wall of the memorial moves people in ways that can be seen: they weep, they hold each other, they touch the names, they stay by it as if by the grave of a loved one. Its reflections create a visceral, confusing melancholy. If, as you leave, you find yourself among the rows of lifelike soldiers in the Korean War Veterans Memorial, you will likely sink deeper into the mire.

In the middle of the mall, the new World War II memorial doesn't have the power of Lincoln or Vietnam. Perhaps it is not possible to commemorate the sacrifice in every theatre of war, or to capture the mind-numbing dimensions of the conflict. The memorial is vast, imposing and inclusive to a fault and yet it's a little short on recognition that there were other countries in the fight. Nothing about it, including the prose, has the elegance of the other monuments, much less the original and complex threads that weave through Lincoln's speech. It's the only memorial in the mall that prompts you to think a small corrective is desirable, just to represent another take on freedom. Perhaps, on a noticeboard nailed to a tree, E. E. Cummings (and with his spacing):

why must itself up every of a park

anus stick some quote statue unquote to
prove that a hero equals any jerk
who was afraid to dare to answer "no"?

At the other end of the mall, Ulysses S. Grant guards the Capitol. He sits on his horse wearing his famous hat: the sort of hat Calvin Klein might make from a hog farmer's. During the riots of 1968, machine guns were mounted on the steps behind him. General Sherman, surrounded by Union soldiers, has been allocated the Treasury, but he's only a two-furlong gallop from the White House. 'Served in the Seminole wars, Mexican wars, occupation of California, Civil War, and was commander in chief of US army until 1884,' it says. It's hard to say if he'd approve of the reference to his service in the Seminole Wars. He thought the whole thing wrong-headed. Instead of herding the Seminoles west to land that white men wanted, Sherman believed the government should have left them there in the Everglades and shipped the Cherokees, Chickasaws, Creeks and Choctaws east to join them.

With all the blood and sacrifice and all the blistering and melancholy rhetoric, I took a wrong turn somewhere and found myself on the wrong side of the river and had to plod a couple of miles in the semi-dark in open parkland and under bridges where shadows lurked. I plunged across what felt like a no-man's land where I might be mugged, or mistaken for a spy or a terrorist in the capital of the empire.

By the time I crossed over the Channel, I had gone off Washington and democracy had soured in my mind. That's when I came upon the fish market, full of shrimp, crabs, prawns and oysters – oysters from Chesapeake Bay which, when the first boatload of Englishmen arrived in 1607, 'lay upon the ground as thicke as stones'. There were stalls selling gumbo, chowder, steamed prawns and steamed corn in a green broth. Folk were coming and going carrying the family fish dinners. The market was alive but smelt of an older economy, and was therefore bound for oblivion.

The whites moved to the Washington suburbs a generation ago and left the inner city to the blacks, who burned a lot of it down after King was killed in 1968. Now, despairing of the commuter grind on clogged roads and unreliable public transport, and feeling the same urges that white middle classes have been indulging for some time in other cities, the white population is moving back. Being on the water and ten minutes walk from the mall, the days of the fish market and Zanzibar are numbered. The Channel Inn can't last. One of the hotel chains will take it out and the place will be to independent hotels what Martha was to passenger pigeons.

As the pursuit of happiness is an unalienable right, and happiness depends to such a high degree on your status, and your status on your school and various material emblems of your progress – including the character and colour of your neighbours – an American's suburb is hardly less unalienable than life and liberty. It was inevitable that a system of material rewards has grown up to make this matter of principle an inescapable fact of life. In Washington I met an English journalist who had been reporting from the capital for twenty years and had raised a family there. The county in which they live has an annual education budget of $2.3 billion; which, by way of comparison, is about one-tenth of the total spending on primary and secondary education by all governments in Australia. They moved there because it would have been unfair to their children to stay in the much poorer counties adjacent. American schools are funded by local property taxes, which means very simply that the poorer the county, the poorer the school. In the county where this couple lived, the schools had 'everything'.

The English journalist believed the United States was, in essence, an 'elective monarchy'. This is a radical view. If Americans know one thing, it is that they live in a republic. Only in the republic can those truths they hold to be self-evident *be* self-evident. But even then it seems they make mistakes. Back in May, a morning talk-show host in Denver told me and his million listeners that many Americans have come to think they live in a democracy. But they do not, he said. It is a republic they live in – a republic with democratic institutions. 'A lot of Democrats don't get it,' he said. 'And the people who carp about the Patriot Act or Guantanamo Bay don't get it.' Only the republic is non-negotiable. This was Lincoln's position, after all, when it came down to it in the Civil War. It is the republic that shall not perish from the earth.

If some Americans fail to distinguish between these two distinct conditions, others find it difficult to grasp how America can be at once a republic and an empire – a respectable republic, that is. On these questions, the facts of history seem clear enough: when Alexander Hamilton proposed an elective monarchy to the 1787 Constitutional Convention, his fellow founding fathers replied with an emphatic 'No'. But then, for the most part, America's leaders have said no to the idea of empire. And if they can build a formidable empire without believing in it, very likely they can live in an elective monarchy while believing they live in a republic. And when you stop to think about it – or to watch it – the more they exult in the republic, the more strenuously they defend it and the more they decorate it with symbols and ritual, the more like a monarchy – and the more like Hamilton's vision, rather than Jefferson's – it becomes.

But it is not Hamilton that the English journalist recommends. When he meets people who are new to the United States or are struggling to understand Washington and the White House, he directs them to the *Memoirs on the Reign of Louis XIV, and the Regency* by a courtier, the Duke of Saint-Simon. In Washington today, as once in Versailles, the only question that matters is: 'Who has the king smiled on today?'

This idea – that the presidency, and the political culture, has more in common with pre-enlightenment thought and institutions than the republic is willing or able to allow – has some illustrious supporters. Tocqueville was struck by the natives' willingness to ingratiate themselves and bow and scrape to gain favour and advantage, even in the frontier towns of Tennessee. Much more recently, Lewis Lapham noted that distinctions between democracies and traditional monarchies had grown blurred. The courtier spirit is 'far more necessary to a democracy than to a monarchy', he wrote: and in many more places than the White House, Congress or the political parties. It is true of the corporations and media, for instance: '[A] democracy transforms the relatively few favors in a monarch's gift (sinecure, benefice, patents royal) into the vast supply of grace and favor distributed under the rubrics of tax exemption, defense contract, publication, milk subsidy, tenure.'

Of course, this is not to say that the parallels are complete in every detail: the president's golf cart is only a rough approximation of the 'box' drawn by small horses in which the last French kings liked to get around their gardens, and his security men are postilions only in the broad sense. The point is rather that the American capital, like the French one of old, seethes with deals, intrigues and cabals, and values character assassination and the truckling arts above all others – and that this is not the mere surface of affairs in the republic, but their true nature.

Then there is the matter of the incumbent: competent presidents are replaced by the less competent and they continue to govern long after a majority of voters distrust or despise them. But the office, like the throne, retains its standing. We might expect democracies to adapt to social, technological and geopolitical change: yet, as the British historian Eric Hobsbawm explains, American democratic institutions live in a 'straitjacket of an 18th-century Constitution reinforced by two centuries of Talmudic exegesis by the lawyers . . . [and are] far more frozen into immobility than those of almost all other states'. No woman, Jew, black, 'Hispanic' or even Italian has yet been elected head of state. True, a woman may soon be made president: and if she is, and serves two terms, the White House will have been occupied for twenty-eight years by members of just two families.

For the English journalist, 9/11 was telling evidence for his thesis. The president was not much loved on 8/11, but on 9/11 he was made a king. Conservative columnists came clanking forth with measures to add stronger sinew and bigger teeth to the republic he commanded. He was granted money and powers as required, including the power to eavesdrop on the conversations of his fellow Americans, much as Louis XIV opened the letters of his minions and subjects. Seasoned and respected journalists became courtiers – what better definition is there of 'embedded'? The less-respected lined up like household servants for their briefings and swallowed any morsel they were thrown without so much as sniffing it. Such independent newspapers as still existed and whole media conglomerations and their proprietors became, in effect, royal retainers, and all the while Democrat leaders did imitations of dukes and duchesses in fear of gory execution. And the people bellowed their support.

'For me the president walks on water,' a Vietnam veteran says in the documentary *Why We Fight*. 'He can do no wrong. But if he lies – what is there?' His son had been killed in the World Trade Center attacks and he was so strong in his desire for revenge that he asked the army to put his name on a bomb to be dropped in Iraq. 'Someone did this to us and we had to hit back,' he said, almost as if it had been an act of sorcery. Then the president told the nation that there was no connection between 9/11 and Iraq and that he had never said there was. That's what devastated the vet. One could feel for him, and yet there was something irredeemably infantile about his reaction. No-one – not his school, nor the army, nor his country – had curbed his instinct for revenge or taught him reserve, and no-one had educated him either about the world or his leaders. He had been misled, but it was like misleading a child. Or a subject. Even if Iraq had been responsible for the attack in which his son died, how can a grown man, a veteran soldier, want his son's name on a bomb? And how can the army agree?

The king had indeed changed his tune. It turned out that he had not invaded Iraq for the reasons given at the time. It was not that he or any of those close to him had lied, fibbed or even misspoken. The reason had just gone – poof! Now the reason was to change the face of Islam, to modernise it and liberate adherents from its dark, repressive creed. *This* – as he'd always said – was the way to fight terrorism. It was a subtle shift and depended on everyone forgetting that Saddam's Iraq was secular, unlike – say – Saudi Arabia. The gambit was plainly hollow and contrived, and yet something about it rang truer than anything his critics could come up with. This was partly because he was the king, and partly because he was a politician and prepared to say that while 'critics' were acceptable in a democracy, 'defeatists' were unconscionable. And, of course, no sooner had he given the sign than a hundred of his most loyal buglers sounded the alarm all across the country: 'Death to the defeatists!'

Up on the hill at Arlington National Cemetery in Virginia, there's a memorial to JFK – a prince if there ever was one. It's a stately place, more elegant than grand, and the simple white cross on the adjacent grave of his brother Robert reminds us of the whole Kennedy family tragedy. It is a memorial to unfulfilled promise. There will never be a monument like this to Bill Clinton: monuments are sometimes built for promise unfulfilled but not for promise wasted. A Clintonite might say Kennedy had more women through the Oval Office than Clinton and that at least one of them, unlike Monica Lewinsky, was a serious security risk. If Clinton was a cad and hypocrite, so was Kennedy, and more so: but no-one chased him down for it. No-one belted him up and down the country and into Congress to impeach him, even when it was obvious to anyone with eyes to see that the president's acts were gross and dangerous. He was, as they say, a man of his time. Put this to Clinton-haters and they might nod, but that's all. You won't get them to concede a thing in the man's favour.

Clinton was a peerless maker of speeches, but none of them will ever be as famous as Kennedy's Inaugural Address, which is inscribed on a wall by his memorial at Arlington. While a great speech, it does not seem enough now to make him great, and it is not easy to see other reasons of substance for putting JFK atop a pedestal so much higher than any that Clinton – or Eisenhower or Johnson on either side of him – could ever scale. The reasons are anthropological. He looked like a prince, and he was assassinated. There are no reasons of substance only if you don't count images – and their power over us – as substance.

History chose JFK in more ways than the assassination: it was one thing in the dawning age of television to know that image counted, but something else to have the wealth and the looks with which to fashion it. He was, as Gore Vidal said in 1967, 'cool'; but as Vidal also said, he was much more concerned with the appearance of things than doing things – about civil rights or health or poverty, for instance. 'If a free society cannot help the many who are poor, it cannot save the few who are rich,' Kennedy said. Today, nothing could sound as hollow. Perhaps, as some of his admirers say, everything would have been different if he'd had a second term. But even with a more imposing record, very likely his name would still speak less for what he was than for what was made of him, and – like a flag or a designer label or an image of the Virgin or a prince – for what feelings his image moves in the beholder.

American liberals are united on Bush, but divided on Clinton. For every half-dozen who adore the sharpness and expanse of his mind, the ease of his speech and the general political genius of the man, there are one or two who despise the ex-president with the passion of the betrayed. As they see it, his preppy self-indulgences and pathetic schoolboy lies gave up the Democrats' advantage and handed the country to the neocons. Everything the Republicans loathe about him, they also loathe – and, loathing the Republicans who profited from his behaviour, they loathe him even more. They will tell you that the Clintons were surrounded by terrible people of their own kind and generation who refused to take advice from other people who might have had a more sensible perspective. They hate them for their failures, the more so because they never called them by that name, preferring to blame the press for every stuff-up and indiscretion and every punishment they received. They hate the Clintons for dissolving their responsibility in the general loathing of Bush.

And if they are old enough to remember, they might hate

the Clintons because they were not Jack or Bobby Kennedy: they did not bring hope and inspiration the way Jack and Bobby did, especially Bobby in 1968, the year he ran for president. They're still waiting for someone like Bobby to reignite the optimism in their liberal hearts, and to help them to get over what happened to him.

It is hard to imagine anyone now promising what Robert Kennedy promised that year, and just as hard to imagine the crowds who turned out to cheer him all across the country: in the rural South, in the cities, in the ghettoes, even in Kansas. On his gravestone are the words of his favourite poet, Aeschylus: 'Even in our sleep, pain which cannot forget falls drop by drop upon the heart until, in our own despair, and against our will, comes wisdom through the awful grace of God.' He quoted them the night he told a crowd in Indianapolis that Martin Luther King had been assassinated. He said: 'Let us dedicate ourselves to what the Greeks wrote so many years ago to tame the savageness of man and make gentle the life of this world.' And two months later, on the night he won the California primary, he was shot dead by an assassin.

One night in a motel room I saw Bill Clinton and George Bush Senior talking on *Larry King Live*. George looks more like the cartoons from his days as president than he did when they were drawn. The years have caricatured his gauntness and the bemused smile of a Brahmin who got just one term as president when his dull-witted son and Ronald Reagan both got two, whereas Bill Clinton – with that phallic nose and the puffy, post-coital eyes, semaphores of his prodigious appetites – might have stepped out of an illustration by Hogarth or Rowlandson. He would have been happier in the eighteenth century.

It turns out, George and Bill are buddies. They have been for twenty years, Bill said – since before the election that Bill won and George lost. Bill and Hillary go up to stay with

George and Barbara at Kennebunkport and they always have a great time. Bill can't understand why George is always travelling and doing things for people when he's got such a beautiful place up there.

For his part, George is impressed by Bill's energy. 'He's like the Energizer battery man,' he said. 'He never stops.'

'Well,' said Bill, 'as I get older I feel I should do more for people.'

Now George and Bill are doing what they can for the people of New Orleans. They have set up a fund in their joint names, and they're talking to the people down in Louisiana. They were not saying anything you could call substantial – not that night on *Larry King*, at least. Bill said they were telling the people of New Orleans: 'We're gonna rebuild your city. We're gonna rebuild your city – and you know, Larry, that's what's gonna get it done.' Larry beamed from suspender to suspender. It was as if all three of them thought there was nothing in the world they couldn't fix by grinning at it.

A couple of months after this, I asked a man who has worked for much of his life as a Washington consultant what two such men would find to talk about: George a decorated World War II airman of the heroic generation, Bill a draft-evading baby boomer; a New England Episcopalian and a Southern Baptist; a Brahmin and an Arkansas rustic; a Republican and a Democrat. He answered without hesitation: 'Pussy.'

Do they watch Howard Stern together? Riding around on George's golf buggy, could they really be communing on the 'immoral and foolish side', as Bill once called it? Is Satan riding with them? For the half of the population that believes in his existence, of course he is. It might be one reason why not only the usual cohort of God-denying liberals but also a consistent national majority never wavered in forgiving Clinton for yielding to the devil in his trousers. Satan tempts.

Man succumbs. It is written. For all the moral bullying of fundamentalist religions, believing that a supernatural fiend is behind temptation might just as well make people more tolerant of those who give in to it; and more affectionate towards those who, by their public suffering and repentance, seem to make the religious drama concrete.

I went to the Four Seasons bar in Washington to meet a heavyweight of the Clinton era, a well-known operator from the Democrat side, a prominent publicist and a man of formidable eloquence and brains. He offered me a big cigar and I took it – 'When in Rome,' I must have been thinking. He was confident the Democrats would win at least the House in 2006 and then commence a series of investigations which would so preoccupy the Republicans that they would not be able to fight an effective presidential campaign. He thought McCain could not win the primaries and would be a bad president anyway, but Hillary Clinton could win the primaries and the presidential campaign, and would be a good president. Already his cigar was an inch and a half shorter than mine. He did not give much credit to Bush for anything. The president's 'no child left behind' education policy, for instance, was a disaster that promoted inequality, and Ted Kennedy had been a fool to fall for it. Talking to Cicero must have been a bit like this.

There is nothing quite like a real political whiz. Some adopt an inscrutable, almost somnolent demeanour and make you beg for their wisdom, while others come at you like a whirlwind. The effect in both cases is the same: even when you think they must be extracting certitude from guesses or cucumbers from sunbeams, you are captive, not only to the verbal artistry but to the weight of the moment, the sense that on these matters to which you are now privy the course of history depends. Politics being civil war by other means, it is fought with the same volumes of smoke and passion and ruthless brutality, and it leaves some of the same psychic wounds. All political environments – democratic, republican and monarchical – have this much in common: it is never more than a short walk in any direction to find someone who disagrees with the last person you spoke to, or who envies or disapproves or wants to thwart him, or who feels thwarted, threatened or misused by him.

As our conversation in the Four Seasons concluded, my friend stubbed out the butt of his cigar. I still had three inches to smoke. I left with it and later that evening I met a consultant, also from the Democratic side, who tried to put me wise to the first man's failings. To be frank, I was left not knowing whom to believe. The consultant told me that these days he thinks it impossible for the US political system to throw up people or parties of true character, vision or integrity. (A businessman from the Republican side once told me the same thing.) Rather, the system is now ideal for hacks, 'yes men' and fodder for lobbyists. Political thinking has become institutionalised and incapable of solving the country's problems. The press has lost character in proportion to the politicians, and accepts their values and arguments almost without question. He thought universal national service with a non-military option might be one way to spread the burden and rekindle a sense of shared responsibility.

The consultant found the culture of Washington DC little short of repellent. That Mark Twain and Henry Adams had the same reaction 130 years ago is of academic interest only: in their time the cast of mind and quality of the system that determined who occupied the White House and ran the Congress did not decide who ruled the world and on what principles. The people of Ohio and Florida – at least, those who think it worthwhile voting – now vote on the whole world's behalf.

There were a few demonstrators outside the White House. They wanted Bush impeached. The Japanese tourists took pictures of them. Sherman would have ridden full-tilt at the whole lot and dispatched them all. 'On no earthly account will I do any act or think any thought hostile to the United States,' he said: the record tends to show that he didn't think other people should either.

A couple of blocks away, a tall black man belted three rubbish cans. He did it with an expression of unappeasable anger, but his rhythm was unbroken. As I tossed a dollar in his plastic bucket I saw that it was half-full with coins. A block closer to the White House, on a marble doorstep under a marble arch, a beggar woman sat with all her possessions piled beside her. She said that so far that day – it was eleven in the morning – no-one had given her so much as a quarter. She was coated in grey grime and looked as if she had slept in a chimney. I gave her five dollars and then wished I had given her ten. She was still there two hours later, just a block away from the president of the United States; and another block away you could hear the man pounding the rubbish bins.

Tocqueville made the point: for democracy to work, the majority of people must own property or have a reasonable prospect of owning it, and if they don't have that, then they need some other kind of possessions by way of compensation. Mark Twain believed something along the same lines. It might depend on your definition of property: sometimes it seems that having abandoned the hope of owning a couple of corner allotments or a tin mine, many folk are content to, as it were, own themselves. Without a field to cultivate or a fortune to grow, they work on their personalities.

Expand yourself. Enhance yourself. Sell yourself. Personality seems to matter more in the United States. Wherever you are, you are never far from a venting self. In a democracy – in this one, at least – everyone has that aristocratic, or merely borderless, privilege. 'Not only does democracy make each man forget his ancestors, it hides his descendants from him and divides him from his contemporaries; it continually turns him back into himself, and threatens, at last, to enclose him entirely in the solitude of his own heart.' That was Tocqueville, appearing, as usual, to be on to something before everyone else.

Americans seem to live between the polarities of Puritanism and theatricality. The first insists on authenticity, the second on display – which, in combination, is a near-enough definition of that very American invention, 'method acting'. The Mexican American essayist Richard Rodriguez recognised it: first, he says, in a theatre, and then, with some alarm, in his own behaviour: 'During speaking engagements . . . I sometimes feel a freedom to weep, to assume voices, to carry on in public, to channel in shameless ways.'

It's the same on the streets. And on trains. Travelling through Connecticut one day, I watched and listened as a young man spoke to his girlfriend in Paris. He wore a stylish overcoat and looked like a guy going places. The first thing I heard was: 'It's much more poetic since you came into it.' He told her how much he looked forward to meeting her in Nantes in three weeks' time.

I could hear *her* voice well enough to pick up that she worked for Canal Plus and had a beautiful bubbly laugh. I liked her. But I did not like him. And if she had been able to see the look I could see on his face – how he did not even smile when she laughed, how his languor was an act – she would not have liked him either.

We were passing fields of sedge bordering crystal bays ringed with the red and golden trees of autumn; but had we gone through Hades on this train, he'd have seen only his reflection in the window. Every now and then he put her on hold to briskly answer an incoming call: and then he paused before reconnecting to his beloved in an insufferable imitation of lovesickness. He missed her terribly; it was heartache every day but the nights were worse. The thing was that he believed it – he was 'inside the character'. That's the method for you. He wanted to go travelling with her. 'I will go anywhere you ask me to go,' he told her. She should have told him to go to hell, but she was reading from a different script.

The Puritan and the thespian might be polar opposites, but those noisy evangelicals issue from Puritan traditions. The First, Second and Third Great (religious) Awakenings in America all had 'ecstatic' origins; as did most if not all religions, for that matter. If that's a fact we would rather not consider, think of James Stewart, the theatrical authentic and authentic theatrical. The truly 'iconic' American is the humble, reserved Puritan obliged by his beliefs to come forth and play the father and defend the good – 'to carry on in public', as Rodriguez says. The Puritan says that God intends every man to stand on his own two feet. So standing is a holy estate. But it's not enough to stand there. A man has to talk, swing his arms – or a rope – around, make an impression; he needs something to sell, and sometimes he has only himself. Watching Americans at large, there are times when we are almost obliged to ask if America is not merely *an* elective monarchy, but a couple of hundred million of them.

The spiritual dimension of American life is founded not in an established church but in the individual and in the state, which, thus invested, are inclined to behave – and to speak – with religious fervour. Lincoln's Second Inaugural, the speech delivered on the cusp of Union victory and inscribed on the marble walls of the memorial, is a withering Puritan sermon in service to a secular cause. Of the warring sides, he says:

> Both read the same Bible and pray to the same God, and
> each invokes His aid against the other. It may seem strange

that any men should dare to ask a just God's assistance in wringing their bread from the sweat of other men's faces, but let us judge not, that we be not judged. The prayers of both could not be answered. That of neither has been answered fully. The Almighty has His own purposes. 'Woe unto the world because of offenses; for it must needs be that offenses come, but woe to that man by whom the offense cometh.'

Lincoln is, in general, and like most of the founding fathers, held to be a deist, if not a full-blown sceptic. But here he is quoting the words of a Jesus whose divinity he doubts, finding in the Civil War the revealed intentions of the Almighty, drawing from the same well of religious metaphor as the Reverend Dr King did a century later. Let us suppose, Lincoln says, that slavery is one of those offences of which Jesus spoke, and it is one that, by this war, God now intends to remove. The people pray that the war will end; yet, Lincoln says:

> . . . if God wills that it continue until all the wealth piled by the bondsman's two hundred and fifty years of unrequited toil shall be sunk, and until every drop of blood drawn with the lash shall be paid with another drawn by the sword, as was said three thousand years ago, so still it must be said 'the judgments of the Lord are true and righteous altogether'.

It is a short inaugural speech – half the length of Kennedy's – and per word makes more references to God than any other in American history. Yet it is not the number of times he mentions God nor the agency he gives Him that makes the Second Inaugural such a 'religious' speech: it is the way Lincoln expresses the war as religious experience.

It reads as if it were a personal revelation. Perhaps he made a conscious effort to give the imminent Northern victory divine sanction, or to wash the Union – and the churches – clean of

Southern slavery's stain. Perhaps it was designed to put the power of the Puritan message to work in the cause of the republic, as an astute political calculation to make the Union a holy cause. But, radical as it was, and as unlike the chauvinism and sabre-rattling we are today accustomed to, the speech was also a chip off a familiar American block. After four years, when it came down to the meaning of the war and the purpose of the Union, Lincoln turned not to Voltaire or Tom Paine but to the Bible. If the greatest American and the most powerful found answers there, where else would the poorest and the weakest go: the freed slaves and their descendants, for whom the war solved next to nothing and the tumult never died? 'The great ambition of the older people was to try to learn to read the Bible before they died,' Booker T. Washington wrote in 1901.

Lincoln's gift for words was that much greater because he was by nature a tragedian. He never doubted the rightness of his cause or hesitated to expand its compass, and he fought the war with unremitting zeal – but not as a fundamentalist. The Gettysburg and Second Inaugural addresses did not shirk complexity or paradox. While he despised the motives of his enemy, he did not call him evil. It was enough to call him wrong. Calling the enemy evil literally demonises him, denies him all rights and sympathy. Lincoln could loathe him yet, as in tragedy, see him as a victim – of time and fate and false ideas. For Lincoln, while political judgements were absolute, life remained relative and men and women fallible. He could not say the enemy was evil without suggesting that he, Abraham Lincoln, was without flaws: an assumption which, even if politics could make it credible, he knew was false.

In those two speeches Lincoln put tragic understanding at the core of American ideology. George W. Bush puts the Manichean there. You can sense the effort of a mind in President Lincoln's words, the seeking after truth. Doubt, including self-doubt, inhabits his prose. In President Bush's speeches we find only glib fantasies of 'moral clarity' – which lead to this sort of thing: 'We have known freedom's price. We have shown freedom's power. We will see freedom's victory.' Soon enough we arrive at 'freedom's enemies'. The more compelling view might be that a love of freedom co-exists with an instinct to throttle it and always shares democracy with multitudes of little tyrannies. This is what Lincoln understood and could admit. But not George W. Bush. His speeches do not allow for the existence of paradoxes. They are shrunk by an absence of doubt. No doubt can live in a cliché. Nothing can, including reasonable hope.

I was driven to the Union Station by a man who, five years earlier, had fled Cameroon to save his life. He had been in Washington for three years and in Paris for two years before that. Life in Washington was hard, he said: he found the language difficult; he felt isolated; he was angry about American foreign policy and American attitudes; he did not earn enough money to save and so could not afford the education he wanted. But despite his grievances, and even though French was his first language and he was much more familiar with French culture, life was much better in Washington than in Paris. In Paris it was harder to get a job and, what was worse, the police and immigration authorities never stopped harassing him. In Washington they left him alone. He had life and liberty and he was pursuing happiness.

———

I went up to New York on *Acela*, Amtrak's express train for business commuters. *Acela* might have represented a vision of an alternative, European-style future for transport in the United States, but it is clear that the enterprise has been less than wholehearted. The trains are only moderately fast, and not as well-appointed as their European and Japanese counterparts.

Once it has abandoned something, capitalist democracies find it hard to go back. Had *Acela*'s designers been able to, the train might be to modern travellers what the Pullman car was to an earlier generation. Not only would they be much faster, they would contain meeting rooms, even boardrooms, with wireless connectivity and all the requisites for PowerPoint presentations. There would be at least one Starbucks, a gym, spa, sauna and masseurs. A team of Japanese chefs would supply a sushi train running from the first carriage to the last. No-one would be seen dead travelling from Washington to New York by any other means.

But America has not put its genius into *Acela*. The only thing today's passengers share with their predecessors in the grand old days of rail travel is the absence of any security check before they board – you can hop on with a suitcase full of plastic explosive and be delivered all the way to Penn Station.

CHAPTER 4

What in all this speaks for man?

Saul Bellow, *Dangling Man*

OCTOBER 2005 WAS THE WARMEST IN RECORDED HISTORY, AND IN New York the wettest. It rained for days on end, and as hard as it rained, the wind blew harder. Gales tore down the canyons of Manhattan and corkscrewed at the intersections. They blew phenomenal quantities of litter up and down the pavements and hurled it down the subway stairs to lie in pools of murky water. But Ahab-like, on street corners, men and women shouted into their cell phones even as they manoeuvred their umbrellas into the teeth of the storm to make it blow them right side out. And often the nylon was ripped from the stays, and the stays from the mast, and their owners abandoned the Chinese-made wrecks to the gutter. Lashed by the rain, still talking on their cell phones and reaching into the pockets or purses for the five dollars to buy one from the next vendor huddled against a wall, they walked on.

On television I saw a limo driver tell an interviewer that every beggar on the streets reminded him of the next week's rent. He was, he said, always just a week away from joining the beggars. In a 'very good week' he earned $400, including tips. His one-bedroom apartment cost him $800 a month. Two million people work full-time in New York's huge service sector and live at or near the poverty line; to stay above it, like this limo driver, a lot of them depend on the kindness – or whatever else makes people willing to tip – of strangers. More than twelve per cent of the US population is poor. In New York City the figure is twenty per cent and rising. Poor means poor. The City is legally obliged to provide shelter for the homeless, but for want of an alternative it has to house them in verminous hotels and rooms for which crooked landlords charge outrageous rents. The mainstream press rarely reports on this, but Jack Newfield – a formidable *Village Voice* journalist now dead – reported on it for thirty years. He found the system 'profligate and brutal'. He castigated equally the real estate elite, which he said was 'power in New York City', and the liberal elite, which concerned itself more and more with gun control and civil liberty and other matters of 'freedom', and less and less with poverty and exploitation and matters of class. Class, he said, was 'a word no-one likes to use'.

The rule is simple enough: where the thing that matters most is personal success, it borders on weird to find common cause with failure. Class is for losers. Success means much the same thing everywhere, but nowhere is it enjoyed as much as it is in the United States. In America it is something akin to a higher state of being. If you watch the way advertisements depict success, or the interviews with successful people conducted by Dave Letterman or Larry King, you will see that that success has nothing to do with class, and less to do with status than with happiness. Success is happiness – and the happiness of others *in your success*. It is always something achieved – like wow! It is immediate: fun, bliss, very heaven. Success is fulfilment. For non-Americans, the absence of cynicism, envy and meanness of spirit takes a bit of getting used to, but once they have it is entirely liberating.

The creeds of hope and deliverance run deep through the realities of American experience. The celebration of success – from which 'celebrity' comes – is the blossom on the entrepreneurial tree, the profitable realisation of the driven, creative self: or, if you prefer, the fulfilment of the plan God has for every one of us. Americans, including the president, sometimes speak of entrepreneurs as if they followed a divine calling, one not mentioned in the Ten Commandments only because God knew an entrepreneur was not the sort of person you can regulate. Or because he covered it in Deuteronomy where it says: 'But thou shalt remember the Lord thy God: for it is He that giveth thee power to get wealth . . .' What more do you need to make a business legitimate – short of one's own name or the company brand substituted for 'thee'?

There is no denying the opportunities that America holds out to men and women of ambition, or the phenomenal economic and technological power their enterprises generate – and much else besides. You know the spirit lives when, perched on a fortieth floor above Central Park, the successful hedge fund manager tells you with unalloyed reverence for his country how he started in New York with the $2000 the army paid him when he returned from the war in Vietnam. And you know it when a radio journalist interviews the first-generation Egyptian immigrant who has a twenty-four-hour street stall in New York that sells lamb and rice with a special white sauce – and turns over $3 million a year.

The Office, the British television send-up of modern working life, was remade for America and lost less in the translation than one might have expected. But it did lose class. The producers took class out of it, and added hope. Americans need hope, they said. But how far can hope stretch? Could it cope with a reality that was, for instance, feudal? Or one in which fifty per cent of all stock is owned by one per cent of the population and ninety per cent by ten per cent? Where chief executives earn millions a year and those who drive them earn five dollars an hour? The gap between the educated executive and the uneducated servant is only one part of the story: the other part is the gap between the educated executive and the educated salary-earner. In New York in 1980, two friends – one a journalist and the other an economist working for a bank – each took home about $40,000 a year. The journalist's salary is about five times that now. The economist, following his career path at the bank, is on $7 million.

In some countries, such inequalities might cause people to protest in the streets. In the United States, the resentment is more likely to find expression in religion, or its cousin, celebrity: in devotion to something more reliable than the system, more realisable than 'the dream'.

With hope – or faith, as all good Christians know – you can move mountains and 'nothing shall be impossible unto you'. But a lot of Americans will tell you that much of the old hope has faded: that no-one any longer takes seriously the proposition that an American can make it 'from log cabin to White House'; that the cult of celebrity is a cipher for the success denied the vast majority; that the rhetoric of freedom and opportunity has never borne less resemblance to reality. If class does not rule America, then it might be some version of Maslow's hierarchy of needs: at the apex the bliss-filled self-actualisers building ever higher gates around their privilege; those below them seeking elevation through credit; and on the bottom rung, a cohort trying to eat their way to a higher state.

Now debt stalks the modern American consciousness. It is not just the debt to China, or the debt to sub-prime borrowers that accounts for a fifth of the mortgage market. It's a kind of empathetic debt: the debt not of middle-class Americans but of their children; people well into their working lives who have no savings, and even if they can finance a home, no realistic chance of paying off the loan. In truth, all hope depends upon their credit cards. For the children the debt is real, the sub-prime a fact of life; and very likely they are often more sanguine about it than their parents, for whom the pain is empathetic and depressing in the way that only parents know. It seems a crime from which they cannot absolve themselves that, having spent their lives escaping from debt, their children are now up to their necks in it. They wonder if their kids will ever know how good it feels to make material progress of the kind that is measured by an absence of debt; how liberating and even ennobling it is to be debt-free. If they do not know this, how will they know the American dream?

There are plenty who think the great days might be over. The opportunities are fewer. The channels for hope are silted up by too much welfare or too little public investment, by too much privilege or too much corruption. Some think they are being kept open only by credit. It's not only poor black taxi drivers in Mississippi who fear a day of reckoning with China, or a mass default in the huge sub-prime mortgage market. They speak of it in the same darkening tones as others speak of the shrinking and oppressed American middle class. The working class might not exist in the general consciousness, but the middle class most definitely does. It must, because it is essential to the health of the democracy and the republic: it may even be their defining element. But wherever you go you will find Americans who say the middle class is threatened or under attack and, like the independent small farmers of the Midwest, not what it used to be.

Amtrak's *Lake Shore* runs from New York to Chicago in a big north-western loop. The brochure lists the many 'scenic high-lights' to be seen on the way: the Hudson River Valley, Berkshire Mountains, Erie Canal, Mohawk River Valley, Lake Erie. But, as the train runs just once a day, winter passengers get no more than a glimpse of the Hudson Valley before darkness falls. Of course, they can see Lake Erie if they buy a return ticket, but then they won't see the Hudson or the mountains. Many other scenic highlights, massive geological phenomena and entire states go unobserved for the same reason. One travels by train across America as a flea travels on a foundering horse: but of course, so long as the sun is up, the view is the same as it would be on a sound one.

The trains that Amtrak runs between Washington DC and Boston, including the *Acela* trains, almost make a profit. The trains that they run on long hauls across the continent run at a considerable loss. This combination of facts appears to be the reason why many economic commentators and, it is alleged, the Bush administration favour privatising the former and liquidating the latter. Trains running in the north-east corridor nearly run at a profit for three main reasons: first, because they serve many millions of people over relatively short distances; second, because a good measure of the population consists of well-heeled business commuters; and third, because there has been investment in the business, the trains are well-equipped, reasonably fast and do not have to give way to every passing loco hauling freight.

On the transcontinental runs, the trains are old and the tracks are owned by freight companies, so they hardly ever run on time and often several hours behind it. According to a freight driver I met, the freight system, which is much cheaper than road transport, is also run down. 'Problem is,' he said, 'we got no more track than we had a hundred years ago. If we had two tracks there'd be no limit to how much freight we could move.'

Even if Amtrak did own its tracks, it's likely that the transcontinental trains would need subsidies – good railways nearly always do. But in the neoliberal age, subsidies are despised – well, sort of: it depends a little on who wants the subsidies and a little on the words chosen to describe them. Subsidies for agriculture are not despised. Large sums of public money spent on roads and airports are not called 'subsidies'; the $15-billion bailout of the airlines after 9/11 was not called a subsidy: but, in the press at least, the money spent on Amtrak is. Whatever you call government money, these days there's a strong political consensus that nothing as ancient as a railroad ought to get it: not even a railroad that runs at eye level across the stupendous plains and mountains of the greatest land on earth, nor a railroad which is itself a shimmering advertisement for American genius and spirit, nor one that provides poorer people in the United States with a safe, comfortable and relatively cheap means of getting round their country. The orthodoxy wishes it gone: they demand it in the name of all that's reasonable and decent. It is as an outbreak of scrofula to a gated community.

On the other hand, there's a bit of a feeling among politicians that some sort of help should be available to a railroad running through places where people vote. These politicians are doubtless as committed as the next person to the proposition that Amtrak should in principle be dead, but they are even more adamant that it should not be killed. A perfect expression of the conundrum came from David Gunn, the Amtrak CEO, after he learned that there was no money for Amtrak in the 2006 budget: 'In a word, they have no plan for Amtrak other than bankruptcy.'

When you ring Amtrak, Julie answers. She says: 'Hi, I'm Julie,' and it takes a few times before you learn not to say 'Hi, Julie' back, even though she tells you that she's automated. Then she says: 'Right, let's get started.' And soon you're answering her questions and doing everything she tells you to do. I liked her. She played it straight down the line. I thought about it often and in the end decided that, were she real, she would be like Carmela Soprano, Tony's wife.

Sooner or later, Julie connects you to one of Amtrak's 'agents'. Why these agents are all helpful, charming and efficient, I do not know: probably it means the company is neglecting the bottom line, or doesn't have a HR department. In either case, we can be sure it won't last long and you should book your trip now. Amtrak agents all seem to be middle-aged at least and to work out of their own homes. I had more than one long conversation with Amtrak agents who were happy to talk as civilised and curious human beings talked before they were trained as parrots. It was in the course of one such conversation, with a woman in Riverside, California, that I learned the reasons for Amtrak's astonishing delays. I knew the freight companies gave their trains precedence over Amtrak's trains – the market has judged that corn and pineapples weigh heavier than citizens – but I did not know until she told me that when freight drivers have an Amtrak train behind them, it is not uncommon for them to reduce their speed to thirty-five miles an hour.

By the time I learned this, the Bush administration had asked David Gunn to step down, and when he refused, they fired him. The Riverside agent told me that, in her view, Gunn had been appointed to break up the company, but once in the job he had decided it was viable and refused to do the bidding of the administration. That's why he was fired, she said.

At dinner on the *Lake Shore*, a woman who had grown up in Kansas and lived in Queens said she had always thought no-one could be worse than Reagan, but George W. Bush made her wish for Reagan's resurrection. She spoke of him with shame. At the mention of New Orleans, she said: 'Five days. How could it take him five days?' This lady thought the Bush administration might be about to unravel, and she hoped the president and the vice president would both be charged with treason.

The compartment conductor makes your bed while dinner

is served in the dining car; while you have breakfast in the dining car he unmakes it, folds it away and makes the seat ready for the day. I would be happy to live like this for months – years. The lower bunk is a few inches shorter, a little noisier and considerably dustier, and it does not sway like the one above it. I slept in the upper one, where a person's nose is about nine inches from the ceiling and it is easy to imagine you are being propelled into the infinite darkness at eighty miles an hour on a mortuary tray. A sleeping pill of some kind helps to convert the sway and racket into comforters, and once this happens, to sleep on a train will remain at least an intermittent desire for the rest of your life.

———

The Midwest woke as if choreographed by the God of that region. We were in Indiana. The sun was just up and lighting the frost on boundless fields of corn stubble. There were reverently mown lawns and plum-coloured barns, and bold, functional farmhouses with Old Glory flying from their porches. Every home was a redoubt of the republic, and pick-up trucks tore up and down the long straight roads with flag decals pasted on their back windows.

Indianans rise to serve their country and their maker, and to grow their share of the country's twelve billion bushels of corn. Half of it is fed to livestock, and some of it is turned into ethanol, some into starch and some into liquor. A lot of it is turned into corn syrup and 'high-fructose corn syrup', which is different and is used to sweeten the nation's soft drinks and just about every processed edible thing in the supermarkets. Forty years ago Americans' food and drink was sweetened with sugar. They had never tasted high-fructose corn syrup. Now, on average every American eats sixty-two pounds of the stuff each year. The switch from sugar to corn syrup – sucrose to fructose – was made because corn syrup is a bit cheaper, and when you're dealing with the gargantuan American appetite for processed food and drink, a few cents' difference instantly adds up to billions of dollars. There are scientists who think the corporate saving might have been made at the public expense. They are coming to believe that the switch helps explain the increasing incidence of type-two diabetes and what the surgeon-general calls the 'epidemic of obesity', and they think it's because in the human body fructose acts more like fat than sugar does.

Not all scientists have reached this conclusion, and the industry hasn't, of course. But there's no arguing with the $25 billion the US Farm Bill pays American farmers each year to produce more corn – along with soybeans, wheat, rice and cotton. When we say 'farmers', that means only *some* farmers: two-thirds receive no subsidies, and of the third who do, ten per cent receive seventy per cent of the handout. The effects of the Farm Bill are felt in all sorts of unlikely places: on the border with Mexico, for instance, where many of the people trying to cross into the United States are doing so because, since the North American Free Trade Agreement, their country has been flooded with subsidised American corn, a disaster that the Mexican government estimates has cost two million farmers and agricultural workers their livelihoods.

The subsidy makes processed foods much cheaper than fresh, which means the poor eat it and feed it to their children, as do the poorer schools. The Farm Bill was introduced in the days when the poor had gaunt and spavined bodies. The subsidies were to put food on their tables and provide a living for the farmers who grew it. Now obesity is as sure a sign of poverty as thinness used to be. Instead of nourishing the poor, the Farm Bill fills them up with carbohydrates and fat. And instead of keeping independent farmers on the land, it keeps agribusiness and the food-processing industry in healthy profit.

But if you want to keep your farmers and their votes, you

have to give them something to grow; or else those beautiful plum-coloured houses and barns will rot, and churches will fall into disuse, and the pick-up trucks will rust under trees and the flags tatter and shred. In fact, that started happening a long time ago. In many places in the Midwest there's just the ghost of a heartland, not a real heartland at all.

The young couple I was directed to join at breakfast had a five-year-old son with Down syndrome. He was cranky and aggressive and soon after I sat down the waiter asked me if I would like to move to another table. The boy's mother said they were defying the advice of experts and friends who insisted that he should be sent to therapists. But if he relied on therapists, she said, her boy would never grow independent. His mother would not believe what the experts told her: that her son with the wily expression was a 'genetic mistake'. They were raising him in a corner of upstate New York, living on the proceeds of a monthly newspaper they had started in fulfil-ment of an old shared ambition. Life was a struggle, but they were not about to give up.

If it was idealism, this was not Kennedy's 'ask what you can do for your country' kind, nor the Bush 'entrepreneurial' variety. These people wore no badges, real or metaphorical, faith-based or secular: they advanced no slogans, were not half as interested in personal wealth as in personal fulfilment. Perhaps they were of the ilk common in American history, literature and film, and essential to all settler societies: the people who believe that reality is only known when the self partakes of it, and that the self is only known and satisfied by experience of that reality. Practical idealists, if you like; and from somewhere in the same philosophy, I'm sure, came their determination to see their son's 'self' realised. The boy's mother's hero was Thurgood Marshall, the great civil-rights campaigner and lawyer in the 1954 Brown v. Board of Education case, which was the beginning of the end for segregation in schools. Marshall started out working for the railroads. Amtrak has always been a place where black Americans could get decent work and find a little self-realisation of their own.

Now, as the black waiters cleared our breakfast table, Amtrak's *Lake Shore* was stopped on the bleak edge of South Bend, Indiana. Chicago was an hour away and the train was already two hours late. We crawled most of the way there, and when we were within just a few miles of the suburbs, we stopped. After ten minutes a mile-long freight train passed. We remained stopped. Forty-five minutes later another mile-long freight train passed us. We began to crawl again. An hour later we reached Chicago.

—

Chicago's Amtrak station lies beneath the streets. Not many winners come down here into the boxing-gym gloom of an age that's almost past. Rupert Murdoch's twenty-four-hour propaganda channel flickers away in the waiting rooms and cafés. The coffee is lousy, but it has been at rail stations since trains were invented. The only difference between station coffee now and station coffee in 1900 is that now it comes in a big cardboard cup. The alternatives are an even bigger cardboard cup or one that holds a half-gallon. Crockery has been withdrawn from American culture below a certain level. Even in smart-looking delis, customers eat and drink from cardboard, plastic and paper and every meal finishes with that last decisive throw into the trash can with the big black plastic liner in the corner. There was a big trash can with a plastic liner in the station café and there is always one up the back of an Amtrak carriage. It may have come down from the spittoon.

'A façade of skyscrapers facing a lake and behind the façade, every type of dubiousness,' E. M. Forster said. Some people can never forgive dubiousness, especially American types of dubiousness, but the present 'façade' in Chicago is a test for piety. You can catch a boat on the Chicago River about a mile from where it used to meet Lake Michigan. It doesn't meet it any more because a century ago, when the river was putrid and a threat to public health, the city fathers reversed its flow southwards into the Illinois, which flows into the Mississippi. So the river that once ran into the Great Lakes now runs through New Orleans and into the Gulf of Mexico. It must do wonders for your confidence when you try something like that and it works – and that's what Chicago has: confidence.

When people say Chicago is *the* great and truly American city and Chicagoans are the real Americans they mean many things, but they always mean, in some sense, a gritty self-belief; trust in imagination allied to invincible can-do, not just a quality of mind but a quality of *ego* necessary for constant growth and re-invention. Chicago's attitude comes, of course, with the implication that the country would do well to follow her example, and Americans would be better if they were more like Chicagoans: Chicagoans with the decency to put a little bar on the river cruise boat, and the barman who gives you an extra shot to keep the cold out as you sail right through the heart of downtown Chicago, as an expert guide tells you how it all happened. If you discovered that mobsters were getting a rake-off on your vodka, would you really care?

When you're looking for the stamp of American genius, this is as good as any other place to start. The genius, of course, is in the buildings, which are very tall and elegant and inspire wonder and admiration in everyone who sees them: but the buildings alone, or even a dozen of them combined, are much less remarkable than the overall effect, which is akin to travelling through a glass and concrete forest, a dream of some Atlantis on the ocean floor or a city fallen from another planet.

Most remarkable of all is the fact that Chicago was built on a swamp and in a fearful climate, and owes its existence to collaboration between (often corrupt) civic authorities and big business that, in most other places, is notorious for creating ugliness and mayhem. If genius is beyond the reach of ordinary imaginations and reasonable expectations, Chicago's architecture fits the bill. More miraculous still, the towers carry no advertising; not even the names of the corporations that built them.

Downtown Chicago is so clean. Not a crust, or a butt or a bubblegum wrapper. You could eat a Krispy Kreme right off the street. Fix your face in the shining glass and marble. If there's corruption, it's not the kind you can smell. The city is as if 'showcased' in museum-like – or Hollywood-like – perfection and, the weather aside, the senses are touched by nothing except awe and the desire to buy. Even the beggars appear to be carefully spaced; and they hold up bits of cardboard on which they have scrawled their pleas in terms that fit neatly in the prevailing doctrines of self-improvement and small government. One may beg but not confront. Walk around the showcase and you might think of Rome. You might even think of the slaves that both Rome and Athens needed. Then you might think that a country which pays legal menials a little over five dollars an hour and illegal ones much less, and which has Chinese workers do its manufacturing for less again, has not left serfdom a very long way behind. Because such order and cleanliness are not natural to cities, a mind soon begins to wonder who and what has been swept away. It looks stupendous, but also a little airbrushed.

It is hard to think of a city that has had more memorable things said about its meanness, toughness and corruption, not least by people who otherwise admire it and even believe that Chicago is the real America – it is 'alive from snout to tail', H. L. Mencken said. Every book I have ever read about Chicago had gravel in the guts. The first was James T. Farrell's *Studs Lonigan*, which nearly forty years later remains a bleak memory. 'Chicago was a town where nobody could forget how the money was made. It was picked up from floors still slippery with blood,' Norman Mailer wrote in the second book I read about the place, *Miami and the Siege of Chicago*. That was 1968, when the present mayor's father ruled both Chicago and the Democratic Party. Martin Luther King said that never in his life, not even in Alabama or Mississippi, had he encountered such racism as he found in Chicago. It is also possible that he had never, not even in the South, run into such ruthless politicians. Within twelve months of signing the Civil Rights Bill, President Lyndon Johnson had been turned against King by Mayor Richard J. Daley. Daley 'cut King's ass off', one civil-rights campaigner said.

There were all manner of obvious influences on Chicago's character, including its bitter winters, but the railway might have been the biggest. When the railways tied the United States together, they tied them at Chicago. In tying the country and the country's capitalist economy together, they tied business and politics together as never before in history. And 'nothing', the historian William Miller wrote, 'so stimulated the bare use of power'. The railways did as much as anything else to make corruption endemic in Chicago. It also made the city famous for its industry, invention, science and a phenomenal capacity to transform itself.

Chicago seems to have more public notices than other cities. They bob up everywhere: in taxis and trains, the walls of buildings, buildings recently constructed and not yet constructed, garbage containers, in the shadows under railway bridges, in places where one does not normally see public notices. And on every one of them there was the name – Richard M. Daley, Mayor. You just know that if he could find a half-legal way, he would mint coins with his head on them. But the liberal, pro-conservation, pro-public transport, pro-urban renewal, pro-gay rights, anti-gun Mayor Daley is held in wide esteem, and having his name everywhere can't be the only reason as many as seventy per cent of Chicagoans have been voting for him since 1989. He must know a thing or two about how to run a city.

Up near the bridge where the river tour begins, a young black man took an old man's begging tin and stood a few paces away, baiting him. The old man shouted at him in desperation and rage. Two classy black women walked past and saw the commotion. The classier of them glared at the young man and said in a voice loud enough for him to hear: 'Some people should have stayed in the South.' Ten minutes later the old man had his tin back and he was begging; but his voice was nothing like the one he used when he was shouting at his persecutor – now it was pathetic, thin and fragile.

There's more than one way to skin a cat. At about eight o'clock one night a man stepped out of nowhere and said, as he loomed in my path: 'Those are beautiful boots, sir.'

I looked down at them.

'But they're fading, sir.'

'No matter,' I said.

'But it does matter,' he said. 'Do you know the advantage to be had from Cadillac Boot Polish, sir?' He dropped to his knees in front of me. 'It restores the leather and the shine is guaranteed for six months. See here, sir, near the toe.'

He looked up and asked without irony: 'You won't kick me, will you, sir?'

Now he drew from the pocket of his overcoat an unlabelled plastic bottle and squeezed a dollop of white goo onto my right boot.

I said: 'They don't need it, you know.'

But he balanced on one knee and spread a cloth on the thigh of his other leg, as if he were a courtier and I some kind of prince, and I found myself obeying his request to put my foot on his thigh and stood there on one leg as people passed and he rubbed the Cadillac Boot Polish into my boot with his hand. 'What's your name, sir?' he asked.

'Don,' I said. 'What's yours?'

'Manny,' he said. 'Manny the shoe mechanic.'

'Do you spend your days doing this?' I asked as he took my right foot from his thigh and put the left one on.

'Just evenings, sir. I don't beg, you see, sir. I refuse to beg. In the daytime I attend the School for African Americans in the Culinary Arts.'

He polished the boots to an average shine with a rag he took from his pocket and asked if I was English. I said no, but he wasn't interested in the answer.

I said: 'Manny, can I give you ten dollars?'

'Eight dollars a shoe, sir,' he said.

He went off with sixteen dollars, looking for another target. He may as well have carried a crossbow or a can of mace.

On the night following, I walked past the same place about the same time, but I wasn't aware of it until a man stepped out of the same shadow. I thought at first it was Manny, but instead of Cadillac Boot Polish this one pulled out a tattered collection of pictures of what he said was an institution for homeless African Americans. He said he was collecting donations for it. I politely told him no, and it was not just because the Cadillac polish had done nothing but darken my boots in the way that liquid soap or hair cream might have. It was because the most gullible fool alive could not have fallen for those photographs. He kept alongside me as I walked until I said it firmly: 'No, mate, not today.'

'You don't care about nobody,' he said, and veered away and shouted something else I didn't catch. So I stopped and turned back to him.

'You don't care about nobody!' he yelled again.

———

It was tempting to read the airbrushed Chicago as a metaphor for the America showcased in the language of post-9/11 patriotism. Like God's manifest guidance and grace, in the Bush republic freedom and opportunity and American know-how (often going by the names 'innovation' or 'entrepreneurialism') are rendered as both ideals and accomplished facts of American life. As the showcased Chicago is not the real one but a kind of museum or Hollywood set, so in its way is the America of neoconservative ideology. They know it's baloney – or at least they did until, as the powerful invariably do, they began to believe their own propaganda.

But it's not all appearances in Chicago. While education and housing remain segregated, and poverty, drugs and crime still abound, a lot of the old slums have gone. There is now a black middle class. Non-profit organisations have invested billions of dollars in projects that promise new generations a better chance than their parents and grandparents had when they came up from the South.

For twenty-three years Gersh drove a Greyhound bus between Chicago and the South. He hated the South, he told me, and nothing would make him go there again. Now he drives for a Chicago limo service whose principal customer is the University of Chicago. A friend who is a professor of history at Chicago told me I should ask him to show me round.

Gersh is in his sixties, I would guess, and his handsome face has aged well around steady, thoughtful eyes and a grey moustache. 'English is my second language,' he tells me, adding that he doesn't have a first. He comes from Lithuanian Jewish stock. His wife is African American. They live in a cottage in the university suburb of Hyde Park. Gersh's father was a wetback: he spent a lot of time in Canada in the late 1920s before he finally made it into Chicago. They lived near the Sears mail-order store. In those days Sears was one of the four biggest industries in the city. From Gersh's old school you can see the original Sears tower a mile away and, in the distance, the modern one downtown. From the school you can also see the old mortuary, which used to be a front for Jewish mobsters.

Of all the places in the United States, why would Gersh's father want to come to freezing, stinking, crime-ridden Chicago, when there was forty per cent unemployment and, as anyone who had read *Studs Lonigan* would know, a mean streak of anti-Semitism?

Well, said Gersh, imagine you've come from some shtetl in Eastern Europe and you reach Chicago which has all these places to go: the parks, the public meeting rooms, the picture theatres, the Conservatory – Gersh's father first saw a banana at the Conservatory, and it was the same for Gersh. Chicago was paradise. He grew up on the south side in an area that was Jewish with a sprinkling of WASPs whom he rarely saw. The meeting halls and picture theatres have gone, the parks are dangerous and the old synagogues – you can see the Stars of David on the fascias – have become Baptist churches. In between his days there and now, the place was Italian and Mexican. Now it's African American. From their front porches, the poor can look across a rail line into the backyards of the affluent.

Gersh is a native pluralist: he loves the ethnic mix and the rivalry between Chicago's north and south sides; but he hates chauvinism. As a blue-collar Jew, he remembers being called a kike by the Catholics, but he also remembers his mother telling him to never reply in kind by calling people niggers or dagoes. There were, he said, invisible lines separating the groups: invisible, but you knew at once when you had crossed them and you didn't stay. He drove me around, explaining the different architectural styles, the history of different streets and build- ings, the places that had been Polish and are now Puerto Rican. He likes flux, he said, but not when new groups destroy the cultural evidence of the people that preceded them.

He showed me where Fermi worked at Chicago University; where Simone de Beauvoir lived with Nelson Algren, who said that 'loving Chicago was like loving a woman with a broken nose'; and Wicker Park, where Algren's *The Man with the Golden Arm* shot up. We passed the statue of Stephen Douglas – 'a real sleazeball', so Gersh said: in 1858 he narrowly beat Lincoln in a Senate race, and the benefit to the Union is beyond calculation. He showed me how the railway viaducts are tied to the stories of the different ethnic groups, and how endemic graft accompanied their arrival through the trading of jobs for votes, and the rise of the 'juice man' – the loan shark – in Chicago's history. Gersh doesn't do this for a living, but no tour guide was ever as good. He painted big and compelling pictures in that clear, clipped Chicago accent, every syllable precise but with missing diphthongs. Most languages don't have them anyway, he said.

There is a lot of paranoia about Chicago, in Gersh's view. These days there was nowhere he wouldn't go – but judiciously. There is a big difference between being paranoid and being judicious, he said.

In May I had stayed two nights at the Drake, which is a sort of grand dowager among Chicago hotels, but this time I stayed at the Ohio House Motel, which has no bar or ballrooms, potted palms, string quartets or dance bands. And no men in livery to help you drag your bags up the concrete stairs. You could feel like a loser at the Ohio House, but where else can you get a place downtown in a city of nine million people with a freestanding 1950s diner in the car park? Where else can you get a place with a car park? The Ohio House Motel is a freak.

Back at the motel I watched *Sin City* – or at least, as much as I could stand before the violence and my situation beside the highways, and the blackness beyond their lights, began to flood my mental corridors with bleakness and fear. In phoney musculature, Mickey Rourke drove a car with the door open and through it held a man's head to the road. I was not stimulated by the satire. I presumed they were taking *film noir* to a logical next step, but I didn't want to take it with them. There is a kind of perverse pleasure in feeling as if you have been dropped into a *noir* plot, even if it's a bit part you're playing and at any moment you may be slain by a gunman in your sad motel room. But the brutality of modern American films – even satirical films like *Sin City* – is to *noir* what a cluster bomb is to military heroism. It lacks the dimension of sympathy, and its effect on the viewer's psyche is of a different order.

Dehumanised cruelty and infantile fantasies of vengeance or masculinity – or whatever you want to call *The Terminator* and all its variants (including V8 pick-up trucks, Humvees and the gear that American soldiers and footballers wear) – might even go back to General Sherman. He was, after all, turned into a tank. President Bush's goofy Texan swagger might have the same origin. Was it Sherman's perennial clash with 'inferior' peoples – the American Indians he hunted before and after the Civil War, the Mexican 'greasers', the Negroes he believed were lesser beings? Vietnamese 'gooks' are part of that continuum, and now Muslims. I wondered if the big brute in American culture came out of all these wars; or if it was the expression of a herd instinct denied fulfilment in the rivalry, individualism and chaos of American democracy – so it has to be imagined, made concrete by anthems and flags, rituals, the pumpkins of Halloween. If you must imagine the collective will, why not imagine it as something huge and indestructible, a Blob to fight the Blob?

Motels can do that to you. It's why they find bodies in them. They must like finding them, or else they wouldn't show films like *Sin City*. It's wrong to blame the film. All the tar and cement outside, the cars spearing through the night, the distant sirens, the beige walls and bad art, the lights flickering in the vertical blinds – these things can do it. Or it could be the little screen itself: the pulverising, discombobulating technology. Mark Twain was on to something when he wrote *A Connecticut Yankee in King Arthur's Court* a hundred years before *Sin City* and fifty before television. Where there is the ability to obliterate there will be fantasies of obliteration. Or is it the other way around? Does America sometimes imagine itself omniscient because Americans fear they are vulnerable, or do they believe themselves vulnerable because they are near as dammit omniscient, but not quite?

I had not read *A Connecticut Yankee* when I saw *Sin City*. I wish I had. The night would not have been so discomposed. Wherever one goes in the United States, one goes there more serenely with Mark Twain.

CHAPTER 5

For an American, insofar as he is new and different at all,
is a civilized man who has renewed himself in the wild.

Wallace Stegner, *The Wilderness Letter*

'OAKLAND . . . IS HIDEOUS,' SIMONE DE BEAUVOIR WROTE IN 1947 when she passed through with Nelson Algren. I spent a night there hoping to see something of the hideousness, or signs of the bruising port where Jack London lived. The train still runs down the main street and right through Jack London Square, but these days it's about as much like London's Oakland as White Fang was like a cocker spaniel. Put it down to another renaissance: it's all warehouse apartments, fancy bars and breakfast places selling wheatgrass drinks and cardboard café latte. But the Chinese restaurant was in the older style. I ate with chopsticks, and all the Chinese used forks.

Stan 'Tookie' Williams, a Los Angeles gang leader found guilty of killing four innocent people in 1979, was about to be executed at San Quentin State Prison. Williams and his thousands of supporters insisted that he was a reformed man. He had written books for children, warning them against gangs, and for adults on the theme of redemption. The president had written him a letter of commendation. But Governor Arnold Schwarzenegger refused to pardon him. As a young man, Williams reckoned life was cheap. Now the State of California was endorsing that view. It cast a pall. At two am I turned on the TV in time to see Don Corleone gunned down. I turned off just as Al Pacino got the gun from the lavatory and re-entered the restaurant. Around the same time the night before, Joe Pesci and Robert de Niro were kicking the guy to death in the bar in *Goodfellas*.

It was a couple of weeks before Christmas. I had taken the train up the California coast from Los Angeles, where I had gone to attend a wedding. Now I was making for Emeryville and Amtrak's *California Zephyr*, which runs from there across the Rockies and the heartland to – of course – Chicago. In the fields outside, hordes of labourers were bent to the ground picking strawberries: inside, Herb with bright eyes, olive skin and a white moustache told me about his most recent Pacific cruise. Herb was deep into his seventies but very fit. He looked like Clark Gable might have, had he reached that age. Herb took a lot of cruises; the last, from which he had just returned, was the eighth he'd taken on the one line. When he wasn't cruising he was riding his six-cylinder Honda motorbike with a trailer that converts to a tent in three minutes. He rides it all over the United States.

The ninety-one-year-old man opposite had written a text book on the law fifty years ago, and it was still paying for ocean cruises. Herb had joined the army just as World War II ended and, though he stayed in it until Korea, he never saw any action. But the lawyer saw more than he cared to recall. He had been in Patton's Third Army and later became a war crimes investigator. In Austria he had had to witness the forced (and frequently fatal) repatriation of POWs to the Soviet Union. Then he'd gone to Korea. He was inclined to laugh at horror, but he also said he thought every act of war was criminal.

His wife was eighty-three. She had once been a marriage counsellor and wrote a thriller called *Motel Murder* in which she killed all the people she didn't like. That 'such a pretty man' as Herb had never married she found surprising. Herb did not blink: it was just a matter of choice, he said. Now, in a broad valley south of San Luis Obispo, hundreds of backs were bent to pick cauliflowers, and thousands of trailers and shacks huddled together on the edges of the fields with American and Mexican flags in a ratio of about twenty to one.

The Supreme Court judge Earl Warren once called Emeryville the 'rottenest city on the Pacific Coast', but it's not rotten any more. It's booming with high-tech. From Oakland it's just a few miles up a local rail line towards Berkeley. Amtrak brought the train into Emeryville right on time, but then a Union Pacific freight train rolled past and we sat there while the conductor recited his drolleries: 'Do not occupy a seat with your luggage. If you wish to buy a ticket for your coat you can do that at the Amtrak office.' We were still sitting in the station half an hour later. Our ambition was to get to Sacramento, where the train becomes the *California Zephyr*. One of the great train journeys begins in the town where the Central Pacific railroad began in 1863.

We sped through marshland where russet grass grew between the channels and half-hid men standing perfectly still with their shotguns tipped back across their shoulders and pointing to the sky, their dogs just as still beside them. The hunters all wore iridescent orange jackets to reduce the risk of shooting each other. In no time we had crossed California's Great Central Valley, which grows two billion tons of rice each year, and unimaginable quantities of almonds and walnuts, prunes, pistachios, peaches, apples, oranges, turkeys, chickens, eggs, kiwi fruit, lettuces, milk and grapes.

At Sacramento a 200-pound, eighteen-year-old youth

flopped down opposite, drew the curtain on his window and loaded a DVD into his player. He played six before we reached the other side of the mountains, and not once did he open the curtain. An historian from the Sacramento Rail Museum came on the public address system to tell us the story of the High Sierra, which we were about to cross. He had a soft, deep voice and it's possible that his cadences owed something to Shelby Foote: 'In 1867 an immigrant train led by Josiah Stevens reached the shores of Donner Lake after a journey fraught with misfortune and ill-advised turnings. Here they were snowed in and a party of the fittest among them set out for Sacramento to get help.'

Somewhere between Colfax and the highest point in the Sierra Nevada we made an unscheduled stop. In the 1870s, our guide said, mining companies blasted the soil off these hillsides with high-pressure hoses and collected the gold salted through it from the gullies below. It was called hydraulic mining: Clint Eastwood used it as the epitome of evil in *Pale Rider*. It was outlawed in 1884, but not before the railroad company was obliged to employ police to stop the mining companies hosing away the ridge on which the railroad ran. We listened to this while looking out at a scene of utter lifelessness. Not a bird, not even a kite or a crow. Conifers. The gates of hell will stand in the silence of a coniferous forest. And the damned will wait for a Union Pacific train to pass.

As we crawled over Emigrant Gap, my youthful companion loaded yet another DVD. People gathered in the observation car to admire American River Canyon and Bear Valley. It was hard to know which to admire more – the grandeur of nature or the efforts of human beings to cut it down to size. On every precipitous and inhospitable hillside there was evidence of mining, irrigation, hydro-electric power or, for that matter, skiing. And there was the railroad itself. We passed some of the wooden sheds that were built to protect forty miles of track from the thirty feet of snow that falls in an average year. And at last the train went through the Big Hole – a two-mile tunnel at 7040 feet – and came out on the other side of the Sierra Nevada. We looked down on the Donner Lake, where more than half of the stranded immigrants died in the snow and, we were told, the living ate the dead: indeed, children ate their fathers, wives saw their husbands roasted. It is a story from Poe's imagination. Or the author of Genesis.

For long stretches Highway 80 snaked along beside the railroad, and at Emigrant Gap it seemed to go under it and bobbed up on the other side. The cars zipped, the trucks thundered, the train edged its way, creaking as it went. The highway is more advanced, no question, but the railroad is heroic; and because its engineers had to shape it to the physical environment, people on the train not only see more of the mountains, they feel them. The sublime thing about a train is that you're always dimly conscious of the engineering.

We passed through Truckee and I seemed to hear the guide say it burned down six times in its first ten years. Truckee was a Paiute chief and his father was Winnemucca, which is a couple of stops after Truckee on the Nevada side of the California border; like Emeryville and Truckee and all the other towns on the line, it was a wild town in its day. So wild, in fact, that the Wild Bunch robbed a bank there. We travelled on in pitch-dark, I presumed across the Nevada Desert. There was an occasional light from a house, or a car spearing through the blackness, and every now and then a Christmas tree with a star on top or a couple of flying reindeer.

I had dinner with people who did not like their president or Mr Cheney. Amtrak travellers are everywhere opposed to them. 'We are all neocons now,' an NPR journalist said soon after the fall of Baghdad. Not on Amtrak, they're not. Not now, and as far as I could tell, not then. Journalists might try to explain the abandonment of their critical faculties after 9/11 as a normal patriotic response. The patriots in the dining car wouldn't buy it.

One of my companions said that, like me, he'd been thinking of Humphrey Bogart in *High Sierra* on and off all day. And the thought led him to recall the *Treasure of Sierra Madre* (an altogether different Sierra) and the bandit who says to Bogart: 'Badges? We got no stinking badges!' which was one of the few times a Hollywood lead was worsted in conversation with a Mexican. The people at the table told me Elko was a cowboy town and famous for its rodeo. I'd heard it elsewhere – Nascar and the rodeo are what every American town wants. Elko also has an annual Cowboy Poetry Gathering.

The lady opposite was travelling to Tampa, Florida. She said to me: 'You could be a cowboy.'

'Surely I'm too old,' I said.

'No you're not,' she said. It was going to take her four days and four nights to reach Tampa.

The train was two hours late into Elko, but there was a taxi waiting at the shed which passes for a station. On the way through the dark to the Stockmen's Hotel and Casino, the driver told me that Elko relies less on cows and cowboys than on gold and gambling. Nevertheless, it was a cowboy I saw when I opened the blinds in the morning: that is to say, he was wearing a white cowboy hat and cowboy boots and a big check woollen coat like the boys wear in *Brokeback Mountain*. He must have weighed 300 pounds and he was picking his way through the ice and snow in the big car park that divides one side of Elko's main street from the other.

The sun shone weakly as I followed the cowboy's trail through the snow to Leotard Corner, and then past some more casinos until I found a laundry about where you'd expect to find the town hall. It had huge washers and dryers, and I left my clothes with one of the half-dozen nice women who worked there. I imagined they were used to cowboys' and goldminers' clothes and I hoped they wouldn't think mine too girly. Then I went round to a little place called Cowboy Joe's, where they make the best coffee in the United States. They knew exactly what I wanted: two-thirds espresso and a third steamed milk. In fact, they had a name for it – a Tony. I had two Tonys at Cowboy Joe's and took myself down to the Cowboy Museum and bought a Cowboy Poetry Gathering T-shirt. I looked at the old photos of cowboys with their chaps and ropes and lariats and hackamores, their rifles, rifle-holders, holsters, boots and spurs and neckerchiefs and fancy saddles, and wondered how long it took them to get dressed and on their way in the morning.

It seemed to me then that this cowboy thing was all about balancing the wild and the tamed. Among the images and objects at Elko's Cowboy Museum were wild horses, wild bulls, wild jackalopes, wild deer, elk and salmon, on the one hand; and, on the other, tamed, dead or stuffed versions of these animals. Tamed nature and cowboys in their taming gear. It's a delicate balance. Too much wild and you can't make progress or money, the two most concrete expressions of freedom and independence. Too little wild and you've nothing on which to exercise those freedoms and the inde-pendence-loving taming instincts which are the hallmarks of frontier experience. The cowboy is caught in this contradic-tion, which might be why some cowboys, like the one I saw walking across the car park that morning in Elko, bear the same kind of relationship to a living thing as a grizzly bear does to its glass case.

A cowboy is a bit of a hoax; and not only because he is grafted on to the Mexican original, the *vaquero*. The brands he burned into the cattle he so expertly roped were not his brands. He was a wage-labourer by any other name, but he could kid himself that he was as free as any man because he was engaged in the essential business of taming wild critters. Sometimes, behind the expression of American freedom, you get a glimpse of an illusion – and not only with cowboys. A man can be robotic, ignorant or vicious. He can be timid and pathetic. None of that matters as long as he keeps saying he is free, or that he stands for freedom or represents freedom. A *New York Times* reporter put it to Larry McMurtry that while cowboys were symbols of freedom and self-reliance, one could hardly say they were 'interested in spreading democracy'. 'No,' said McMurtry, the great novelist of the species, 'they were interested in spreading fascism.'

I liked Elko. The women, in particular, were very pleasant. I went into an optometrist's shop and asked the lady there if she could straighten my glasses. She was a handsome, intelligent, middle-aged woman, and when she put the spectacles back on my nose I asked her whether Elko was a good place to live. She said she couldn't honestly say that she was happy there, and after nine years she was leaving.

Around five-thirty pm I rang Julie. It was dark and the moon was bouncing light off the snow in the car park. Julie said the *California Zephyr* to Chicago – due at 9.40 pm – was now due at 12.10 am. As it was several degrees below zero and the station was just a shed three miles out of town without so much as a kerosene radiator, there was nothing for it but to kill time in town.

I went over to the Commercial Hotel and Casino and ordered the prime ribs and salad for $7.70 and a glass of red wine. The vegetables came in a bowl of hot water sitting on the plate, with some garlic in a plastic cup and the meat juice in another plastic cup and a potato in a piece of silver foil. I ate every morsel. The wine they brought was white; when I told them I'd asked for red they brought me some and said I could have the white as well, because there was nothing they could do with it now. I drank the red and washed it down with the white, and I was playing a machine when the thing began to jangle and gurgle and spit out coins and an alarm went off. Next moment a young woman appeared at my shoulder and told me I had won eighty dollars. Half an hour later I'd lost it, and another half-hour later I was eighty dollars down.

I walked back across the car park to the Stockmen's Hotel and Casino and lost another fifty dollars, so I sat at the bar in the gloom and drank vodka and read the *Elko Daily Free Press*, whose headline read: INCREASED PROFITS AT ELKO CASINOS. Then I read the back of a Go Mega Bar wrapper: it contained twenty-eight different ingredients, including sixteen different fruits and berries. It had vitamin A and vitamin E and omega 3, folate, iron and calcium. A poker machine was inlaid in the bar. I lost some more money on it.

I rang Julie again and this time she said the train would be in at ten-thirty pm, which gave me about twenty minutes to get there. The shuttle driver was in the lavatory. He must have taken a book with him because it was fifteen minutes before he came out. We raced out to the shed by the tracks, but the train wasn't in. The driver went back to town. A few snowflakes were falling. There's no place as dark as a railway track in the middle of the night, the killer says in *Double Indemnity*. I waited an hour, thinking about the immigrants at Donner Lake; then I rang Julie again. Just as she said 'Hi, I'm Julie', I heard the whistle blow and I saw a light in the distance.

———

The next stop was Salt Lake City, but I had taken a sleeper and missed it. I missed Utah completely. At some point in the night, when I peered through the curtain, we seemed to be skimming across ice, as if on a frozen lake – or a salt lake, I wondered.

In the morning, as I looked out at the landscape west of Grand Junction, Colorado, cowboydom became seductive.

The land dares you, it murmurs freedom, stirs your most basic desires. You want to get out and hear whips crack and cattle bellow and horses gallop after them. 'No hour of life is wasted that is spent in the saddle,' Winston Churchill said. Interstate 80 was running beside us again. I wanted to get a car.

The conductor said: 'You may have noticed that we're a little late but think of all that time you've spent on Amtrak at no extra cost.' He hoped we had not been 'too greatly discommoded'. There is a fruit stall at the station at Grand Junction and a postbox and a little shop where you can buy a toothbrush. Why it is the only station in the United States with these simple amenities is a mystery.

We slid creaking up into the red mountains towards Glenwood Springs. Through the window on a bend I saw a dozen elk career across the line, and I heard the whistle blow and I'm sure I felt the driver brake. The gunslinger and dentist 'Doc' Holliday went to Glenwood Springs to try to recover from TB. He died there. Al Capone liked to take the waters at Glenwood. And Teddy Roosevelt came here to watch birds and hunt bears and mountain lions; to write imperial tracts and withering letters to Southern racists; and to dream both of shooting elephants and of saving them.

At lunch, a lady from Indiana sitting opposite said Spanish would be the language of the United States in ten years' time. Already people had to speak it to get a job in a bank or a school. Something would have to be done, but she didn't know what. She asked me if she was right in thinking Australia was 'ruled by the Queen of England'. Her husband didn't say a lot, just that Indiana wasn't doing so well these past fifteen or so years. Independent farms used to be the backbone of America, 'but not so much now', he said. He did not express it as a grievance, but in the way someone familiar with Ecclesiastes might.

The president had made a few speeches in recent weeks

and gas prices had fallen, and the most recent poll had him up one point to forty-two per cent. But one kept thinking: how long will they put up with the body count, the generation that doesn't remember when wars killed a lot more than this one is killing? If they don't care so much about the dead, does the $8 billion a week concern them? How long before these concrete facts begin to outweigh the abstractions on which the case for the war was built?

That night I stood by the lavatories for an hour and a half and talked to two veterans of the radical student movement. One of them retained a Kurt Vonnegut moustache and dressed in 1960s denim. He lived in Denver for the snowboarding. He had decided years ago that politics made him angry and aggressive, and he'd drawn back – not so much to a position on the fence, he said, but so far beyond it that he could not see the neocons or hear their voices. He loathed George W. Bush for all the familiar reasons and one more: Bush was so bad, he said, that he had been unable to ignore him and he'd again become the angry radical he didn't like.

The other man was a university accountant and teacher of tai chi who had studied history in the days of the radical revisionists like Christopher Lasch, William Appleman Williams and Eugene Genovese: the historians whose critical take on American history morphed somehow into political correctness, which in turn, it seems, created the conditions necessary for the rise of the new conservatism and the culture wars. It seemed appropriate to be having this conversation in a huddle by the lavatories out of sight on an underused train.

I had dinner in the dining car. Catfish. A little after six-thirty I was the only one left. I heard a waiter hawk and spit a gob big enough to make an audible thud. Beside my table the seating attendant confronted the waiter about it.

'Man,' he said, 'did I just hear what I think I heared?'

'It come up,' said the waiter, 'and I got rid of it.'

'Man, you can't do that in the dining car,' said the seating attendant.

'You need to dump, you ain't got no can to dump in, you gotta dump somewhere. That's what I did. Had no choice.'

The attendant laughed and shook his head: 'But man. You can't do that.'

'It's all over now, man,' said the waiter. 'Why make a fuss about it?'

———

It was eight am and the cold grey sky seemed to be crowding down upon the wide, empty streets of Omaha, Nebraska. My hotel was on Harney Street, three blocks from the corner of Eighteenth Street, where in 1919 a mob hanged Will Brown, a black man accused of assaulting a young white girl. As Will Brown's body hung on the rope, the mob riddled it with bullets. Then they took it down, cut the legs off at the knees and burnt it. The mayor, who tried to intervene, was also hanged but someone cut him down before he died. Photos show the men standing around the fire as the body burns in the flames. You can see their faces as clear as can be. Some are smiling. Some pose earnestly for the camera. Fourteen-year-old Henry Fonda watched it all from the second-floor window of his father's printing works across the street.

Henry Fonda, Marlon Brando, Montgomery Clift, Nick Nolte, Dorothy McGuire and Malcolm X all came from Omaha. Johnny Carson started in television there. *Boys Town* was in Omaha. It still is, but now it's Girls and Boys Town. Fred Astaire came from Omaha. *Mutual of Omaha's Wild Kingdom*, the prototype for all television wildlife programs, hosted by Marlin Perkins and Jim Fowler, the Steve Irwin of his day, was essential viewing for families and dope-smokers in the 1960s. Union Pacific has had its headquarters in Omaha since 1862, which was just eight years after Chief Blackbird of the Omaha gave up the prairie for a reservation on Blackbird Hill and the land speculators arrived. Warren Buffett, the second-richest American, who is said to pay himself a mere $100,000 a year and to have given $30 billion to charity at a single stroke, was born in Omaha and still lives there in what is generally described as a modest house.

The two aircraft that dropped the bombs on Hiroshima and Nagasaki in 1945 were built just south of Omaha at a place called Fort Crook, after Major General Crook to whom Geronimo surrendered. Fort Crook became Offutt Air Force Base and headquarters of Strategic Air Command from the beginning to the end of the Cold War. Now it is home to Air Combat Command and the Fightin' 55th. The US Air Force mission statement reads: 'To fly and to fight in Air, Space and Cyberspace. To achieve that mission the Air Force has a vision of global vigilance, reach and power.' On 11 September 2001, when no-one quite knew where he was, the president was waiting and weighing his 'sovereign options for the defense of the United States of America and its global interests' in a bunker at Offutt Air Force Base.

Something about Omaha is definitive. Parked out there on the plains by the banks of the Missouri, it was once the great railhead to the West. It was also the great slaughterhouse and the great packing centre. And a great mill town. Founded in 1919, the Nebraska Consolidated Mills eventually became ConAgra, one of the biggest food companies in the world with sales of $20 billion or so and 40,000 employees. ConAgra is Latin for 'with the earth', though between the earth and Jiffy Popcorn, Golden Cuisine Ready Made Food for Seniors and many of the company's other eighty brands, quite a lot happens. At some stage in the 1980s, ConAgra became the biggest player in the US chicken industry, which accounts for about ten billion birds a year. The 270 million turkeys – about one for every legal citizen – are a separate item. The company claims to have a product in ninety-five per cent of American homes, and the CEO once boasted that his was the only company to 'participate across the entire food chain'.

Omaha is another one of those American cities undergoing what is called 'urban renewal'. It's a pity they didn't start before 1988. That was the year that ConAgra knocked down most of the warehouse district, despite the fact that the precinct was on the historic register. With what remained, however, Omaha has done impressive things. Not a lot of cities with half a million people have concert halls that seat 2000 and a fine theatre, art gallery, museums and zoo. Sometimes these renaissances mean taking a tough old part of town with a bit of character and turning it into a place with none: unless you think being able to drink wine under a Campari umbrella on the footpath and buy handmade soaps and candles or an American Eagle shirt with a deliberately damaged collar make for character. Renaissances generate clichés and gimcrack at will: but they also replace drab paddocks of concrete and lifeless malls, they keep some cars out and they reconnect cities to rivers cut off fifty years ago by freeways; well, almost – I went looking for the river in Omaha and got lost in the ConAgra complex.

I rang Julie to check on the train. She said the *California Zephyr* scheduled for 5.49 am was now due at two pm. A while later Amtrak rang and said it would be four pm at the earliest. I went back to bed and wondered again what Julie would be like if she existed. Would she drink whisky or gin?

When I woke and put on the TV, Don Imus, the startlingly cadaverous national talk-show host in the cowboy hat, was interviewing George Carlin, an ageing New York comedian. Carlin didn't like the way the country was going. Imus didn't disagree. Human beings are good at two things, Carlin said: being cooperative and being competitive. But in America these days it was all competition and no cooperation. Imus didn't disagree with this either. Carlin said he didn't like the execution of Tookie Williams. Imus said: 'Yeah, it seems a good idea sometimes, until they do it.'

Like other Union Stations across the country, Omaha's has been converted into a museum; an unfussy one that is neither jubilantly parochial nor tiresomely 'correct'. Passengers waiting for Amtrak trains to arrive at the prefabricated shack out the back can kill time in the museum and learn how trains used to be the last word in comfort, speed and efficiency. It contains a Pullman car with an oak dining table and chairs, sleeping compartments more ingenious and comfortable than any I've seen on the modern trains, a sumptuous bar, and beds that had been shaped to accommodate a mother and child. Americans should look at this carriage and weep, not for the past but for the future.

The museum presents a portrait of Omaha that might be likened to the way Henry Adams presented Silas P. Ratcliffe in *Democracy*: as typifying a category of Americans with 'a certain bigness; a keen practical sagacity; a bold freedom of self assertion; a broad way of dealing with what they knew'. Omaha has been visited by most of the calamities, man-made and elemental: tornadoes, blizzards, floods, depressions, riots, strikes, locusts, lynch mobs and the global economy. The place gives the impression that, much as Henry Fonda used to with those blue eyes, it has stared them all down.

At half past four in the afternoon I sat in the profoundly stationary train and listened to a man on the radio explaining to his listeners that they did not have to know *why* Billy Graham had Parkinson's disease: they need only know that God is sovereign and give thanks to Him. 'If a drunk runs over my child,' the preacher said, 'there is no knowing why he drank that six-pack; but we do need to know that God has taken note.' The age of atheists – by which he meant the Beat Generation – was over. 'Hear not on your own understanding,' he said. This was not a counsel of despair or total self-denial. Not at all. 'I enjoy a good Dr Pepper and some rocky road ice-cream. I like to go downtown and work out in the gym, run thirty-five minutes on the treadmill, visit with some guys and have a good coffee,' he said. It was impossible not to hope that God had also taken note of this man's insufferable smugness. We were skimming over snowy plains, now shining in the dark. The wide Missouri had a thin crust of murky brown ice.

The train was late because it had collided with a truck near Moab, Utah. The driver of the truck, a twenty-six-year-old Coloradan, had been killed. At dinner, people wondered if he had committed suicide. Several passengers said they heard a thud but felt nothing. Some of them saw pieces of the truck cabin flying across the fields. They sat in the train for hours waiting for a new locomotive to arrive.

By the time the train reached us in Omaha the kitchen was down to a beef stew that was nine-tenths gravy. The cook had put some carrots in it and they were dishing it out free. The young people opposite were vegetarians and made do with mashed potatoes. They had fallen in love on an organic farm in Colorado and were going back to Illinois to tell their parents. The young man, pale with a blond goatee, said he hoped to lease some land of his own out there and the two of them would farm it. When the mash was on their plates he said: 'If you don't mind, we will say a prayer before our meal.' And he took her hand and they bowed their heads in silence for about ten seconds, then looked up into each other's eyes and smiled. We smiled on our side of the table too.

All across the land the Christmas lights were blazing. They came into the train. Stars on the left side of the train were reflected in the windows on the right; and reindeer on the right sailed though the air on the left.

Chapter 6

*So long as he owned his own car he could always be in
control of his own fate – he was fated to nothing. He was
a true American . . . second generation to no one.
He was his own ancestors.*

Joyce Carol Oates, *Them*

In chicago station we sat in the train for two and a half
hours. The conductor said the problem was 'no engines'. He
believed they had located two and they'd be bringing them up
shortly. Two tables of Amish people – men and boys at one,
women and girls at the other – were eating catfish, an Amtrak
staple. Soon after we got going, a man fell ill in the dining car
and we lost another half-hour in the suburbs as two ambulances came and collected him and drove away with their lights
flashing in the snowy night.

The lady from Smyrna, Georgia, sitting next to me said it
was like déjà vu – a metro train she'd been travelling on that
same day had run over a pedestrian. Then she told us about a
man in Lafayette who raped and strangled a ninety-year-old
woman. The strange thing about it was that he had not forced
his way in. It meant the old woman probably knew him, she

149

said. 'Can you imagine that?' And he had stayed in the house for twenty-four hours after the murder.

The man sitting opposite asked if he had robbed her.

The woman from Smyrna said: 'No sir! Just raped and strangled her.'

'That's sick,' the man said with a smile.

He came from California and he was on his way to catch a cruise ship in Miami that would take him to Costa Rica and Panama. He was Polish by birth and still had the accent: and he had dark, Satanic eyes that might nail an innocent soul to a wall.

The woman from Smyrna was reminded of 'that man who disappeared from a cruise ship on his honeymoon. All they found was some blood on the sheets!'

'A lot of people go missing on cruise ships,' said the Pole. 'People plan these things for years.'

'Who?' asked the woman from Smyrna.

'Husbands. Wives,' said the Pole. 'That's why I stayed single.'

'And who gonna look after you when you're too old for philanderin'?' asked the woman.

'I'll go back to California, take the money from my investment account and get a facelift and my teeth done. Then I'll go back to Panama and the young girls,' said the Pole.

The lady from Smyrna took a breath and smiled.

'How young's the girls?'

The Pole was a master of the pause.

'Twelve,' he said.

At this the fourth person at our table, a young man with a pasty brow and a wispy black beard who had been silent during dinner, spluttered.

In New York, as Christmas approached, the city's transit workers went on strike. The people waited in the bitter air; they rode bicycles; they trudged across the Brooklyn Bridge. As if the underclass had replicated overnight, the people going nowhere shared their fate with the successful. The three-quarter black coat or full-length Burberry mingled with the nylon parkas and polyester fur. Everyone was snagged in the same river, the limo passengers and those who drove them for five dollars an hour. Everyone was at the mercy of the next log that floated by.

The imposing Roger Toussaint led the union in what he liked to call a 'strike for respect'. For every New York transit worker, he said, the 'number one passion is to come to the day when you're no longer a transit worker'. Retirement and dignity went together, and they demanded both at fifty. Seventy-three per cent of his members voted for this strike, spurred on, Toussaint said, by Mayor Bloomberg calling them 'thugs'. Toussaint said his union members kept public transport running twenty-four hours a day: they were good New Yorkers and Bloomberg had no business abusing them. The workers did not have a legal right to strike, but Rosa Parks did not have a legal right to that seat on the bus in Montgomery.

The media reported general outrage and went looking for cases of anger and hardship and price-gouging by cab drivers, but instead of rancour and misery, their pictures and words depicted something more stoic and inspiriting. In a cab crawling up Broadway with six autonomous selves squeezed into it, the consensus was for the strikers. Even the young woman dressed in the mandatory black of business, her phone somehow to her ear and telling her friend in Tel Aviv that she was sick of New York and its strikes and its weather, said she thought the strikers had a case. They had lousy jobs and the Transit Authority was corrupt. Besides, what sort of public authority made a billion dollars profit in a year?

Friends had me up to their place in Connecticut for Christmas and a couple of days later we edged into the cease-less tide of cars for the seven-hour journey to Washington DC. The more we drove, the more we became like rats or krill: but heroic rats, ingenious krill.

In Washington I rented a white Pontiac G6 and steered it gingerly onto the highway that runs south towards Richmond. I did not want to go south. I wanted to go west and eventually reach Yellowstone Park, but people I knew persuaded me to go down to Williamsburg first. I don't like tourist towns (and I never met a tourist who said he did), and I especially don't like historical pageants and colonial recreations. Williamsburg is in a different league, they said. And it is the site of the 1607 settlement; and you will see the College of William and Mary, which was designed by Christopher Wren. And Jamestown, the birthplace, they said. So I went. I don't know why, but the highway south was jammed, and this made me resent Williamsburg before I got there.

I left early the next morning, desperate to make progress westward, but I missed the James River ferry by thirty seconds. Still, the sun was warm as I waited at the head of the queue for the ferry to return. Just a mile away was the site of the settle-ment where those first Europeans pitched their tents and prayed. After half an hour a red pick-up truck parked behind me. In the mirror I could see it flew a Virginia flag on one side of the hood and an American flag on the other. The whole unit sparkled in the morning sun.

The driver caught me watching him. He had massive shoulders and no neck, a gleaming pink face under a red baseball cap with many badges sewn onto it, and a red silk jacket with more badges. He looked like a giant child dressed as his mother might have dressed him when he was eight years old. He stared at me until I dropped my gaze. Next time I glanced he was reading *Life* magazine. He seemed to be reading it aloud because his lips were moving. He glanced up again and, still watching me, pushed the little finger of his right hand into his nostril.

Once over the river, I took a back road in the hope that it would be the fastest way to Interstate 85, but soon found myself stuck behind a farmer enjoying the sun as he puttered along on a tractor. A turkey buzzard hopped aside from some roadkill. Swarms of kites circled over swamps. Blow-up Santa Clauses still stood guard outside many of the houses. A banner with the Three Wise Men on it had been strung across the verandah of one, and a banner with a Santa Claus and reindeer on another. A hand-carved Jesus hung from a cross twenty feet high at the entrance to a ramshackle house. The cross was painted yellow. Two shorter crosses stood on either side, unpainted. There were other massive crosses along the way and many churches, including the massive new Living Tabernacle in a clearing in a pine forest near Buckskin Creek.

I finally reached Interstate 85 and went flying down it and turned west onto 40, whereupon the sun struck the left side of my face and stayed there for the next ten days. The road swept through groves of trees and well mown verges, past the burgeoning towns of the 'new South' – Durham, Greensboro, Winston-Salem. I drove with the guilty exhilaration of a schoolboy, as if I'd stolen the car. I was desperate to get there, though I didn't know where 'there' was. Every hundred miles or so, rest-stops offered a variety of vending machines, the cleanest toilets in America and uncanny tranquillity to cool the ardour of one's flight. At the first I visited, not a scrap of rubbish fell that was not at once picked up by a wiry old attendant who moved about with such measured steps and a smile so fixed it seemed possible that he'd been through the heavenly gate, and this sunny rest-stop and pick-up stick and dust coat were his for eternity.

Thomas Wolfe was a native of Asheville and put it on the

literary map with his novel *Look Homeward, Angel*. The book, though often called a 'classic', is not much read these days – a fact which might be put down to its considerable length and the not unrelated matter of Wolfe's relationship with adjectives. Thus (on the same page): 'Fluorescent with smooth tight curves, the drawling virgins of the South fill summer porches ... [they] watch the summer crowd of fortunate tourists and white cool skin virgins fly by the sidewalk in thick pullulation.' In the summer perhaps, but on 30 December 2005, there was no pullulation on Asheville's sidewalks.

The centrepieces of Asheville's famous Pack Square are a large fountain and pool and a considerable obelisk to a Confederate governor called Vance. In his novel, Wolfe is always going back to this square, as if these (probably unconscious) fertility symbols had a magnetic effect on him. General Lee is also acknowledged by a plaque, and there are statues of turkeys and pigs, a homage to the days before Asheville was judged one of the most 'vegetarian friendly' cities in the nation. But it is the architecture that makes Pack Square. At one end stand the pink art-deco City Hall and the fifteen-storey Buncombe County Courthouse. Down the south side there are several 'skyscrapers' in various styles, all dating from the first three decades of the twentieth century, when Asheville – and the Vanderbilts who lived there – spent up. It is hard to say if it is the inherent beauty of these buildings that is so pleasing or the mere fact that they survive. It would not be very much more surprising if they were Etruscan.

They survived because, with so much money poured into the city in the good years, the Great Depression sank Asheville into the highest per capita debt in the country. For more than forty years it stagnated. Developers didn't get cracking until the mid-1970s, when they knocked down several blocks and highways were driven through in the usual way. But by then the people of Ashville had lived with the buildings long enough to be fond of them and recognised their value. So they stopped the developers before their city went the way of other places. Very soon the idea of heritage tourism took hold: 'rehabilitation tax credits' followed and, as a consequence, many of Asheville's wonderful buildings were not only saved but restored. The place is now a damaged jewel. It is also, according to a national survey, 'one of the 50 most desirable places to be' in the United States.

It was also desirable a hundred years ago, when the wealthy and fashionable went to Asheville to escape the summer heat. Others came to find cures for their respiratory diseases, including tuberculosis. Zelda Fitzgerald came, was diagnosed with schizophrenia, and died in a fire in an Asheville asylum in 1947. In 1958 Robert Mitchum came and made a film called *Thunder Road* about the battle between the whisky distillers in the Smoky Mountains and the Alcohol and Tobacco Board.

People still come in droves, both as tourists and to set up homes and businesses in a city that looks, and probably is, unlike any other in America. Arty, green, new-age, vegetarian Asheville gives the impression of a hippydom that, like the buildings or an asthmatic cured by the mountain air, somehow managed to hang on and now enjoys a second chance at life. These are just impressions, of course. For more concrete evidence of success we best turn to the housing market, of which a columnist in the *Asheville Citizen Times* wrote at the end of 2005: 'Sales from such homes as busked up West Asheville bungalows net profits that would allow their sellers to settle comfortably in Malibu.'

Oscar Wilde quite liked the idea of socialism but he doubted it would work: he reckoned that not enough people would be willing to give up their nights. His opinion was a distant echo of Tocqueville's sober observation of American democracy as a 'mild' form of despotism that 'would degrade men without tormenting them'. All the frontier-levelling was fine, he thought, but what happened when the people were too busy procuring 'the petty and paltry pleasures with which they glut their lives' to take a useful interest in governing themselves? As he saw it, they shook off their state of dependence just long enough to select their master, and then they relaxed into dependence again. For the aristocratic Tocqueville, American democracy threatened to impose upon the people a power that 'compresses, enervates, extinguishes and stupefies' them. Not tyranny – but 'an immense and tutelary power' that would keep the people 'in perpetual childhood and spare them all the care of thinking'.

There are times when just an hour in front of the television seems to justify Tocqueville's darkest apprehensions of American democracy. Driving for an hour through poor communities with flags flying from every porch can provoke the same thought: 'It [the "power" granted by the people] is well content that the people should rejoice, provided they think of nothing but rejoicing.' Yet there are also times when American democracy – and American television – seems more alive than any other; when the people, again in the words of Tocqueville, 'are hindered by no permanent obstacles from exercising a perpetual influence on the daily conduct of affairs'.

By way of illustration, when I turned on the television in a motel in Asheville on 30 December at seven pm, the first channel was showing a hearing into a proposed rezoning in Tunnel Road. Various residents stepped forward and made their cases against the proposal. A disabled woman told the tribunal that she had renovated her home to make living in it possible and now the tunnel might drive her out. Her argument was very clear, though she wept while making it and so did a few in the room – and doubtless some who were watching in motels. The next three stations were screening evangelical programs of one kind or another. On one, a woman said that in her church the people dance and sing to 'contemporary gospel', which had taken her from 'a situation of devastation to a situation of victory'. On the fourth channel, C-Span, there was a program about the Atlantic slave trade, and C-Span Two was rescreening the 6 December Congressional Hearing into Hurricane Katrina.

Ishmael Mohammed told the panel, chaired by a Republican from Connecticut, that eighty black citizens of New Orleans were shot by soldiers instructed to shoot to kill. He said the 'looters' were getting food for their people. The chairman said he had some sympathy for such people, but not for those who took television sets. He asked what should be said about the people who were too frightened to go outside because of violent mobs. The three black witnesses all said that racism was at the core of the response. The chair said: 'The mayor didn't do his job, the governor didn't do her job and the president didn't do his job, or the people around him.' The black witnesses said they wanted the government to investigate the many reports that the levees were deliberately breached with explosives. The panel was concerned that the levee story was taking on the character of a conspiracy theory to rank with the assassination of John F. Kennedy. One of the witnesses told how his father returned from Europe at the end of the war an army captain, and went back to a society where he was not allowed to stand in bus shelters. His father told him: 'Never has a country I loved so much treated me so bad.'

———

Through grey, leafless hills I wound down into the town of Cherokee from the Maggie Valley, wondering if it was smart to come this way and not take the scenic route through the Great Smoky Mountains on the Blue Ridge Parkway. These settlements, now devoted to tourism, outdoor sports and gambling, have grown out of the remnants of the Cherokee Indians who hid out in the mountains when the rest of the tribe was removed to Oklahoma and eventually won title to some land. You know you're in Cherokee when you see a vast hall with a sign saying: TRIBAL BINGO. Then there are a series of grim motels called Chief Motel, Warrior Motel, Cherokee Motel. There's Big Chief Gift Shop, Running Bear Den and Cherokee Casino, which is so big it's out of all proportion to the rest of the town and the valley it lies in. Then come the novelty shops and Tomahawk Mall, Big Beaver Camp Ground, Hiawatha Park, Praise God Coffee. For fifteen or twenty miles it was like this, all the way to Bryson City, North Carolina, where the first thing you see is a pink sign saying: BARBEQUE with a pink pig on top of it. There were signs saying: CONSULT YOUR ELDERS ABOUT DIABETES, and one on a bend in the road that said: AND AFTER DEATH, WHAT?

The road runs beside a beautiful wide stream, and when it reaches Bryson City you can get your nails done at 'Nails by Judy'. (In Asheville, you could get them done in a *drive-in* nail salon as big as a bank.) Bryson City is not a city but a town of 1300 people, ninety per cent of them 'white or Hispanic', with a median income of $23,000. It has a town hall and a war memorial and a great many churches, including one with a flag and a big white crucifix and a nativity scene in a box. There's the Hillside Baptist, the Midway Baptist, the Evangelistic Tabernacle and many more, and in among them there's the Hillbilly Mall.

In summer the people come here to go canoeing or fishing or hiking, and from tiny shacks hardly big enough to make a family-sized pizza in, the locals sell them boiled peanuts and hickory-smoked ribs. A funeral went by; all the mourners were driving pick-up trucks or SUVs and many of them showed their support for the troops in Iraq with yellow ribbons. Some of the ribbons were draped around a cross, and some had a red ribbon as well as a yellow one to indicate the wearer's love of country. One always has a choice. On the radio, a preacher with an Australian accent said that a lot of 'research' his church does was bringing more and more people to accept the 'new creation' and be freed from the bondage of sin. He quoted Psalms, Revelation and Isaiah as 'absolute authority' for 'some form of catastrophic event coming in the future'. But those who took up Christ's offer of salvation had nothing to fear, so long as they took it up today. 'Don't put it off,' he said, as if the offer were for a limited time only, and referred listeners to 2 Corinthians 6: 'Now is the day of salvation.'

In a place that seemed to have just a handful of permanent residents, the number of churches was bewildering. Many of them were new. Some were huge, their crosses towering over countless faded advertising hoardings, used-car lots, spare-parts operations and tattoo shops: as if some new culture was just now overrunning a fading one. It was New Year's Eve, but on both sides of the border with Tennessee, Christmas decorations still adorned the houses. They had, presumably, gone up soon after Thanksgiving, and now on many front lawns the inflatable Santas were detumescing. Some had tipped forward and lay sadly on their noses.

—

There was a Starbucks in Broad Street in Chattanooga, so I parked the car in a nearby side street. As I pulled up, a black man in a baseball cap was talking to an Asian couple on the pavement. They walked away, and he turned and gave me unnecessary directions for parking. That he was hustling I knew for certain. He tapped on the window, looking cross. I asked what the matter was.

'Those guys,' he said, 'don't believe Cleveland's in Tennessee. They say it's in Ohio.'

'Well, most people think that,' I said.

He was looking in the back of the car. 'Cleveland's twenty

miles from here,' he said. 'Cleveland, Tennessee.' He needed to get there because he had a wife and child there and he wanted to spend New Year's Eve with them. He had no money for gas. I knew it was bullshit but I gave him five dollars.

'God bless you – if you believe in God, as I do,' he said.

'I don't,' I said.

'I've got a jeep,' he said. 'Neat for the jeep.' And he walked away with a smile.

I re-parked the car two blocks further on and walked back to the Starbucks. The hustler was sitting on the step of an Italian restaurant with a white companion, laughing. He was still there when I came out.

Further down Broad Street, where the aquariums and big river redevelopment are, they were setting up for the end of a long-distance run. It was the Tocquevillian dichotomy. At one end of the street we had the communitarians, the people who were prepared to give up their evenings. They ran singly, and as couples, and as families. Some ran pushing their children in strollers. Christmas carols were playing on loudspeakers, as they had been all over the land since early November. At the other end of the street were the other kind of citizens – the ones who would not participate, but who knew enough about those who did – the wife, the child, the god, the jeep and Christmas – to make do grifting.

Chattanooga is another city having a renaissance. The volunteer attendant at the aquarium told me that, in this case, it was much needed. Fifteen years ago, he said, the city was a wreck of a place, very nearly a slum. You need travel only a couple of blocks down M. L. King Boulevard to see bail bond offices, pawn shops, boarded-up businesses and the grey decrepitude to get an idea of Chattanooga unrenewed. The contrast with the business district is almost as striking as it is with the sweeping curves of the impeccably kept gravestones at Chattanooga National Cemetery, further down the Boulevard.

Americans have no equal when it comes to cemeteries – and few surpass their renaissances. With the help of Coca-Cola money, downtown Chattanooga sparkles with a new arts centre, a new stadium, a new bridge across the river, a newly renovated wharf and, of course, the aquariums which, with the help of 450 volunteers, attract a million visitors each year. When you add a university, Bessie Smith Hall and an African American museum, for a city of 100,000 people it is magnificently endowed.

A railroad is all it lacks. The last train ran from Terminal Station in the 1970s, and the old Union Station was demolished years before that. The Chattanooga Choo-Choo is now a Holiday Inn and diner.

They tamed the Tennessee River with nine dams built between 1918 and the 1960s, the bulk of them constructed by the Tennessee Valley Authority in the 1930s as part of the public works undertaken in Roosevelt's New Deal. The railroad came from Atlanta in 1849, 'mingling the waters of the Atlantic and the Mississippi', as someone said at the celebrations. Needing command of both the railroads and the river, the armies of the Civil War clashed repeatedly round Chattanooga until the Union won and Chattanooga became the 'gateway to the lower South', the staging point for the assault on Atlanta and beyond.

Chattanooga has a river aquarium and an ocean aquarium. I went to the river aquarium. In one section visitors are as if in a primeval forest on a bank of the Tennessee River, somewhere high up where it gathers force for the descent to the Mississippi Delta. Birds twitter and fly about; terrapins, cottonmouth snakes, copperheads and rattlers snooze among rocks and rotting logs; otters tumble-turn. The aquarium contains life in immeasurable variety – mammals, fish, frogs, molluscs, reptiles, birds, butterflies – all kinds of creatures of which very few are mentioned in connection with Noah's Ark. For a thousand years the mysterious tribes of horseless, corn-farming 'mound-builders' lived along the banks of the Tennessee River. For much longer than any race of people, catfish, salamanders and the cartilaginous, caviar-bearing *Polyodon spathula* – or American paddlefish – have been swimming here; the paddle-fish with its mouth wide open and electro-receptors in its snout. It was swimming up and down the river with its mouth open fifty million years before the last of the dinosaurs.

When getting to grips with the concept of creation it is useful to observe creatures that seem to be immune to time. A young female alligator lay motionless in a corner of a great glass tank. Several little pieces had been bitten out of her tail by the 140-year-old snapping turtle that for three days had occupied the space between the corner where the alligator was and the corner where she wanted to be. The attendant who told me this explained that the aquarium tried not to interfere with the course of nature. Sometime in the next week or so, he said, the turtle would likely nod off and it would be up to the alligator to seize the moment. Of course, she might not be brave enough or swift enough; she might lack the necessary self-belief. It is possible that even now, the alligator is still there in a place that does not suit her: in which case, in truth, she cannot be counted among the fit. It was official policy to apply the Darwinian principle, not the lesson of the Beatitudes.

CHAPTER 7

'Did you think you had educated the superstition
out of these people?'
'I certainly did think it.'
'Well, then, you may unthink it.'

Mark Twain, *A Connecticut Yankee in*
King Arthur's Court

IN A CHURCH THAT LOOKED LIKE IT HAD BEEN DECORATED for a debutantes' ball, with golden columns and a mighty red and gold velvet crown, the Rock Trio strummed their banjos and sang: 'We'll soon be on the other side and see the face of Jesus.' I turned it off. From the next room I heard a preacher on another channel: 'The gentle mother comes to him and says, "My daughter is grievously vexed with the devil."' It was eight am on New Year's Day in Chattanooga. 'And Jesus,' the preacher said – and paused. 'Jesus said, "The children must come first."'

All in their pyjamas, or in combinations of sweaters and sleepwear, smiling and smelling of talcum and sleep, a family of six crowded into the lift, on their way to the free continental breakfast downstairs. The television in the breakfast room had

165

the preacher too: 'A seven-year-old schoolgirl . . .' he said in a theatrical hush. 'She cannot bring that name into school because of the so-called separation of church and state.' Here another well-practised pause, and loud microphone breathing, then: 'Talk about Buddha all you like. Talk about Mohammed all you like. But you can't mention' – he paused again, till they were craving the name – 'Jesus Christ.'

The congregation murmured their protests.

'Enough is enough!'

They cheered.

'I'm gonna say it,' this preacher said, as if he might be burned alive by liberals for the heresy. And did he say it: 'This nation was founded on the word of Almighty God!'

His audience cheered and shouted hallelujah.

'This nation is a Christian nation! It is not a Moslem nation!'

That brought the house down.

———

Every day of the year, many millions of Americans spend an hour or more in the Holy Land of 2000 or more years ago. Twenty-four hours a day they can hear the voice of Paul on the road to Damascus, or the Good Samaritan, or Jesus raising Lazarus from the dead. Or they can learn what is meant in Isaiah when it says: 'Behold, at my rebuke I dry up the sea, I make the river a wilderness' – and they can hear it as if Isaiah had been a guest on *Larry King Live*.

Religion is seductive in America, even to the unreligious. 'When you do the will of God you *cannot* lose,' says Dr Charles Stanley of In Touch Ministries. You can go with Dr Stanley on a cruise ship to Alaska and take in his wisdom and the 'unparalleled beauty of God's creation' all at once. And you *want* to go. 'And Paul says, "Lord, why did you knock me off my jackass?"' It's as good a question as you're likely to hear that day on the radio or television. It stays with you. Listen again tomorrow and you will hear another one. It might be from Job or Genesis or Revelation. If you do not have much else to do, or if what you're doing does not demand much thinking and you're sick of political questions, it will occupy your mind a good deal. It will keep it active and alive.

You don't have to listen to it. In a democracy the propaganda competes in the marketplace and the listeners have choices. If you choose to listen, you have more choices: between churches, personalities, formats and music. It's the competition that makes them so good at what they do. Competition obliges them to put a lot of money into the marketing and presentation. They contend for your attention. If you do not like Fox News or country music, or if you're out of NPR's reach, usually there are a dozen or more radio stations that will give you religion. Move up and down the AM and FM dials and after a while you can imagine you're living in a theocracy. But it's a multi-party theocracy wherein God is always present and on duty and the people spend their days figuring out his meaning and intentions, or having it figured for them. *This* is the life of the mind in large parts of the United States, and before people in the other parts say it is a travesty, they need to ask if there is any comparable spirit of intellectual inquiry in the places where they live. Who are the humanist equivalents of the preacher taking the concept of grace or the exegesis of Isaiah or the shape of Armageddon to the porches of the South and the Midwest every day?

Of course, these preachers also tell people how to behave and who or what is wicked and dangerous; what will be forgiven and what is unforgivable. For the most part, the model of behaviour is a kitsch conglomerate of largely imagined values they call Judeo-Christian. West of the Appalachians in the winter of 2006, the model was manifest in the person of President George W. Bush. It sounded sometimes as if he were a semi-divine, as if he sitteth on the throne. Of course, everything that was alleged to be good about the president was held to be bad by liberals, humanists and secularists. But no-one who knew Jesus as he is known in these parts would be listening to them.

Fifty miles north of Chattanooga I came to the little town of Dayton, Tennessee. In the window of the new Republican Party office the sign said: MOVING TOWARDS THE FUTURE. But not so much as a dog moved in Dayton on New Year's Day. Nothing in the street, nothing on the freight line. The two policemen leaning in the doorway of the new Rhea County Jail might as well have been statues. The Three Wise Men on the front step of a nearby house *were* statues: alabaster miniatures looking down at a little nativity scene, all beneath a sign that hung from the spouting saying: HAPPY BIRTHDAY JESUS. And in front of the redbrick Rhea County Courthouse there stood a statue of William Jennings Bryan. The inscription on the plinth described him as PRESIDENTIAL NOMINEE, SECRETARY OF STATE, CONGRESSMAN, AUTHOR AND ORATOR. His hand rested on a lectern inscribed with his watchwords: TRUTH AND ELOQUENCE.

Eloquent he was. It was said that on an average day on the stump between about 1890 and his death in 1925, he gave four one-hour speeches and filled another two hours with shorter addresses. He once spoke for twelve hours during a fifteen-hour period. Most of these orations were performed without a microphone; indeed, the introduction of the microphone helped Bryan's rivals to compete with him. Known as 'the Great Commoner' because he believed that truth – secular truth, at least – resided in the people, Bryan dominated Democratic Party politics for three decades. Three times he was the party's presidential nominee. He did more than anyone else to get Woodrow Wilson elected in 1912, and Wilson made him secretary of state. He was anti-trust, anti-gold standard, anti-railroad company, anti-Wall Street, anti-big city (especially

New York) and anti-alcohol. Nor did he like imperialism. No-one ever put the argument in plainer terms: 'A republic cannot be an empire, for a republic rests upon the theory that governments derive their just power from the consent of the governed, and colonialism violates this theory.'

Bryan was the most devout of Christians, but as a Southern Presbyterian, he would likely find the rise of the modern fundamentalist churches and the liberalism of the modern Presbyterian equally confounding. (What sort of Presbyterian Church entertains the thought of homosexual marriage, and calls on all its members to be carbon neutral?) He remains America's most famous creationist, but he thought along significantly different lines to the contemporary variety.

He was not quite the fool his liberal-humanist opponents made him out to be. Books about the Great War persuaded him that the Germans had fallen under the godless spell of Friedrich Nietzsche, whose philosophy he traced to Darwin – and Darwin he could not accept. Even less would Bryan accept what became known as 'social Darwinism': the theory that human societies are governed by the same evolutionary laws that guarantee the survival of the fittest in nature. This Bryan saw as a 'law of hate': 'I choose to believe that love rather than hatred is the law of development,' he said. Bryan's supporters might say that he was vindicated by the rise of Nazism and the widespread fashion for eugenics. The argument would have more force, however, if he had ever raised his voice *against* the eugenicists, or occasionally directed his Christian love and his wondrous oratorical skills to the cause of black Americans.

A sign on the edge of the lawn explains Bryan's presence in Dayton:

Here, from July 10 to 21, 1925, John Thomas Scopes, a country high school teacher, was tried for teaching that man descended from a lower order of animals, in violation

of a lately passed state law. William Jennings Bryan assisted the prosecution. Clarence Darrow . . . the defense.
Scopes was convicted.

The flow of the language tells you the sign is an old one. But the statue of Bryan, sponsored by Dayton's Bryan College ('a highly ranked, nationally competitive college that puts Christ above all') was unveiled only in 2004, and the Republican Senate Majority Leader from Tennessee, Bill Frist, sent greetings. Two months earlier Frist, who is a Harvard-trained heart surgeon, said he believed that 'intelligent design' – the doctrine that the intelligence of an all-powerful creator can be detected in patterns that exist in nature – should be taught in schools on an equal footing with the science of evolution.

The front doors of the courthouse being closed, I went to the back and found the entrance to the Scopes Trial Museum in the basement. The door was closed, but it opened when I pulled. A note on the door behind it said CLOSED but I pushed and it, too, opened. The basement was dark. I felt around for a light and when I found the switch and the fluorescent tube stopped flickering, there before me under glass lay a family Bible open to Genesis and the words 'Let there be light'. On the wall next to it there was a sign that said: PLEASE TURN OFF BEFORE LEAVING BUILDING. And beside the Bible, also open and under glass, was Darwin's *On the Origin of Species*.

The Scopes trial was only held because a couple of Dayton's businessmen thought the publicity might drag the town out of decline. They recruited Scopes, the twenty-four-year-old biology teacher, as their stalking horse; but the stars were to be God, represented by Bryan, and Darwin, represented by the near-celebrity Darrow and two other distinguished lawyers. As an active anti-evolutionist and, according to Darrow, the man responsible for the Tennessee law, Bryan self-selected. 'If evolution wins, Christianity goes,'

Bryan said: and he repeated the message in a sermon at a local church attended by the judge and his family. Darrow got the nod to appear for evolution only after H. G. Wells declined. He told Bryan he wanted to deliver the country from 'your fool ideas that no intelligent Christian on earth believes'. The trial, Darrow said, was 'the first of its kind since we stopped trying people for witchcraft'.

For the first time in the history of the world a court case would be broadcast live on radio. Hordes of journalists arrived in town. Among them, from Baltimore, was H. L. Mencken, a Nietzschean who believed God was dead, religion a sham and democracy a system for keeping a country's few intelligent people under the boots of its inexhaustibly plentiful morons. He called Bryan 'a sort of Fundamentalist pope and an idol of Morondom'. The contending forces set up stalls and the Anti-Evolution League unfurled a banner proclaiming: THE CONFLICT – HELL AND THE HIGH SCHOOL. Someone brought some chimpanzees – to give evidence for the defence, the creationists joked. The courtroom was scarcely able to contain 500 souls sweltering in the July heat, much less the 5000 who turned up; so at length the judge, a conservative Christian like the twelve male jurors, moved proceedings onto the lawns. Lemonade-sellers did well. Darrow called Bryan to give evidence and, with the press cheering him on, drove the old crusader to concede that the 'days' of creation were 'periods' that 'might have continued for millions of years'.

The defence planned to demolish the anti-evolutionists' arguments for the purposes of entertainment and public education, but to lose the case and appeal to a higher court that would surely find the legislation unconstitutional. The jury obliged, the judge fined Scopes and the defence appealed to the Tennessee Supreme Court: the court found for Scopes, but only on a technicality, so the case was closed without reference to the principle at the heart of it. William Jennings

Bryan dropped dead a week after the Dayton trial ended, and that was the only thing to be resolved decisively. 'I have been so well satisfied with the Christian religion that I have spent no time trying to find argument against it,' he had once said.

Eighty years on, despite the government-inspired surge in science teaching after the Russians stole a march in space, the creationists are stronger than ever and their opponents are still smart-asses. Among the creatures of the Galapagos Islands that confirmed Darwin in his theory of natural selection was the *Nannopterum harrisi*. It is a cormorant in all respects, but its wings are pathetically small. The physical limits of its habitat and an absence of natural enemies have caused it to lose the ability to fly. It might be the same with the creationists. So long as their habitat is secure and they are left in it unchallenged, the 'reason and free enquiry' that Jefferson said were the only useful agents against error might go the way of the cormorant's wings.

The policemen hadn't moved when I came out. I could have loaded the whole display into the back of the car and driven away with it. In a sense, that's what I did. A sponsor invited radio listeners to join a retail plan which would make them 'part of a revenue stream that will advance the kingdom'. A preacher extolled the work of Christian missionaries in places devastated by the tsunami. The way had never been so open in Indonesia, where there were 500 different language groups who have never heard the Word until now. Progress in India was phenomenal. In Cambodia the ravages of communism and civil war had created 'marvellous opportunities for the gospel to go forward'. What with Hurricanes Katrina and Rita, in the last year the Lord had been prodigiously kind to those who had chosen to do His work.

From Dayton I drove out through the land of the falling-down shed, the stark clapboard house, the Church of Christ and cemeteries so bedecked with flowers they looked a bit like quilts. There's a family out there by the unusual name of Measles: there are letterboxes with Measles on them and the Burrell Measles Bridge. Up in the forest, bulldozers were clearing the way for the Eagle's Bluff Gated Community. All alone, high on the rise at Little Mountain was a barbershop, a clapboard shack with a hand-painted barber's pole out the front.

McMinnville radio was broadcasting live from the Chamber of Commerce, where a choir was singing *Amazing Grace*. There is something about old hymns. In certain circumstances they seem to bind the various bits of you together. I listened as I drove down the long main street, which was adorned with yellow ribbons. They stretched between power poles, hung from fences, tree branches and traffic lights. On the Jesus' Name Pentecostal Church a sign said: GET RIGHT OR BE LEFT. The choir sang *Blessed Assurance*, a hymn composed by a couple of Methodist ladies from New York back in the 1870s:

> *This is my story, this is my song,*
> *Praising my saviour all the day long . . .*
> *Perfect submission, perfect delight!*
> *Visions of rapture . . . And so on.*

The McMinnville transmitter didn't reach much beyond the town's borders, but the echo of those plain voices took many miles to fade. After hearing Methodists sing *Amazing Grace* and *Blessed Assurance* in McMinnville, it is hard to know why modern Christians feel the need to sing anything else but those two and perhaps *Abide with Me* and a couple of psalms. Even if they need more hymns, they don't need more denominations. McMinnville, which is home to just 12,000 souls, has 107 places of worship.

In *A Connecticut Yankee in King Arthur's Court* and elsewhere in his writing, Mark Twain expressed a deep democratic loathing for an established church of any kind. He professed no faith of his own, and wondered aloud why believers asked us to love God as the author of all things when so many of those things were gross cruelties for which we would hang a fellow human being. Nevertheless, Mark Twain thought religion good for the health of society. He believed in a spiritual world beyond the visible and so thought it natural for men and women to commune with it. Religion was fine so long as it issued from personal conviction and not from authority vested in an established church. Like Winston Churchill, who described himself as a buttress rather than a pillar of the church, Twain supported it from the outside. Not one church but many: he was adamant that there must be enough for them 'to police each other'.

But Twain would have thought 107 churches too many for McMinnville. Forty free sects, nationwide, he reckoned ideal. Many more than this and he must have seen that they would not so much police each other as create a riot of their own: that for every hundred 'sincere and right hearted' priests going among the people, there were bound to be fifty frauds and crooks fighting like ravens over the carcass of reason and generating half the country's fantasy and humbug.

I heard five or six preachers on the radio that morning, the voices of the Fourth Great Awakening in America. They interpreted elusive metaphors; they found in scripture the answers to the pain of loss, the confusions of love and the wages of infidelity and lust. They offered a world in which God and Satan are perpetually – and demonstrably – at war, and Jesus is as real and constant as the sun, the sky and the supermarket. They are not all creationists – at least, they don't all say they are – and they do not all declare a loathing of Islam or fealty to the president. But they all wrap their listeners in a fantasy, a never-ending soap opera in which the heroes never die and antiquity never fades. It's easy enough to imagine how it grips, particularly when the comfort comes in familiar forms like those of country music. Jesus seems at home in country music, or at least in what is called 'inspirational country music':

> *Have you asked Him to forgive you?*
> *Have you laid your burdens at His feet?*

All day and all night they wail melodiously. It is radio religion's state of grace.

The signs of grace come less easily to the preachers who seem permanently agitated and warlike and who are forever hounding and abusing their enemies. This posture they share with the secular shock-jocks, who might once have believed in enlightenment and reason, but you wouldn't know from listening to them. Pentecostalist and talk-show host alike rant as if locked in a fight to the death. They make a pretence of truth and eloquence, a great show of good old American common sense, but they appeal exclusively to the emotions. They prey on what their listeners feel. Your feelings are real; perforce they must be true. They may indicate possession by Satan or by liberalism, in which case we will help you drive them out. If, however, your feelings are at one with ours, you are saved. This is 'faith-based' thinking. The phoney word 'values' does well in such an environment. What we're really talking about, however – and what it 'feels' like after a few days' listening – is propaganda. 'There is no argument in the world that carries the hatred a religious belief does,' Will Rogers said.

It was dark when I reached the town of Savannah, Tennessee, and saw the illuminated cross in the distance. I drove out of the town, over the Tennessee River and there it was, by the massive Pentecostal church on the hill in Crump (population 1521), which must have been named for Ed 'Boss' Crump, who ran Tennessee politics and the Tennessee Democratic Party for most of the first half of the twentieth century. It was a towering cross and if a fire had been burning at the base of it and figures had been gathered there in white hoods, the scene would have been more menacing only by degree.

A little further on, in Adamsville, the Love and Truth Church was not that much smaller than the Pentecostal. It was a 'Last Days Church' and its mission was to 'bring in the end-time harvest'. I turned back in the dark, crossed the river again and booked into a motel adjoining the old courthouse of Savannah. I could hear the giant flagpole rattling down by the bridge at the BP station, next to the Cherry Mansion where Ulysses S. Grant set himself up before the Battle of Shiloh, a bloodbath staged a few miles downstream in April 1862.

The motel-keeper recommended the Mexican restaurant a couple of miles out of town, but when I got there it was full of broad-shouldered policemen, so I went to the 'family' restaurant on the other side of the road. It was late and, being a Sunday, a lot of families had been in; I never saw so much mayonnaise and fries on one carpet. I picked my way through a catfish, drove back to the motel and decided to walk down to the BP with the rattling flagpole to get a beer or wine or something to wash the taste away. But of course it was Sunday, so all the liquor was chained up. By the flagpole there were two cannon and a pile of cannonballs, worn smooth by children playing on them.

A car went by and someone put his head out the window and unleashed an appalling, withering scream that truly reached into my very bowels. It was the descendant of a Rebel soldier, most likely, and the 'Rebel yell' handed down through the generations. Henry Morton Stanley, who later found Dr Livingstone in Africa, fought at Shiloh on the Rebel side and said the yell 'drove all sanity and order from us', which is what you want in a battle like that. My hair was still on end when I reached the courthouse and came across the monument erected – in the mid-1990s – to the 'Gallant Confederate Soldiers of Hardin County': they were 'defending their homeland', it said.

In nearby Nashville that night, 8000 Christian youths had gathered to join in worship. They formed circles and prayed for the television cameras and praised the glory of the Lord for reporters. The half-burned body of a woman had been found on New Year's Eve. If it turned out she had been murdered, that would make one hundred murders for the year in Nashville. Meanwhile in New York, Mayor Bloomberg congratulated his people on the *decline* of crime, including homicide; and to cheers from his audience he went on to say that every kid in New York now received an education in the arts.

A man from Tennessee rang the station I was watching to say that 'those people' on *The New York Times* who revealed that President Bush had been tapping telephones should be charged with treason. Whatever they might wish for in New York, he said, 'out here we want to be safe from terrorists'.

In the morning the Indian proprietor of the motel was sitting in a big armchair wearing just his pyjama shorts and watching flamenco dancing on TV. He'd been in the United States for ten years, and he liked it. He had started out in California, but he liked Savannah because there was less crime. His father had another motel a few miles away. Discovering I was Australian, he went out the back and returned with a cricket ball and asked me to show him my bowling grip.

The 2000 census showed that more than twenty per cent of the residents of Savannah were living below the poverty line, twenty per cent were over sixty-five years old and there were twenty per cent more adult women than adult men. But it looked pleasant in the daylight, without the flagpole clanking and the cross alight on the hill: 'a fine old town, unruined by commercialism', as the brochure said. There were good old homes in various styles: Queen Anne, Classical Revival, Colonial Revival, Greek Revival and a mode that is called simply 'Southern' and has a real charm about it. The Cherry Mansion had either antebellum grace or ostentation, depending on the angle and how its evocation of the old plantation days played upon your mind. Until the mid-nineteenth century these parts were all woodland, full of wild turkey, bears, beavers and deer. In 1838, a party of Cherokees went through on their way west along the Trail of Tears. They were being removed to Indian Territory. Some people in Savannah gave them soap and biscuits. By then *Amazing Grace* had been translated into Cherokee and had become their unofficial anthem. The story goes that they sang it as they trudged along.

I drove west again through Crump, where flags flew by the Pentecostal Church. The cross did not look as menacing as it had in the dark. A genuine Vietnam-era chopper with shark's teeth painted on it and the full complement of weaponry made the centrepiece of a little roadside park. And then I came again to Adamsville and its big Piggly Wiggly store – 'America's first true self-service grocer store . . . founded in Memphis, Tennessee in 1916 by Clarence Saunders', who was a political rival of Ed Crump. And a little later, a hand-painted sign: ELECT JAMES MILLS SHERIFF (of Hornsby, that is, population about thirty). On the radio a woman sang:

> *How do you like the paper plate*
> *And the pork 'n beans you're eating?*
> *You should've thought of that*
> *Before you started cheating.*

Suddenly the highway floods with cars and you know you're close to Memphis, and when you've skirted the city you reach the banks of the Mississippi, where the ancient mound-builders left a famous mound. But now there's a glass pyramid, which makes a kind of sense when you think about it. The pyramid is the last thing you see before you cross the river and enter Arkansas, the state Mencken once called 'the apex of moronia'.

⸻

Eastern Arkansas was dusty and dry and the roads were not so good. The Winnebagos – the word comes from the Indian tribe of south-west Wisconsin – ploughed happily on. You have to love them: Pop driving, Ma with her feet up, reading. Most of them tow an SUV behind. Some days you pass one and later stop somewhere, then find you're passing them again – and maybe she's driving this time. You can get attached to them, as if you're extended family.

It must have been the same on a wagon or a horse, the way the sun never stops burning the left side of your face, but no-one ever said so in the literature. To escape the ceaseless burning, I turned south down a quiet road to a sort of town that seemed to be more of a car park than anything else. In the diner, old people – women, mainly – in baseball caps and check shirts sat around drinking Coke and eating fried catfish, chicken tenderloins and fries on plastic plates with plastic 'silverware' (as the signs above the trays said). The people did not say much to each other, but seemed to be communing just the same.

Somewhere out on a tiresome plain east of Little Rock, a voice said that each year American kids buy $15 billion worth of goods and influence the purchase of another $700 billion worth. This remarkable information faded into the ether, and then there was a man shouting, as if he had been accused of some enormity: 'What do you mean? What do you mean!? You people! I don't know how you can do it!'

The caller said something about Joe Lieberman and something else about John McCain, and the announcer paused a second, then fired in all directions: 'The trouble with Democrats is that they don't have any joy! They don't have optimism or hope! A woman phoned yesterday and she was the most miserable woman on the face of the earth! I tried to tell her a joke, but she didn't laugh! She *won't* laugh! This is the way they are! They're all like this!'

The caller had been cut off by then, but the announcer kept firing in case he was still in the precinct. When they went to an ad break, the announcer was identified as Rush Limbaugh.

It is difficult for a halfway reasonable person to drive in a straight line while listening to Rush Limbaugh. There are no shades, no variation, no circumlocutions. Barking and shouting and grunting, he rushes at your very being like a gorilla rushing to the end of its chain. The effect is concussive, spirit-crushing. At least, that is the effect on non-believers. For those who share his point of view, no doubt he is a tonic.

In silence, I passed the astonishing First Pentecostal Church on the fringes of Little Rock: like a wonder of the world in lemony cream and white marble with a huge rotunda, fluted marble columns and soaring windows, it is a building to accommodate thousands of worshippers – and miracles, no doubt, in proportion.

It was a long, unedifying drive. I should have veered into the Ozarks, just to see something. I imagine if you drove around the United States every day for twenty years, you would still be left feeling that, if only you had turned down that road, or gone straight on instead of turning, you might have found something essential or unforgettable – like the Buffalo River in Newton County, Arkansas, which Bill Clinton says is 'one of the most beautiful places in America'. There, perhaps I would have found something essential about Bill Clinton.

West of Oklahoma City, fires had been burning for a week. East, the land was parched, the leafless trees like kindling waiting for a match. Clouds of dust slipped across the land: ghosts of Oklahoma's past. Dreary as the scene was, no-one over fifty can arrive in Oklahoma without the words of the song sweeping into his head like the wind that comes sweeping down the plain. It would not be so bad if it stopped there, but *Oh, What a Beautiful Morning* and *The Surrey with the Fringe on Top* and *The Farmer and the Cowman Should Be Friends* and pretty well all the others come back in much the same order as they appeared in the film and on the record. Indeed, the night you saw the film aged seven comes back, and you wonder by what freak of culture this faraway and unexceptional place grafted itself onto your brain when so much of importance never took hold.

An Oklahoman once said that his state was 'to sociology what Australia is to zoology'. He meant a place where political and administrative attitudes and institutions seemed to have escaped the evolutionary process, like platypuses. It was 1959 before they gave up prohibition in Oklahoma. That the state held on long after the rest of the country abandoned it might have had something to do with the people's attachment to the Baptist, Methodist and other churches of the communitarian kind. On the other hand, for every Oklahoman attached to religion, another was attached to bootleg liquor, and no doubt some were attached to both. A natural balance might have evolved and expressed itself in the popular referenda by which the state decided many things. 'Oklahomans vote dry as long as they can stagger to the polls,' Will Rogers used to say.

I met an Oklahoman judge, an open-hearted and liberal man with a deep knowledge of his country's political and intellectual history, who believed Will Rogers was the greatest twentieth-century American. In his day he was certainly the most popular. He was the archetype of the good citizen. Rogers made seventy-one films, including the first film version of Twain's *A Connecticut Yankee in King Arthur's Court*, and John Ford's *Judge Priest*, which contains the imperishable: 'First thing I learned in politics was when to say "ain't".' Rogers combined Hollywood film stardom with radio broadcasting and newspaper columns syndicated in 500 papers. His mother was a Cherokee. It could be said that the two greatest Oklahomans were both Cherokees, the other being Sequoyah – the Noah Webster of his people. As Webster's *American Spelling Book* and *Dictionary* were to the general populace, Sequoyah's alphabet – or syllabary – was to the Cherokees. It spread literacy among them.

Will Rogers had a bit in common with that other ingenious American Mark Twain. He didn't have Twain's intellect, and he was not oppressed by the same anger and despair; but then Twain couldn't ride a horse or do tricks with a rope like Rogers. Both had the same kind of tolerant, liberal, secular, democratic, laconic American soul. 'Liberty doesn't work as well in practice as it does in speeches' pretty well sums up the Rogers style. Perhaps it had something to do with his being half-Cherokee, though what happened to the Cherokees might just as well have made a man vicious. Rogers said that the most important thing he inherited from his Indian forebears was humour when facing adversity. 'My ancestors didn't come over on the *Mayflower*,' he said, 'but they met 'em at the boat.'

Back in the 1920s and 30s, Rogers didn't hold with a lot of what holds in the United States now. He didn't hold with Republicans then and he'd hold with them even less now. He didn't hold much with religion. He preferred horses. His idea of a perfect Sunday afternoon was 'to get on old Soapsuds and ride off up a little canyon'. He was a teetotaller and a family man and not a particle of scandal attached to him. When news went round that Will Rogers had been killed in a plane crash in Alaska, someone said that 'a smile passed from America's lips'.

'I never met a man I didn't like,' Rogers once said, and he was always very proud of having said it. It's inscribed on his gravestone at the Will Rogers Museum in Claremore, Okalahoma. By one account, he first made this strange remark in 1926, in reference to the communist revolutionary Leon Trotsky. Okay, he could like Trotsky, but would he have liked Rush Limbaugh? Did he like Andrew Jackson, the president who engineered the Indian Removal? Or all those other people who lied to his ancestors and cheated them out of the land they'd been granted in the south-east of the country and 'removed' them to Indian Territory on a march that killed about one in ten? Or the people who, when the tribes – the so-called Five Civilized Tribes – had established themselves in tolerable prosperity on this much less fertile land, cheated them a second time?

You can think about it for hours and still not work out what he thought was so good about that remark. If his columns are anything to go by, he didn't much like John D. Rockefeller, or warmongers, purveyors of automatic weapons, or people who he thought exploited or oppressed the poor. Rogers was a supporter of FDR and the New Deal and some of his opinions were not so far removed from those of a fellow Oklahoman, the radical singer-songwriter Woody Guthrie. He even wrote in measured praise of the Soviet Five-Year Plan – it was a plan, he said, and in 1930 that was more than the United States had.

Perhaps it was just a homily along the lines of 'It always helps to meet a man and see things from where he's sitting', or 'There's a little good and bad in everyone'. Coming, as he did, from a prosperous mixed-blood landholding family of a class that before the Civil War often owned slaves might have taught Rogers that the moral universe is complex and does not submit to prejudice and dogma. Maybe he was getting at the bigots by a circumlocution, rounding them up with a sort of moral rope trick.

The museum in Claremore has enchantments but doesn't offer much sense that Will Rogers was a great deal more than an American Candide or everyone's archetypal pal. Still, to go there is to know not only why Americans mourned him when he died, but why they should be mourning yet. He was immune to paranoia and curious about people and the rest of the world. And he was funny: a president who could play the Connecticut Yankee or Judge Priest, the droll and decent Southerner, *and* rope a steer or a duck or a girl's little finger is a president to dream of in the current climate. The most popular man in America was a liberal. He believed the United States was liberal. 'Europe don't like us,' he said, 'but . . . they give us credit for being liberal.' It was 1931 and Rogers was speaking up for unemployment relief. 'I don't know about America being fundamentally sound and all that after-dinner hooey, but I do know that America is fundamentally liberal.'

Tell that to Rush Limbaugh. Or Sean Hannity – shock-jock and author of, most recently, *Deliver Us From Evil: Defeating Terrorism, Despotism, and Liberalism*. Or Fox News's Bill O'Reilly. Or Anne Coulter. These folk and a dozen more like them, who could no more rope a calf or say something funny than recite the Koran by heart, are paid many millions of dollars and given access to all forms of media to make sure America is fundamentally *illiberal*. By the way, if ever you're in the United States and you want to ring Sean Hannity, don't forget to say 'You're a great American'. It's not compulsory, but like tipping waiters and doormen, it is expected. He's likely to say 'Thank you, ma'am, you have a good day, now' or 'Well, someone's got to save the country' and get right back to the job of tearing liberals limb from bloody limb. 'The ground occupied by the skeptic is the vestibule of the temple,' Emerson said: but to hear the evangelists of Jesus and patriotism you might think they were swarming all over the altar. If Will Rogers (or Mark Twain) wandered into one of their studios and said America was liberal, they'd slap him straight in the grinder with Ted Kennedy.

Jim Thompson also came from Oklahoma. Among *noir* writers, he was the blackest, bitterest and, at his best, the greatest. 'I hopped off a freight in Oklahoma City in a bitter November night, a half starved and filthy bum. And almost immediately I was taken into custody by two patrol car cops.' That was the general tone. Thompson reckoned the state of Oklahoma was the 'rottenest, politically, in the country'. He was far from alone in that opinion. The rorts and looting were extraordinary – though, to be fair, the temptations were greater in Oklahoma. Oklahomans merely 'seized the greatest opportunity for wholesale looting that was ever placed before any American population'. There was all that land the Cherokee, Choctaws, Chickasaws, Creeks and Seminoles had been living on for three generations: that had to be taken from them. And then there was the oil. It was no fault of Oklahomans that it turned out the state was filthy with it; that even the city they built was sitting on a huge reservoir of the stuff.

In the winning of the West, Oklahoma was not the only place where idealism and indomitable courage were mixed in with greed, trickery, betrayal and brute violence – not to mention the .45 Colt and the repeating rifle. For every acre honestly 'won' another was got by corruption, force or pure serendipity. It is to be expected that in the end, in Oklahoma as in the nation at large, the people could not tell one thing from another and believed only harm would come from trying. They preferred myth: frontier societies always do. Myth was more convenient than history; it was practical and at the same time indispensable to spiritual needs. It contained both more lyric and more commercial possibility. It was protean and unbreakable. In this as well, Oklahoma imitated the rest of America.

There are oil wells in the grounds of the Capitol, which has a new dome, like a cherry on a sundae. If Oklahoma has a lingering sense of shame or inferiority, as the historian Angie Debo suggested, the Capitol is not about to own up to it. In the atrium there are paintings of Coronado's arrival; of the Indians; of the small farmers; of Will Rogers, of course, with a plane rather than a horse; and of Wiley Post, the famous aviator who died with Rogers in Alaska. Woody Guthrie and Jim Thompson are not there. The names of the donors who made the dome possible are inscribed on the base inside. It's a mighty thing; dizzying when you look up from the floor below. The last name I saw before my neck cramped was Halliburton.

Elsewhere in Oklahoma City there are gleaming monuments to pioneers and cowboys and a vast new historical centre. In 1964, downtown Oklahoma City was redesigned by the famous modernist architect I. M. Pei. He left it looking very modern, but with nowhere to eat. In other words, he 'malled' it. He dropped the architect's equivalent of a neutron bomb, leaving Oklahoma City with many memorials to its rowdy past but unable to reproduce the life from which it sprang. Still, cities everywhere are prone to do themselves these injuries, and we must remember that wealth is created in the doing. And when they undo it and have a renaissance, there will be more again.

Out in one of the malls I met an elderly man who twenty years ago gave up a very successful career in the corporate world to start a bookshop. He reckons the next generation might think that Borders and Barnes & Noble are the only bookshops there ever were. A few years back he stood for mayor. It had always been a non-partisan contest, he said, but in the last two days of the campaign his opponent ran some concerted push-polling with the aim of linking the bookshop owner to the mayor of San Francisco, who permitted same-sex marriage. He doesn't know the mayor of San Francisco, but 25,000 new voters turned out in Oklahoma City and the push-poller won handsomely. The only way the Democrats can beat the religious right, the bookshop owner said, was to engage them on theology: to demonstrate the tendentiousness of their interpretation and the falseness of their beliefs.

—

At nine am on the morning of 19 April 1995, as Oklahoma City's office-workers settled down in front of their computer screens, Timothy McVeigh parked a rented truck in a drop-off zone outside the nine-storey Alfred P. Murrah building in downtown Oklahoma City. He walked away leaving two timed detonators ticking. At 9.02 the truck full of ammonium nitrate and nitromethane exploded. The blast measured six on the Richter scale. It was felt fifty miles away. It ripped the north face off the Murrah building and killed 168 people, injuring more than 800. Nineteen children died because McVeigh – unwittingly, he said – had parked the truck beneath the building's daycare centre. He called it 'collateral damage'.

As the news spread across the country and the world, it was generally assumed that this act of terrorism, at that time the most deadly to have occurred on American soil, must have been committed by outsiders, people possessed of a foreign ideology, probably radical Muslims. But within two hours of the explosion Timothy McVeigh was arrested and, three days later, Americans learned that the terrorist was a twenty-nine-year-old native of a rust-belt town in western New York State who declared he had acted in defence of American freedom to 'put a check on government abuse of power'. 'Borrowing a page from US foreign policy, I decided to send a message to a government that was becoming increasingly hostile,' McVeigh said.

Soon the public also learned that McVeigh's mother had left the family home when he was ten; that his father gave him his first rifle when he was thirteen; that he'd had no luck with girls, couldn't get a decent job and so had joined the army, where he learned to switch off his emotions; and that he had served with distinction in the first Gulf War. They learned that he came back from the Middle East disillusioned, in particular by the US forces' slaughter of the fleeing Iraqi army. Failing in his effort to become a Green Beret, he became a member of various right-wing 'survivalist' groups. He witnessed the siege of the Branch Davidian religious cult at Waco, Texas, and the killing by federal agents of more than eighty of its members, including as many as twenty-five children. It was partly to avenge these people that he bombed the Murrah Building, and he did it on the second anniversary of the Waco massacre. The T-shirt he wore that day proclaimed, as Brutus had at Julius Caesar's death and John Wilkes Booth at Lincoln's, SIC SEMPER TYRANNIS – 'Thus always to tyrants', as well as the words of Thomas Jefferson: 'The tree of liberty must be refreshed from time to time with the blood of patriots and tyrants.'

McVeigh was charged with eight counts of murder, conspiracy to use a weapon of mass destruction, use of a weapon of mass destruction and destruction of a federal building. About 300 survivors and relatives of the victims watched his execution by lethal injection in Terre Haute, Indiana, either as official witnesses or via a special broadcast transmitted on encrypted fibre-optic cable to a room where they were gathered in Oklahoma City. McVeigh's chief accomplice, Terry Nichols, was also a Gulf War veteran. He is serving a life sentence in a Colorado gaol.

During his trial, McVeigh compared his own atrocity not only to the Waco massacre, but also to deadly actions taken by American forces against civilians or hopeless soldiers in full retreat in Iraq and Serbia. In so far as it was common to hear people say that Americans had lost their innocence with the Oklahoma bombing (we heard it again after 9/11), McVeigh had a reasonable point – though it would have been better made by just about anyone else, including a Cherokee Indian. Of all the pleasing qualities that issued from the mouths of the founding fathers or that leap from the pages of American (or Oklahoman) history, innocence is not one that immediately stands out; nor does it come at you from the streets, or the media, or Congress, the White House, Wall Street or Hollywood. But clichés and fantasies tend to have their way regardless; the fact that terrorists often fortify the most self-deluding of them might be counted part of the damage they inflict.

Though McVeigh insisted that he and Nichols and a third man – presently at large on a witness protection program – had been the only conspirators, since his execution various conspiracy theories have been put about: Nichols might have had a connection to al Qaeda cells in the Philippines, for instance; McVeigh might have met the al Qaeda operative Jose Padilla when they were both in Florida. The FBI is accused of bungling the case, losing essential documents, failing to make a proper forensic examination of the site, covering up evidence. The truth, a lot of websites want us to believe, is just beginning to emerge.

The Oklahoma City National Memorial, erected on the site of the Murrah Building, manages to transcend both the clichés and the conspiracy theories. Set behind two great walls, one marked 9.01 and the other 9.03, with the gate between them representing the moment of the blast, the memorial consists of 168 bronze and glass 'chairs' set in nine rows facing a reflecting pool. The chairs represent the slain officeworkers, everyday folk who sat at desks. Nineteen chairs are miniatures that represent the dead children. Reflected in the pool by day, the chairs also look like tombstones; and lit from within at night, like candles in a cathedral.

The winning design was chosen by a committee of survivors of the bombing and victims' families, all of whom subscribed to a 'mission statement' whose terms had been painstakingly agreed: 'May all who leave here know the impact of violence. May this memorial offer comfort, strength, peace, hope and serenity.' The words are inscribed on a wall, and if they are not as compelling as they might have been, most visitors would likely say the memorial itself succeeds. It is sufficiently abstract to avoid sentimentality and concrete enough to jolt the senses.

Next to the memorial a museum was built, and across the road a new white statue of Christ looks towards the scene with his hand to his eyes. It's inscribed: AND JESUS WEPT. On a fence outside the museum people hang all sorts of votive objects – soft toys, bits of clothing, badges. The museum tour begins in a re-created room of the Oklahoma Water Board, where on the morning of the blast a meeting began at nine am. The Water Board was on the other side of the street. Visitors hear a recording of the meeting for two minutes, then the blast – and the lights go out. The museum also contains glass cases full of items gathered from the wreckage: more toys, car keys, spectacles, computer screens, venetian blinds, filing cabinets. It's a Pompeii of office life circa 1995. And there are the thoughts of survivors. The bombing taught one that she 'must always be ready to meet Christ'. Another says: 'For one moment in time, it didn't matter whether a person was white, black or brown; a Catholic, Baptist or Jew, rich or poor – everyone was joined by a common band of brotherhood.' They thank God and they wonder at the kindness of strangers who came forward to help when they might have turned and run.

It is a strange museum: by no means all sentimental, but with a bit of the communal solipsism of daytime television shows. The memorials at Hiroshima and Nagasaki, which both express the same instinctive fascination with the moment

190

of annihilation, do it on behalf of a quarter of a million dead civilians, tens of thousands of children. Somehow at the Oklahoma Memorial a sense of scale has been lost. At the same time, in the religious homilies and the unrestrained grief, the altruistic and the narcissistic become inseparable – a paradox that just might have been the root of the evil in Timothy McVeigh.

CHAPTER 8

The Lord has promis'd good to me,
His word my hope secures;
He will my shield and portion be,
As long as life endures.

John Newton, *Amazing Grace*

I HEADED NORTH TOWARDS THE KANSAS BORDER ON INTERSTATE 35.
There was no very good reason to see the Dwight D. Eisenhower Presidential Center at Abilene, but Eisenhower was the first president of my conscious life, and 'I Like Ike' was my first political slogan. He was the last president of the railway era, the last to do a whistlestop tour of the country. He was also the last general to be president, and the last president of unimpeachable common sense and reliably in control of all his faculties and instincts. Perhaps it was because his parents were pacifists, or because he never actually fought in a battle, but compared to Patton or Macarthur or Montgomery – or Churchill, for that matter – he was a sane sort of general as well. Because he looked a bit like a favourite uncle of mine, I *did* like Ike, and I find that I still do.

Late the night before, in Claremore, the TV news

announced that thirteen miners trapped in a West Virginian coalmine had been found alive. The people of Sago declared it a miracle. One miner's wife said she had never lost faith and everyone had prayed and God had delivered them alive. The governor and congresswoman joined in the prayers and celebrations. They gathered in the church hall and sang *How Great Thou Art*. Next morning *The Oklahoman* and dozens of other newspapers across the country headlined their early edition: ALIVE! But by then the mine manager had told the families that twelve of the thirteen men were dead.

All day, the story of the Sago mine unfolded on the radio. It was true, as some said, that the media should have exercised more caution. But then, the media might take more care with what it feeds the public if the public were not so prepared to swallow anything it's fed. The story unfolded in the manner of a modern fable; the local priest completed it when he said he could understand the families being angry, even with God. And God, he said, would forgive them for it. As the company had been cited for more than 200 health and safety violations in the previous year, and as there was evidence to say that the Mining Safety and Health Association had been less than rigorous in enforcing the regulations, and as the price of Appalachian coal had doubled in the past ten years, it seemed possible that God and the media were not the only ones involved in the disaster at the Sago mine.

In Abilene, two signs glowed in the dark: the adult bookstore's and one placed right in front of it: JESUS HEALS. Christmas decorations were still hanging in the street. The town where Eisenhower grew up is slap-bang in the centre of Main Street USA. 'The proudest thing I can claim is that I come from Abilene,' he said. There's a statue downtown that portrays him as the all-American thirteen-year-old boy. Not a particularly bright kid, he grew up in a happy Mennonite family on a farm on the Great Plains, headed off to West Point and, without firing a shot in anger, became America's first five-star general, commander of the greatest military force the world has ever seen, the liberator of Western Europe. Later, as president of the United States, he was not only the most powerful man in the world, but the most powerful in all of history – the first man ever to have the power to end all life on earth. Implausible as it seems, this was the story we grew up with – the president of the United States, whoever he was, could end everything at a single stroke.

Eisenhower's reputation as a president was buried under the Kennedy mystique, Johnson's Vietnam disaster and Nixon's corruption. Yet his record is not too bad. Here was a president who began his first term by reminding Americans that every dollar spent on weapons was 'in the final sense, a theft from those who hunger and are not fed, who are cold and not clothed', and who ended his eight years by warning them about the dangers of the 'military-industrial complex'. He was wise enough to see that Vietnam was a trap, and that Britain, France and Israel were wrong in their 1956 Suez adventure. He was liberal enough to maintain much of the spirit of the New Deal; and if his record on civil rights was not particularly impressive, the Southern Democrats in the Democrat-controlled Congress have much more to answer for.

Eisenhower built the highway system, expanded the national parks, kept a firm grip on the budget – and despised Joe McCarthy. With these policies he'd be about as welcome in today's Republican Party as Fidel Castro. It's possible that the liberals never forgave him for defeating the intellectual Adlai Stevenson, or for lacking the glamour of the Kennedys. He never pretended to be profound, yet he had as much gravitas as any of his successors and a lot less trickery, solipsism and baloney than most of them. And after you have walked around the somewhat overblown Eisenhower Center for a while, something tells you that he would have done things differently after 9/11, and very likely before that day as well.

As I headed west on Highway 70, the great contest for America's soul continued on my radio. The secular right bashed away at the liberals and the religious right at the secularists. I turned off the highway and made for North Platte, Nebraska, on the back roads. The houses along the way had no shelter against the wind. They sat on the bare, brown grass, many of them with a primitive sculpture of a lizard, a coyote, an Indian or a creature of the imagination for company. Cut-out metal Indians and lifesize horses and riders stood on the uninhabited rises. The sign on a little Baptist church said: THE LORD HAS MADE KNOWN HIS SALVATION. THERE IS NO PEACE UNTO THE WICKED. Everything was bare and plain. A truck ground its way through this landscape with a load of hay: there was a heart attached to it, and a cross, the American flag and the flag of Kansas, and a sign saying: HEARTLAND HAY.

These small towns put their names on the water tower, and sometimes they put a cross on it as well. They're sad-looking places, but there might be something in them the visitor doesn't see. Civic pride, for instance. Plainville (population 2000 or so) had a pretty little park and a well-kept cemetery laid out like Arlington and with more graves in it than there seemed to be people alive in the town. There was a monument to the Grand Army of the Republic, the offices of a newspaper called *The Plainsman* and a supermarket. A few oil pumps were forlornly working and a few had stopped with their necks at various angles to the ground, like animals that had suffered a sudden seizure. Angus cattle waited in the knackery yard. A weather-beaten two-room shack wore a sign saying: INDUSTRIAL DEVELOPMENT CORPORATION.

The shops in Plainville had no verandahs: a sign, perhaps, that they had been badly modernised at some point, or that a fire once went through and they'd been rebuilt without them.

Beginning in the 1870s with a few sod houses and a sod hotel, it became known as 'the Queen City of Paradise Flats' and was regarded as a great place for hunting buffalo and elk. The difference between Plainville and hundreds of other towns on these plains is that it still has people in it – the Great Plains are running out of them. Various ecologists and geographers think they should be given back to the buffalo.

It seemed essential to have seen these Great Plains and to have felt the freezing wind that blew across them on that sunny day. It's not hard to imagine the excitement they held for settlers, or the fear: plains are one thing, but plains with enemies upon them are another. And as easy as it is to sense the fear, it's easier to understand the religious dimension of life in these places. In fact, it's hard to imagine how these communities could have grown *without* religion. The towns were nothing much and yet, standing in that palpable emptiness, the impression they left was indelible and moving. And then you see the furrows rippling as you fly along the road, the sun sinking into the earth, and seven planes racing towards the Pacific coast.

North Platte has the biggest freight yards in the United States and, driving in after dark, I imagined I could smell cattle. Maybe it was blood-and-bone fertiliser on the lawns. It was animal, whatever it was, and whenever I think of North Platte I will think of that smell. It consolidated the impression I had of a plain and practical place – a view that was reinforced by reading somewhere that half of the 25,000 people who live there are Catholic or mainstream Protestant, and there are no more than thirty churches of the evangelical variety. Like little Plainville and many other places on the Great Plains, about a third of North Platte's citizens are descended from German settlers.

Not that it makes the slightest difference to town architecture and planning. North Platte was malled and looked much the same as every other town its size. The motels and fast-food chains were, as usual, congregated on the highway out of town. There was a Days Inn, a Quality Inn and a Comfort Inn. While driving across the country I often recited the names of all the inns from memory, and then I'd recite the fast-food franchises that spring up around the motels like thistles round a cow-yard. The traditional inn was inclined to nestle – into high streets, on the banks of streams, at the feet of hills, in groves of oaks – and the name implied a homely shelter from the elements and robbers. The chain inn does not nestle: it projects. If it nestled, no-one would see the brand. The wind and rain and sun fairly belt them; confidence men, embezzlers, runaways and hitmen frequent them; and only the homeless could think them homely. Yet they remain a miracle of convenience and, as places in which people can enter a kind of existential holding pattern, a boon not only to life on the roads but also to the nation's psychic health.

Within days of the United States' declaration of war on the axis powers in December 1941, troops started passing through North Platte on their way to the battlefields: travelling east if they were to fight Germans in Europe, west towards the Japanese in the Pacific. By Christmas Day the local people had established a food canteen. People drove in from a hundred miles away, bringing food and drinks and magazines – and company. They provided music and a floor on which, in the half-hour or so that each train stopped in North Platte, the soldiers could dance with local girls. Over five and a half years the North Platte Canteen served six million departing and returning soldiers.

—

Driving from North Platte to Fort Collins, Colorado, and from Fort Collins to Cheyenne, Wyoming, you can understand why most Americans don't bother to get a passport. Why go to Turkey or Patagonia when you have Wyoming? The Pony Express used to gallop across these plains – it cost five dollars for a half-ounce letter, delivered to Sacramento in ten days. It only lasted eighteen months. The men behind it were crooks but the idea was pure gold. There are statues: the horse at a breathless gallop, the rider pivoting in the saddle to flog the horse's rump as if outrunning a storm of arrows, an avalanche or the demons of his past.

Some of the land is designated as Pawnee Native Grasslands and drivers are advised that collecting arrowheads and spear tips is forbidden. The Indians lived on these plains for 8000 years. They lived on bison: bison meat fed them; from bison hides they made their shelters, their clothes and vessels; from bison bones their tools and weapons. Bison were the basis of their material culture and their religion.

In 1870 about fifteen million bison lived on the plains. According to Angie Debo, a train in 1868 travelled 120 miles through a herd of them. Within little more than a decade, they were gone. A male bison weighs near enough to a ton. In pure body mass, it must have been the greatest slaughter of one species by another in the history of the planet. Five million were killed in 1873. They were hunted for their meat and hides and for sport. In one year Buffalo Bill Cody supplied labourers on the Kansas Pacific Railroad with 4280 hides. When the track was through, the railroad company sold tickets for the privilege of shooting them out the window of their trains. Sport, perhaps, but hardly sporting. An old hunter recalled how they took advantage of the animal's better instincts: 'When a buffalo was hit, the others would mill around it, and if there was a hundred or so in the bunch, the hunter could get nearly all of them.'

In the Old West, Cheyenne was a rail depot, and a jump-off point for prospectors heading for the mountains and soldiers going to fight (among others) the Cheyenne Indians. This is country the nation had to fight for: they had to wrest it violently from the Indians. 'God only knows when, and I do not see how, we can make a decent excuse for an Indian war,' said General Sherman somewhere to the east of here in 1866. In due course an excuse was found. They were fighting for the grasslands and the gold and silver and the railway and commerce in general, but it seems possible that they were also acting on some primal need for dominion over nature. They had to have it for the same reason that Ahab had to have the white whale. The Indians talked about the Great Spirit, and the grass and the earth and the wind and sky speaking to them, and what they said became a cliché or a joke in Western lore. Yet White Antelope's death song – 'Nothing lives long / Except the earth and mountain' – might have been the Pony Express rider's as he hightailed it towards the Sierras.

The map of this region reads like an old TV guide. After Cheyenne I thought I'd see Laramie. I was driving through the Medicine Bow Forest, listening to Fox News, when Abraham Lincoln loomed out of the scrub on the side of the road, glowering like some fearsome raptor. In the second or so I had to look, it seemed to be carved of wood and about twenty feet high. A big maroon and white pick-up tailgated me all the way down the hill. As we reached the bottom it overtook me, then abruptly slowed me down: two grinning cowboys, with lank fair hair hanging down from their hats, a badge on their back window saying: WYOMING NATIVE, and a yellow ribbon and a red one and a blue one – an unbroken spiritual chain with General Custer, who rode these hills on the way to doom at the Little Bighorn.

———

In winter, entering Yellowstone National Park is possible only from the north. You have to drive up through Wyoming with the mountains of the park on your left and on your right the high rolling plans. It was a battlefield in the nineteenth century, and all the fading Bush–Cheney stickers make it feel a bit like a battlefield now. On the radio for sixty miles or so, two men from Wyoming discussed environmentalists: they meant people who had infiltrated government and other institutions and now exercised a sinister and pervasive influence. Environmentalists were dedicated to destroying American freedoms, especially the freedom to hunt. Environmentalists threatened the American way of life. Their precious bison threatened the American cattle industry with brucellosis. Their precious wolves marauded among the herds. Well, not any more. These guys were fighting back against the environmentalists, like the creationists were fighting back against the humanists, like the White House was fighting back against the terrorists.

You drive through Wyoming and wonder about the origins of life, because in Wyoming's landscape it's as easy to imagine dinosaurs as sheep, and somewhere on the radio someone will be talking about intelligent design. A pastor or a priest will be talking about it; or there will be something that you might at first mistake for a conversation between scientists. Their method is the same one used for colon cleanser and gym equipment: an enthusiastic novice asks questions of an expert who has all the answers. The expert, you can bet your boots, is a member of the Discovery Institute's Center for Science and Culture.

The Discovery Institute is a front for the intelligent design movement. Most, if not all, of its leading lights are evangelical Christians, and when they address religious audiences they like to show how their arguments provide support for Biblical creationism. But when they address secular audiences they speak in secular terms; in fact, they avoid naming God as the intelligent designer. There is a very good reason for this. The movement's goal is to establish ID as valid science and to get it into science classrooms alongside evolution.

You won't necessarily hear the Sean Hannitys and Rush

Limbaughs and Bill O'Reillys rooting for intelligent design, but you won't hear them denouncing it either, or standing in the way of paid-up members of the movement who want to get on the radio. And had you been listening in January 2006, you would have heard O'Reilly calling organisations opposed to teaching ID in school science rooms 'Taliban'. 'Fascism', he called it. 'Hitler would be a card-carrying member. So would Stalin.'

The ID movement is Scopes and the old Anti-Evolution League in new and hipper garb. Of the fifteen states that wanted to ban the teaching of evolution in the 1920s only two went through with it, but folk weren't going to give up the creator because big-city lawyers, the American Civil Liberties Union and the east coast press made fun of their ideas, or because some know-it-all judge overturned Scopes' conviction on a technicality. The creator has outlived a lot of better men than them, and lot more technicalities. Now they're back in force, and where the media used to be against them, now the big ones are on their side. A lot of the media hate the same smart-asses they do; they hate the ACLU just as much; they hate all liberals just like them. They even have the president on their side now. And everyone in Washington wants things to be 'faith-based', just like they always should have been. And the smart-asses can't use science to confound them any more – because now they've got some smart-asses of their own, what you call intelligent designers.

Paul Nelson, 'an able spokesman for the intelligent design movement', had the floor for a hundred miles or so. He spoke to Hank Hanegraaff, whose radio show, *The Bible Answer Man*, is heard in all states daily and on the internet. Hanegraaff is president and chairman of the board at the Christian Research Institute International. Both men were 'exuberant' about recent 'scientific discoveries' which demonstrate the 'fact' of intelligent design, though Hanegraaff made the point that they were not talking about any new theory here, but rather a position reached by history's best minds, including Plato, Heraclitus and Cicero. Our expert agreed and saw no need to remind listeners that those guys didn't have a telescope, much less a cyclotron. He also agreed with a woman who called to say she only needs to look at a fish to know Someone must have created it. Nelson asked her to consider something even more miraculous: namely, the development of a human being from conception to birth.

Hanegraaff asked Nelson what he thought of the Discovery Institute's new DVD called *Unlocking the Mystery of Life*. Nelson thought it was a knockout. Hanegraaff said it was just fascinating, and the great thing was you could sit down in your lounge room with the family and a bag of popcorn and you would get 'a view of biology that you'll never get on PBS'. Nelson said that today Darwin is where Marx was twenty-five years ago – on the verge of eclipse. Science was discovering 'that it made a wrong turning with evolution' and it was about to correct itself. In another couple of decades, evolution – or 'naturalism' or 'Darwinism' – would be in the trash can.

Unlocking the Mystery of Life is taking off around the globe, we were told. It has been 'widely translated', most recently into Mandarin and Russian. 'Just last year,' Nelson said, the DVD 'created a firestorm of controversy in Australia'. This Australian didn't notice it: it must have been one of those little firestorms that sneak past. God moves in mysterious ways, as everyone knows. No-one knows why he created paddlefish and salamanders, for instance. Or Pluto. Why did he create us with weak knees and sinuses that would work better if we walked on all fours? The thirty-seven million Americans with sinusitis might ask themselves if their design shows much intelligence.

The Medicine Bow River was frozen and ice lay around in the sage brush hills. The sign on the biggest building in the town of Medicine Bow reminded travellers that it was

The House of the Virginian and that the Virginian said: 'Smile when you say that' before he shot the cattle rustler. The rest of the town looked as if it had been left behind with its 270 inhabitants by the retreating ice age. People come to hunt pronghorns, elk and mule deer, to visit the nearby dinosaur beds or perhaps just to stand under that immense sky, which was forever changing from grey to blue to black; at its most startling, it was black over the snowy mountains and bluffs to the west, and blue over the grassy hills to the east.

A few miles out of the town a patrol car flew past me. By the time I got over the hill, the policemen were talking to the driver of a car resting on its roof in the snow. Twenty miles further and a Winnebago was lying on its back, all eight wheels spinning in the breeze. Another patrol car went past and didn't bother to look.

The Lincoln Highway roughly follows the Bozeman Trail, which Custer came up in pursuit of the Sioux and Cheyenne. Sixty years before Custer, Lewis and Clark travelled through the Sioux country and returned unscathed. But by 1867 the Plains Indians had learned the truth of things and turned ugly. They killed and robbed settlers and lured companies of troops into ambushes. The troops were there to protect the expansion of white settlement, which was driven principally by lust for gold. As the gold-diggers pushed into the reservations, whose boundaries the Sioux were themselves not inclined to respect, the troops followed. They drove Sherman to declare: 'We must act with vindictive earnestness against the Sioux, even to their extermination, men, women and children.' But Sherman never got to do his execution: when Grant became president, he was recalled to run the US army. Little Bighorn, where the Lakota Sioux and Cheyenne annihilated Custer's soldiers, is just a short drive from the town in northern Wyoming named after another Union general, Phillip Sheridan, who was sent to replace Sherman.

It is easier to be on the Indian side; not only because we like to see a bully get a bloody nose, or even because it was Indian land and culture the Indians were defending. It is also because we know what was coming. At Little Bighorn, the United States got an unexpected mugging of a kind it wouldn't experience again until 1941. For the Lakota, the Cheyenne and the Kiowa, it meant the end of everything.

I came to Billings, Montana, and finally to Livingston: and on the industrial edge of town, in the snow and sludge at the back of a gravel car park where you'd expect to see a pawnbroker or a bail bond agent or a junkie, there was the Café d'Art. It was a shed with a window on the side and two women serving drive-in customers espresso coffee and homemade cakes. They told me to watch for ice on the roads. You cannot contain the good in the world forever. Not in America. Not in Montana, where there are one million people, six million guns and the Café d'Art.

About three blocks of Livingston's 'historic downtown' is intact. As you leave you pass the new Christian Center, next to Rubber Ducky River Rentals, then the food outlets and motels, and then you bend south through southern Montana till you reach the big gates by the Yellowstone River, where you pay your twenty dollars. The river was half-frozen. The biggest swans on earth, white trumpeters, glided in the current as if born of the ice and snow, made of the same elements, moulded from them. Snow lay three feet deep on the ground. It spattered the yellow cliffs and the pines that sprout from them. A herd of bison grazed on the river bank, using their colossal heads and necks and shoulders to knock the snow aside and find the grass. Clouds of gas rose from the hillsides. Sulphur filled the air.

Bounded by three states – Wyoming, Montana and Idaho – Yellowstone is huge – 2.2 million acres – but in winter you can hire a snowmobile and a guide and, if you set off early in the morning, you can go a hundred miles into it and return, five-sixths frozen, by dark. You will see the Yellowstone Falls and Canyon, wide snow-blown plains, fearsome cliffs, coniferous forest burned and unburned, hot spring terraces in colours of extraordinary brilliance and subtlety, frozen lakes. You will also see bison, elk, deer, bald eagles, red-tailed hawks, turkey buzzards, coyotes and – if you're lucky, as I was – wolves. In my case, it was one wolf, a lone wolf in the white silence, indifferent to our gaze and two watching bison, as if lost in thought, loping along the snowy banks of a stream towards the forested hills two miles away. Theodore Roosevelt claimed he'd seen them white, red, yellow, brown, grey and grizzled. This one was dark-grey; a 'grim elder brother' of the coyote and much, much bigger. Wolves are big. Some of them weigh 160 pounds.

Set aside in 1872, Yellowstone is the world's oldest national park and probably the most familiar. Even under snow and on such a strange machine it was hard to throw off the sense of déjà vu. I had been there before with Donald Duck. I had seen Yellowstone, the palest pink in tooth and claw, on Disney's *Adventureland*. I saw a flock of birds eating green pine cones and at the moment I began to wonder if they were the birds I'd seen on one of David Attenborough's programs, which follow every feed of the acid pine with a dose of alkaline limestone, they confirmed it by taking to the air together, as if all getting the gripe at the same instant and heading for the limestone cliffs.

'Be fruitful, and multiply, and replenish the earth, and subdue it,' says the Book of Genesis. Having subdued twenty million or so bison, a couple of billion passenger pigeons and much else besides, some Americans established Yellowstone to preserve one small part of the natural world from these ravages. Even then, it took years to stop the poachers. By 1902 there were only twenty-three bison left in the park and they were living as farm animals. By the 1930s Yellowstone's wolves had been exterminated. The park's managers, it seems, could not quite control their instinct to subdue nature: they wanted to improve upon it and protect it from itself. Into naturally fishless lakes they introduced sport fish that spread into spawning streams and ate the native fish on which bears and eagles depended. They smashed the eggs of white pelicans because pelicans ate fish. All through the twentieth century they culled elk, in the last decades using helicopters to drive thousands of them into yards for butchering. They dedicated themselves to preventing and putting out bushfires and became expert at it until, after a huge blaze twenty years ago, they realised fire was essential to the organic renewal of species.

Difficult as it sometimes is to subdue nature, it comes to us a lot more naturally than letting it take its course. But now, in the blackened forest, a new breed of happy rangers – evolutionists all – will tell you how woodpeckers love the dead trees, how the elk thrive on the burned bark and how the new trees are already two metres high. They will also tell you how several wolf packs, descended from fourteen grey wolves set loose in the park ten years ago, are culling the elk, deer and bison, and that because they take the weakest they will make each species stronger. Their kills create food for coyotes, bears, eagles, ravens and foxes. And the sight of them thrills the tourists.

But the park cannot be fenced and wolves see no distinction between wild and domesticated prey. Roaming into sheep and cattle ranches, they at once become varmints: not just wolves, but creatures of an insidious, un-American ideology. Across the three states that border Yellowstone, in the previous year they had killed no fewer than 112 sheep and ten calves. The owners received full compensation for each dead beast.

Some sights, once seen, stamp themselves forever. In Yellowstone there were three. The wolf was one. The second was a coyote, sitting in the snow fifty yards from a herd of bison, his big ears listening for the footfall of a mouse. They wait for hours near the herds, hoping the beasts will disturb some morsel. 'He is always hungry,' Mark Twain wrote. 'He is always poor, out of work, and friendless.' And that's how this one seemed – a despised outsider, a junkie of the natural world.

The third vision some ravens led us to: they were sitting in the pines on the edge of the track and below them, at the bottom of a steep bank, was a bison carcass. A few days earlier, wolves had crippled but failed to kill it, so the rangers ended its misery and rolled the body down the bank. As my guide and I looked down, a coyote trotted away. It was not really a carcass. The skin on the massive head was untouched, though the ears were gone and the mouth was eaten out: there were no ribs, just the spine and legs with faint pink specks of flesh. The creature had been flensed.

The ranger came from a farm in Idaho. He decided to join the service after seeing a documentary called *Yellowstone: America's Sacred Wilderness* and reading Barry Lopez's *Of Wolves and Men*. He thought the farmers and the hunters were crazy. He preferred the universally abominated but tough and brave coyotes. He told me that in Idaho the people hunt mountain lions, though there are not a great many left. The hunters put microchips in the collars of their hounds, a measure that gives them a crucial advantage in their contest with the beasts: it means they can stay in their pick-ups until they get the signal that the dogs have one cornered. The Yellowstone ranger told me about the hunter who received an order for a mountain lion from a man on the east coast. While his client flew west to whatever was the nearest town and settled into a hotel, the hunter drove out and released his microchipped hounds into the wilderness. Upon receiving the signal from his dogs, he phoned the client and told him to get on out there. So the man from the east got to shoot a mountain lion and take it back, stuffed, to his apartment. Thus was the spirit of the frontier kept alive.

The ranger was moved by the idea of the park as a place where people might experience elemental, primal nature and find excitement in its wonders, clues to existence in its mysteries; where they might establish some faint touch with the truth of their own natures. He was passionate about it. Yellowstone *does* inspire in the way of a religion. It might be when they sense this that some visitors interrupt the ranger as he describes the course of evolution in the park. Evolution is just a 'theory', they say, and insist he should not present it as a fact.

The ranger would like to tell them that evolution is something that we know and can demonstrate; that it is the essential key to scientific understanding and advance, including medical advance, and to our understanding of woodpeckers, bison and humans. He would like to tell them that intelligent design might be a useful bulwark for religion, but as science it's pure hokum. Yellowstone, however, is a public institution dependent on public patronage, and so the ranger has taught himself a form of words that sound more respectful than he feels. The creationist is mollified. The ranger has adapted to his environment.

Yet, if 'belief consists of accepting the affirmations of the soul; unbelief in denying them', as Emerson said, who is the believer in this encounter? The ranger, whose heart is moved by nature for what it is? Or the visiting Christian, who can only accept it amended by doctrine? Perhaps some of us are too susceptible to nature, but it seemed quite reasonable to me, and not altogether terrifying, to imagine that if the origin of life teemed in that mud, so might a soul – or millions of them.

The most recent poll I saw said fifty-four per cent of Americans disputed the theory of evolution. Yet, as wolves chased elk and the mud volcanoes hissed and farted in Yellowstone, as millions of Christians united in loathing and Bill O'Reilly ranted away, in Dover, Pennsylvania, a judge found for the eleven parents (represented by the same combination of the ACLU and big-city lawyers that defended Scopes) who had sued to have intelligent design removed from the public school science curriculum. The judge ruled ID to be religious in nature and not science. He also found that its proponents in this case demonstrated 'breathtaking inanity' and 'ignorance' and that two of them had 'lied outright under oath on several occasions . . . to cover their tracks and disguise the real purpose behind the ID Policy'.

While this was happening, a Darwin exhibition in New York attracted crowds of people who did not seem at all disturbed by evolution's implications. Across the country, the world's best and richest research institutions proceeded on evolutionary principles. And it continued to be true that if you didn't turn on the clowns and thugs of radio and television in the United States, you could go a long way in most directions with no reason to doubt that you were in an enlightened, humanistic and, yes, liberal country.

CHAPTER 9

In daily life, human relations are established on an equal
footing; each person's pride in his title of American citizen
creates an aura of ready understanding. Each person can
disguise the mediocrity of his fate by thinking that he
participates in the life of a great nation. And each person
recognises others as his fellow creatures and wants the
dignity of man and of the American to be affirmed in
his fellow creature just as it is in himself – hence the
generosity, the benevolence, the atmosphere of friendship
that is America's most endearing feature.

Simone de Beauvoir, *America Day by Day*

I DROVE ON THE ICY ROAD IN A SEA OF SNOW AND FLYING
slush and grit, past towering mountains and frozen lakes, and
billboards advertising Wal-Mart Supercenters and the Church
of Jesus Christ of Latter-day Saints. Every moment of every
day in America, someone refers to 'this great country of ours',
and they're right: it *is* great and it *is* theirs, though what it is,
what is great about it and whether it is everybody's equally are
matters in permanent dispute.

'This great country of ours' is an incantation of the

patriotic heart; and when someone loses control of his car on the ice and spins into a truck or flies off a bridge, he dies with it there, along with the Lord, and lust or greed or desperation. They die in battle, soldiers in the never-ending crusade, carrying their banners on their cars: yellow, blue and red ribbons; NRA badges; the nation's flag; stickers declaring their love of God and their oneness with their Saviour. PROPERTY OF JESUS, one said on the back of a Winnebago outside Idaho Falls.

A couple of radio preachers were trying to help people 'struggling with lust or addiction'. They had a book that provided both practical advice and assurance that the lustful could be forgiven. A man phoned in to say that he was 'one with God and one with my spouse', and that they prayed together in bed each night before setting the alarm clock.

I drove down the west side of Yellowstone, through Idaho and into Utah, then east to Colorado and south to New Mexico: a gruelling drive. I found consolation in imagining how much harder it must have been for the homesteaders, the miners, the cowpunchers, the women; or for the Nez Perce Indians, who were pushed into Yellowstone and out the other side by Europeans determined to put them on a reservation. I tried to remember every western I had ever seen. I tried to remember every character in the TV series *Deadwood*, and which recent president they most resembled. It was easy enough until I came to George W. Bush: he seemed to be without a spiritual ancestor.

In *Deadwood* Samuel Alito would have been Seth Bullock, the self-righteous sheriff ruled by a bruising superego. The Senate hearing on his nomination played all the way to New Mexico; and all the way, the radio and television host Sean Hannity beat the living jeepers out of the Democrats for questioning Alito's fitness for the job. In particular, he beat up Senator Edward Kennedy. In fact, he did not so much beat him up as feed him to the pigs. Those pioneers had it hard to be sure, but at least they did not have Sean Hannity riding them to the grave.

A citizen rang from Louisville, Kentucky, to tell Hannity that he was a great American, and Hannity told him he appreciated it. The caller said that 'some of these characters are disgusting', and Hannity said: 'I'm glad you're out there – and don't worry, we're winning.' The Democratic Party, he said, was in the hands of radical left-wingers. Alito was a good man. The Patriot Act was a good act. The war in Iraq was being won. The Dow Average was up. Unemployment was down. He was talking to people all over the country.

The culture wars went on: actual blood was not let, but there were times when one felt nearer to understanding why, once the shooting starts, civil wars are so savage and so hard to stop.

Among all the mountains, lakes and billboards there was a picture of two happy men holding the head of a moose. An American flag flew behind them. UNITED WE STAND, the logo said. The flag must have been there as a kind of sanction for going out into the woods and shooting a moose and sawing its head off. In these parts, every town has a taxidermist: railroad stations are rare, but there are plenty of taxidermists. It seems strange to love God and insist He is the author of all creation and then cut off the heads of His creatures. But it's an old tradition and it shows the blood is strong.

In 1861 a stagecoach in which young Sam Clemens was a passenger reached the Big Mountain Pass in the Wasatch Range in Utah. Later, when he had become Mark Twain, he wrote that from the elevation of 7000 feet 'under the arch of a brilliant rainbow . . . all the world was glorified with the setting sun and the most stupendous panorama of mountain peaks yet encountered burst on our sight'. Fourteen years before him, Brigham Young led a band of 144 Mormons, including his twenty-seven wives, through the same pass and declared that what he saw was the Promised Land. They dammed the creeks and very soon had thousands of acres under cultivation. The Mormons had a genius for irrigation: within fifty years of their founding, they were watering six million acres in several states. They built the Tabernacle and it became Salt Lake City. I approached it from the north in a Pontiac, and from about thirty miles out I saw a lustrous glow in the sky, a grey-blue shimmering mist and a golden aura above it.

About twenty miles out, a massive mall has been constructed. I ventured in to find a Starbucks and perhaps a Barnes & Noble for a talking book with which to drive across Utah. Despite getting directions from several people, I never found either of these places, and for three-quarters of an hour I could not find my car either. America can make you feel like a king: just as quickly it can also reduce you to a puddle of inadequacy.

And then it makes you believe again. That evening, just south of Salt Lake City, I missed a sign and found myself going west in heavy traffic when I wanted to go east to meet a friend who was holidaying in the ski resort of Park City. For the moment I could see no way of turning back. It was six pm and, as the evening tide of commuters surged along the freeway, I angled through the traffic and pulled over to look at a map. I'd been sitting there no more than thirty seconds when I heard a knock on the window. A man was peering at me, his face yellowish and shadowy in the flickering light of the passing cars. He smiled reassuringly, which seemed to make it more likely he was a psychopath than a policeman.

Too tired to resist whatever was in store, I put the window down. And this man in a suit and tie with a kind, plain, conservative face – a Mormon, I presumed – said he'd seen me pull over and thought I might need help. He told me how far it was to the next exit, how to find my way to Park City and what pitfalls to avoid. I was not lost and would have found my way soon enough. But if instead of walking back to his car he had fluttered on gossamer wings, I would not have been surprised. No ordinary person notices someone edge out of commuter traffic, and even if they do notice, they do not think to stop. There is no kindness on the road – but there was this man.

—

I reached Park City. It was the week before the Sundance Film Festival and the place was filling up with film types, as recognisable as cowboys, setting up deals and meetings on computers, mobile phones and BlackBerrys. I wanted to make a film about a man who even from a great distance and travelling at high speed can sense a motorist's despair. He's working one side of the moral freeway while the other side is worked by a shiftier angel, like a man I met in the foyer of a motel in Kansas. I was looking at my computer screen when he sat down beside me on the couch and asked what program I was using. His moustache looked a little moth-eaten and his eyes were sunk in dark-blue holes, as if he hadn't slept for a week. His approach was nothing more than a pretext for telling me that in *his* laptop he had a program that could deprogram the programs in the big semi-trailers. The freight companies have their prime movers set up so drivers cannot exceed sixty-five miles an hour. This man cruised the highways and at roadside stops looked for drivers willing to pay $500 to reset their trucks to eighty-five miles an hour. He found one or two every day, he said.

I set off east across Utah feeling warm about the Mormons, who make up more than sixty per cent of the population, and enchanted by the snow-spattered cliffs, stupendous walls of rock, pine trees poking from them: it's as if the whole thing had been done by an interior decorator. I took the route that runs south-east to Highway 70. After a couple of hours I reached Carbon County and then wound down into Price River

Canyon, where there's a brutish looking carbon plant on the river and the little town of Helper. A month before, the *California Zephyr* had stopped here when I was sleeping. It's called Helper because, in days past, an extra engine was required to get coal-laden trains up the canyon. Butch Cassidy, having fled the Mormons to become an outlaw, stayed in the town before he robbed the coal company. It was an inconsequential act in the greater scheme of things – Helper is reckoned to have enough coal to last the United States for 300 years.

When you get on Interstate 70 and head east, the mesas loom before you. An hour later they still loom, but now they're beside you as well as before you. Utah is a still life; the drama is in the shapes and their textures and their arrangement. In Utah you might think a sticking plaster has been torn from the earth's skin, taking lumps and layers of flesh with it. You drive on ancient scar tissue. From the hill of a roadside stop you can see the snow on the Rocky Mountains of Colorado in the east, and all around vast plains and bizarre red-brown cathedrals of rock that dwarf every living thing – including freight trains a mile and half long.

Utah's Mormon settlers were bound to see a likeness to the Holy Land. Job might have sat down here with his boils. The poet Wallace Stegner saw it in 1960:

> It is a lovely and terrible wilderness, such a wilderness
> as Christ and the prophets went out into; harshly and
> beautifully colored, broken and worn until its bones are
> exposed, its great sky without a smudge of taint from
> Technocracy, and in hidden corners and pockets under
> its cliffs the sudden poetry of springs.

A little oasis south of Highway 70 on the Colorado River became Moab, probably after the son of Lot from his eldest daughter, and the town of idolaters he founded east of the

Jordan who 'shall not enter into the congregation of the Lord'. Ruth came out of Moab with her daughters. Some, however, say that the Moab in Utah is derived from an Indian word.

Modern Moabites depend on tourists coming for the rafting and trail-biking and filmmakers wanting John Ford settings. The important thing is that the name not be associated with the world's biggest satellite-guided weapon, the 'Massive Ordnance Air Blast' (or the 'Mother Of All Bombs'), the terrifying MOAB. Moab's city fathers have asked the Defense Department to change the acronym. They also hope that the world's biggest uranium tailings dump, lying beside the Colorado River since the world's biggest uranium mine left town, does not leak. At Moab the river turns south on its way to the Grand Canyon and the Hoover and other dams which water Las Vegas and much of Arizona. Those dams, and the cities and farms dependent on them, have reduced the Colorado delta in Mexico to five per cent of the size it was in the mid-twentieth century. Now the wondrous river does not even reach the sea.

This country at once stimulates a person with its grandeur and annihilates him with its relentless scale. You want to go faster, like Sir Donald Campbell did in his supersonic car, Bluebird, on the Bonneville salt lakes in the 1950s; or give in to it and stop altogether. It might be better crossed on a mule, to allow the forlornness it provokes to form itself into a philosophy or a religion. In me it provoked – for the first time in decades – some species of homesickness. I wanted green undulating hills, drizzle and mothering. After travelling the Overland Route to Salt Lake City in 1861, Mark Twain wrote of seeing, east of the Green River, many graves of emigrants and skeletons of mules and oxen that 'gave forth a soft, hideous glow' in the night: 'It was the loneliest land for a grave.' The old route looped north of what is now the Utah–Wyoming border: had it stayed south and crossed the Green River where

Interstate 70 crosses it in Utah, one imagines just as many graves and bones lighting up the nights.

For a while, after you cross the Colorado, the country is much the same, and then it rises and becomes something that looks like it is made from some element harder than any rock. And spread out below the highway, a vast lonely plain. And then you come to Grand Junction.

There's a little more left of Grand Junction's core because the train – the *California Zephyr* – still stops at the old station and a few buildings of the same era remain. The place has been malled, but not entirely, and because of the train and the railway yards, it feels in touch with both its past and its geography. It looks and feels real and muscular.

I wanted to wait around and see the train pull in, and the passengers get out and smile and stretch and visit the canteen for apples and bananas. I wanted to see my own experience from the other side. In fact, I wanted to leave the car and get on the train. Failing that, I wanted to hear its whistle blowing as it came into Grand Junction. But it was an Amtrak train: I might have been there till dark.

———

A person who has tired of Utah's scenery has likely tired of life; but Colorado revives him. He comes to the mountains and follows the rail line up through the snow-smudged red rocks. He glances down into the plunging ravines and wonders how many old goldminers are down there, their bones mixing with the dinosaurs'.

The deeper into the mountains I went, the deeper became the grilling of Samuel Alito – and the deeper the hole, out here at least, the grillers dug for themselves. In her syndicated column in the local Grand Junction bugle, Maureen Dowd put the sceptic's view of Alito, while another commentator dismissed these views as Manhattan ideology. Those for Alito portrayed him as a man who had grown up with no greater desire than to honour his father and live by his code and that of all the decent families of New Jersey. He was a good son in a world abounding with transgressive youths who desired only to *dishonour* their fathers (and mothers) and live by any foreign code they chose. In other words, psychologically speaking, he was pretty close to a perfect fit with the president and the men around him.

Listening to the hearings, you could tell Alito aroused the deepest instincts in Edward Kennedy and his colleagues. Politics has *natural* enemies: people who, like some dogs, cannot stand each other on sight. Alito sounded like a man whose Oedipal reflex had failed to function. This is anathema to people in whom it is still sputtering long after it should have stopped. Just to sense such a person in the same room makes their necks harden and their teeth clench. No doubt something like this also happens to the conservative when some flag-burning, father-disgracing, intolerably late-maturing liberal enters the chamber. This is the fuel rod of the culture war, the clash of the good son and the rebellious one. The Alito nomination made it clear again.

In fog and ice and snow, cars crept over the mountains past other cars that hadn't made it. Trucks loaded with cars that had rolled or slid or spun chugged east towards the panelbeaters. Finally, after a long tunnel, travelling behind a car with stickers saying FREEDOM ISN'T FREE and SECURE OUR BORDERS, I came over a hill – and Denver with the sun shining on it looked like the Holy City, the Promised Land. Three million people (or four million, depending on what adjacent parts are counted) live in Denver on a mile-high plain. All across the low, rolling, grassy rises that fringe the city, housing developments were spreading. In landscapes from *Gunsmoke* and *Wagon Train* there were miles and miles of neat rows of new two-storey houses in beige and cream. This was apparently the new 'City of Lone Tree': built out there under the big sky and looking at the Rockies, on high plains still redolent of mules and cowpokes. Sherwood Anderson believed these places imparted a 'semi-religious' feeling to the people who lived in them:

> Mystery whispered in the grass, played in the branches of
> the trees overhead, was caught up and blown across the
> American line in clouds of dust at evening on the prairies . . .
> I can remember old fellows in my home town speaking
> feelingly of an evening spent on the big empty plains.
> It had taken the shrillness out of them. They had learned
> the trick of quiet . . .

Who can say whether the technocratic residents of Lone Tree will hear the same mystery and have their shrillness taken?

Denver grew on the wealth from mining, oil and transportation, and it still depends on them. The new Denver airport occupies more than fifty square miles, which makes it the biggest in the United States, and it's the fifth-busiest. The building has a resoundingly new frontier feel on the inside and, with a roof that at once suggests the peaks of the Rockies and a cluster of Indian teepees, an old frontier look on the outside. If you buy in Lone Tree – and you will need an income of around $100,000 if you want to blend in – the airport is just minutes away. Denver is diversifying, especially into telecommunications. If it doesn't, one day all these new communities might have tumbleweed blowing through them. For now it is a phenomenon of urban growth, and on that evening it was astonishing to behold.

—

I left Interstate 70 and went south down 25. The sky was cloudless; a full moon shone in the east. Pikes Peak, 14,000 feet high, glistened with snow in the west. The country felt like its essential self – blessed. Pastor Benny Hinn was selling prints of a special painting he'd had commissioned. It was called *The Lord Bringing in the Souls* and listeners could have a copy for $100.

In his novel *Cain's Book*, Alexander Trocchi, a Scottish drug addict who lived on a scow in New York in the 1950s, wrote that under the influence of heroin 'the organism has a sense of being intact and unbrittle, and, above all, *inviolable*'. Unlike marijuana, which makes external things seem 'more enchanted or detailed', with heroin 'the perceiving turns inwards . . . the blood is aware of itself'. He could almost be describing Clint Eastwood.

For the attitude born of this sense of inviolability there is the word *cool*. The United States divides along many lines: race, religion, politics, geography, gender and class. But it also divides between the cool and the uncool. This is not the same as fashionable and unfashionable, although to be fashionable is one way of being cool, and therefore inviolable. But fashion is a surrogate. Real cool comes from something deeper – as it must, because inviolability, intactness and unbrittleness are, if not essential, at least a great boon to existence in America. They come with the self-possessed, plain-speaking, matter-of-fact American turf. They are the first thing the visitor feels he lacks.

The 'cool' are those who know who they are and what they want, and how they will get it. Jefferson, Jackson, Lincoln, Sherman, Gatsby, Bogart, Mitchum, Don Imus, all the heroes of *noir* – the archetypes of American masculinity – are not just cool, but timeless models of intactness, unbrittleness, inviolability. The archetypes didn't use heroin, of course, but a lot of them used hard liquor, which at first makes you feel inviolable, intact and unbrittle. True, the method school created brittle characters, but their brittleness was another form of intactness.

It was an identity, a way to confront the world on *their* terms, yet consistent with being American.

For most of the last half of the twentieth century the term 'evangelical' and the name Billy Graham were all but synonymous. Graham is now in his late eighties and leading a quiet life in North Carolina. His views have quietened as well, though his faith is undimmed. He believes that the Messiah will come again but he does not know when, and while 'nearly all' the signs are 'being fulfilled right now', he concedes that this might have been 'true throughout history'. Graham believes Jonah was literally swallowed by a whale, but that the Biblical days of creation are figurative. His son Franklin is much less accommodating, much more political. Billy still talks to presidents, but it's Franklin who declares Islam 'a very evil and wicked religion' and that the Democratic Party runs to a 'gay agenda'. Billy seems to feel that politics is not the main game for evangelists. He can leave that to someone like Jerry Falwell, a pastor who is not an evangelical and who sees it as his duty to 'confront the culture'.

Billy Graham reflects the general mood more than his son. Despite the palpable strength of the religious right in US politics, the polls are beginning to suggest it might have reached the limits of its influence. The Pew Research Center finds that ninety per cent of Americans believe in God; but as well it finds that sixty-six per cent of them want the nation to reach the 'middle ground' on abortion, and among evangelicals about the same number want 'compromise' on the subject. Forty-four per cent of evangelicals support stem cell research. These might be signs of self-correction, that American pragmatism is reasserting itself over American religious zeal.

But probably not in Colorado Springs. Colorado Springs is a good deal more than a mile high and growing faster than Denver. The people have Pikes Peak to look at and fresh mountain air to breathe, at least when they're not on the roads – Colorado Springs has grown too quickly for transport to keep up. They have jobs at the big army and air force bases – NORAD has its headquarters there, which puts it on a par with Omaha should the intercontinental shooting ever begin. Telecommunications is big business in Colorado Springs. And although only twenty per cent of residents go to church each week (the national average is thirty-five per cent) and the divorce rate is staggering, the other business is religion. There are more than eighty different religious organisations in a city of 350,000 people. There are literally hundreds of places of worship: among them, a dozen Assemblies of God, two dozen 'Charismatic', nine Churches of God in Christ, a dozen Nazarene and at least eight Pentecostal churches. There are plenty of Catholic and Baptist and Presbyterian and Methodist as well, but the religious zing in Colorado Springs comes from the new churches; the most famous are James Dobson's Focus on the Family and Ted Haggard's New Life Church.

The 'father of the modern faith movement' was Kenneth 'Dad' Hagin, a self-taught preacher from Texas who would have looked more at home on an oil rig than on a pulpit. Dad was born with a bad heart, and when he was about sixteen years old it stopped beating. Three times it stopped, and three times he was drawn close enough to the gates of hell to see inside. And each time he came back. That – understandably – converted him.

Pentecostalism is not much more than a hundred years old, but some of its practices, such as speaking in tongues and driving out demons, are very much older. So is Gnosticism, of which Hagin was accused by some clerics. Others, including Hank Hanegraaff, accused him of the even older crime of heresy, but that didn't matter to the faithful thousands who came to Dad Hagin to be healed. At these sessions, whole churches full of normal-looking people all descended into lunacy at once. On a wave of Dad's hand, they would begin to laugh and then fall backwards into the arms of their brethren or slide off their chairs in convulsions. 'Holy laughter', Hagin called it. His own laugh sounded like something he overheard on one of those visits to hell. The technique was also known as 'slaying in the spirit' and 'spiritual drunkenness' and was said to be very good for all kinds of common afflictions. It was a bit like a tarantella for people who can't dance.

Dad Hagin's heart caught up with him in 2003, but not before he taught 'holy laughter' to Kenneth and Gloria Copeland, who now carry on the tradition at Word of Faith Ministries. They combine it with an aptitude for tying the promise of eternal salvation to the prospect of financial success: 'As the seeds of prosperity are planted in your mind, in your will and in your emotions they eventually produce a great financial harvest.'

The prince of modern evangelicals is Benny Hinn. 'Pastor Benny', who was born in Israel and raised Greek Orthodox, has a television show seen around the globe five days a week and runs 'crusades' all over the world. He comes on in a white suit while a massed choir sings *How Great Thou Art* – blessed are the meek, not. God speaks to Benny. He gives him the names of people in the audience who need healing, and Benny calls them from the stage. He does 'slaying in the spirit' in the style of Dad Hagin, and when he's finished driving out the cancers, HIV, rheumatism and blindness up to sixty people will be left lying on the floor. Even as they lie there, the money is collected and out the back ministry workers count it.

God told Benny not to appear on the *Dateline* television program. Benny says his ministries support tens of thousands of needy children around the world, but *Dateline* could only find 247. *Dateline* also found people who had died soon after Benny healed them. The man is as phoney as his hairpiece. He lives in a $10-million mansion in California, pays enough for a suit to feed an Indian village for a year, drives two Mercedes, travels the world in a private jet and takes layovers in famous resorts in $3000-a-night rooms.

However we define Pastor Benny – zealot, ratbag, conman, cultist – religious history has seen plenty just like him. Usually they thrive in places and at times of desperation and abandonment. They find their followers, as Jesus did, among outcasts and the poor. So why do these Pentecostal churches thrive in places like Colorado Springs, where the median income is a healthy $45,000 a year? Perhaps their mortgages and credit cards make them *feel* poor. But if they felt poor we might expect more preaching on the themes of the Sermon on the Mount. 'Slaying in the spirit' doesn't seem to offer consolation for the meek or a recommendation for the pure of heart, but it might offer something for people who don't feel inviolable: a remedy not for the meek but the uncool; not for the down-at-heel but the down-on-confidence. The people who can't dance. It tells them that they need not be vulnerable and brittle; that the Lord knows who they are and what they want to be. The Lord brings them in.

On a perfect winter's day, through the window of the Garden of the Gods motel, the mountains were very close and the sun shone on their snowy crests and on the bungalows in tree-lined streets. Good oatmeal was served by people as friendly as people can be, and there were people just like them walking up and down with no outward sign that God or Satan moved in them. It made you wonder why so many Americans feel such a need for God's presence. Give thanks. Seek grace, of course. But why hound Him all the time? Why will they not leave Him be? Is it because in a place where everyone wants – even needs – an identity, it comes hard to know you don't have one? There are the self-possessed, and there are those possessed by others – Jesus, Satan, Benny Hinn, Wrestlemania. Not everyone can be cool: and the condition of uncoolness is like enough to leprosy to create ample and fertile ground for faith-healers of all kinds to work in.

But the thought remains: what will it do to America if, one day, the evangelists decide to put their powers to some social purpose? If they should say: 'Pick up your cross and follow me to the mall'? It's not impossible that someone will come to see more in the New Testament than personal healing, personal satisfaction, personal closure, and opposition to abortion and the 'gay agenda' of the Democratic Party. What if they begin to pursue the kingdom of God and decide that empire is as it was in Christ's time, the opposite of God's kingdom; that the mall is what the temple was; that the politicians, moguls, media hosts and evangelists are hypocrites and false prophets; that the worship of celebrities is idolatrous; and that the flag offers all the reassurance and moral force of the Romans' SPQR? What if the corrupt and reactionary evangelists and their political parasites have created the conditions for their own demise?

To the extent that history is tragic repetition made sufferable by irony, it is almost preordained that the temples, built inevitably on moral compromise and falsehood and blasphemy even against their own tenets, should be torn down from within by a new breed of radical Puritans intent on the kingdom of God. Now there was another idea for a film – a Biblical epic set in Colorado now.

—

The Sangre de Cristo Mountains were in spectacular view, and with good old country music playing instead of good old Sean Hannity, life was good. There's something in that hooting sound – the semi-yodel – that sends a shiver down certain kinds of spines, especially in places like southern Colorado. It's not a yodel, but an echo of it. It has to be at least related to a mating cry. Down here you cross the old Santa Fe Trail, and there are memorials and museums to the mule trains and pioneers of the Southwest, and it is striking that when they paid their respects to them, the writers of a generation or two ago did not feel obliged to invoke the Lord on the pioneers' behalf.

Trinidad is the last town before the border of New Mexico. You put your credit card in the petrol pump and a sign flashes: REMOVE CARD QUICK. On the ATM inside they've stuck on a sign that says: REMOVE CARD VERY SLOW. It's just a little town of about 10,000 people. Bat Masterson was sheriff back in the days of the Santa Fe Trail when people were called Bat. In the 1960s a doctor started performing sex-change operations in Trinidad and the place became known as the 'sex-change capital of the world'. It's a conservative town, but the people must have reckoned being the capital of something was better than the capital of nothing.

The surgeon's name was Stanley Biber, and he said he'd honed his cosmetic skills as a MASH doctor in Korea. He did his first operation in Colorado Springs in 1969, when a community worker asked him to. Once his reputation was established, he did an average of four a day. He was five-foot-two and got around Trinidad in a big cowboy hat and cowboy boots. But he wasn't *all* hat: he had a ranch and cattle, and it was on the way back from a cattle sale in Nebraska that he caught pneumonia and died, aged eighty-two. This was in the week that I passed through. The radio report I heard said that he was tolerated because it is a tradition of the West to let people do what pleases them.

In the information centre, where I went to buy a map, I got into a conversation with the woman behind the counter and a man who seemed to be on general duties. They were telling me about the Battle of Glorieta Pass and the boundaries of New Mexico before Sam Houston redrew them on behalf of Texan interests. The lady thought Mexico had extended to the present border of Wyoming, but the man said it stopped at the Arkansas River – and she laughed: 'I guess you'd be right, you always are.'

While I browsed, I heard her say: 'Oh did you see that poor woman? They made her cry!' She was talking about Samuel Alito's wife.

The man said: 'Yeah, and look who made her cry! That man from Massachusetts. That man who should have been in gaol for life. That poor girl drowned when he was drunk. They should have thrown away the key.'

It was just what a talk-show host had said about Edward Kennedy and the night the girl died in his car, but the host had also observed that the 'outcome would have been different' today. Today's media would have properly destroyed him.

———

A person can have too much scenery. An occasional modest house with the Stars and Stripes flying was the only interruption to the dull, brown undulation of the plain – if that is not unfair to the several rocks that saved it from complete formlessness. One of the rocks was called Wagon Mound and a little town had grown around it. It was mid-afternoon and, on American Family Radio, someone sang:

Lord, I'm tired of crying,
Carrying all these tears,
Carrying all this pain alone . . .

I knew how she felt. Las Vegas glistened in the sunlight – Las Vegas, New Mexico. I wanted to visit it, see where Doc Holliday lived with Big Nose Kate and practised dentistry. But sometimes nothing can make you stop. You can no more pull up and commune with the living or the dead or the landscape than those planes streaking across the sky.

I thought I might ring Julie, just to hear her voice. I wondered if she liked country music. Was she a Pentecostalist? On the radio someone called from his car and began by saying where he was, and the announcer said: 'Oh, did you see that cactus on your left? And there's a good rock about ten miles further on. Keep your eye out for it.'

Soon after, I passed a big Dutch Star Winnebago with a jeep in tow. Driver and passenger sat in glum silence. It was a Vermeer on wheels. I got the feeling they hadn't spoken since they set off six months ago; that he might have been counting her failings, she remembering the hymns they sang as children; that they were silently winding back their lives, sifting through the grievances, the names and faces of other ones they might have married. And then one day they'd go home.

Now there was scrub all around and more houses, some of them adobe. Poking out of the bushes in front of one of them, a sign warned passers-by against 'Hellary' Clinton.

D. H. Lawrence said that in New Mexico 'a new part of the soul woke up suddenly, and the old world gave way to the new'. A case could be made for not going there unless you are prepared for a personal cataclysm and have a few years to spare: to visit the ruins; to study the Clovis and later Indian civilisations; to comprehend the mind of Coronado; to read all Cormac McCarthy's books twice and Willa Cather's *Death Comes to the Archbishop* three times; to learn Spanish, if you don't know it already; and to get over the melancholy brought on not only by the history, but also by the architecture of the Pueblo Indians.

In the late 1960s, following the great American tradition of religious migration, thousands of hippies moved to New Mexico, particularly to the Sangre de Cristo Mountains. They took a stand against the commercial culture, because commercialism had destroyed many of the sensory perceptions human beings needed to live in nature. That was an old notion. The newer one, shared with Aldous Huxley, was that they could rediscover those perceptions by ingesting various drugs. They established communes, built adobe houses, burned pinon cones and, with the aid of peyote and jimson weed, peered through the doors of perception at 'the miracle, moment by moment, of naked existence'. Hardly any of them stayed more than a year or two, but in Santa Fe you still see people with something peculiar in their gaze that suggests they once took Carlos Castaneda very seriously.

Santa Fe is still a seductive place. It's the colour and scale of the buildings, the soft air, the scent of smouldering pinon and the palpable sense that there's more to life than commerce, religion and the flag.

It is a tourist town and there's nothing a visitor can do but be a tourist and ignore the occasional signs of disdain from the locals. So you go to the Palace of the Governors, and it *is* remarkable; and you wander among the Indians selling rugs and jewellery; and you visit the cathedral built by the French archbishop who is the hero of Cather's spellbinding novel; and next to it you see the chapel with its 'miraculous' spiral staircase. The chapel had been built without one, and finding no-one in the town who knew how stairs could be erected without ruining the building's interior, the sisters prayed for deliverance. That evening a stranger arrived, riding on a burro. Using only the hammer and saw he brought with him, he built the beautiful pillarless staircase. The sisters believed it to be a miracle, and why not? The story would sit well in the New Testament and just as happily in Gabriel Garcia Marquez.

There is evidence from as early as the thirteenth century that drought shaped the history of settlement in the South-west, and there was a drought in January 2006. Phoenix had gone eighty-five days without a drop of rain. It was much the same in Dallas. And it was the same in Santa Fe. 'We needn't worry,' said the man at my motel. 'We have a president who talks directly to God.' As did the bull-rider at the rodeo I saw on TV that night. Rudy Lortsch stayed on Lazy River for the mandatory eight seconds, and he'd no sooner hit the ground than he was on one knee with his head tilted up to the firmament.

The Spanish took the place in 1540. They brought the Franciscans on the spiritual side, and sheep on the practical. More than a century later, the Pueblo rose up and drove the Spanish out. Then the Spanish came back. It was part of New Spain until the Mexican War of Independence made it part of Mexico. Then the United States took it from the Mexicans in 1846 and fought with the Apaches, Comanches, Utes and Navaho, until Geronimo – the last of them – surrendered in 1886. New Mexico has a history of the most terrible massacres, brutality and ordeals of other kinds, and it is almost certain that this concentrates its appeal. The violence has not been concreted over; more has been left in the air.

CHAPTER 10

Señor, señor, do you know where we're headin'?
Lincoln County Road or Armageddon?

Bob Dylan, *Señor (Tales of Yankee Power)*

IN MAY 2005, WHEN I FIRST ARRIVED IN ALBUQUERQUE, NEW MEXICO, on the *Southwest Chief*, a derailment closed the line and Amtrak deployed three buses to take us the next three hundred miles to Winslow, Arizona. They gave each of us a box of Golden Pride and a large Coke, and through landscapes of red mesa and sage bush we zoomed along the old Route 66 in a fug of fried chicken. Mock dinosaurs waited at the edges of the roads. We passed the scene of the derailment, and all the way to Winslow long freight trains stretched out in silence on the plains, as if they had been snuffed out by alien intervention or thermonuclear blast or Apache raid – all of which New Mexico has known.

A lot of Californians are moving to Albuquerque to escape the rat race and the smog. About 800,000 people live in the city and surrounds, but Albuquerque's growing so fast that they have to move still further. The city nestles beneath the Sandia Mountains, which manage somehow to be both low and imposing. There is an art museum, a natural history museum and an atomic museum. The art museum had paintings by Spanish masters of the seventeenth and eighteenth centuries and, on permanent display downstairs, a life-size conquistador in armour on a life-size armoured horse. Four centuries ago, these aliens in their hundreds marched across the plains and into the Zuni and Hopi settlements and did what was necessary to honour the name of Jesus. Shock and awe was the strategy.

The natural history museum has a thirty-five-metre seis-mosaurus (so called because the earth shook when it walked), 'locked in mortal combat' with something a bit smaller from the Triassic age. New Mexico is the primal state: the dinosaur capital and the atomic capital. The Atomic Museum has replicas of Little Boy and Fat Man, the bombs developed a hundred miles north at Los Alamos, tested two hundred miles south at Alamogordo, and dropped on Hiroshima and Nagasaki in 1945. These days at the Los Alamos National Laboratory, they are preparing for a new production run of seventy nuclear warheads with an explosive yield equivalent to 2200 Hiroshimas. Added to the existing 10,000 warheads, it should be enough. Los Alamos also seems to be the place where the 'Rods of God' and the 'Divine Strake' are being developed, the latter as a possible conventional alternative to the 'Robust Nuclear Earth Penetrator'. The Rods of God, as one would expect, will be fired from space.

This time in New Mexico, I did the driving. South of Albuquerque the radio played *The Tracks of My Tears*, then *Band of Gold* and *Knock Three Times*. Smokey Robinson writes songs every day of his life. He's always thinking about songs, he says. It's a national habit and always has been: the human heart is one more frontier to be discovered, fought over, conquered, ploughed, evangelised, and turned into a car park or a poem. No people on earth make music like the Americans – no-one else comes close. It's one more place where socialism can't compete: a couple of rousing anthems against 10,000 songs of love and anguish. When anti-American feelings sneak up on you, when you think the democracy is a bit of a sham, the people are ruled by ignorance and fear and no good can come of the place – think of the music.

I drove south past Albuquerque and turned east off Highway 25 and into the little town of San Antonio, New Mexico, where no more than a couple of hundred people live by the banks of the Rio Grande. It was a sudden whim, a last-second decision to veer left instead of going where I had intended at the beginning of the day – which was to El Paso. At the San Antonio gas station, I found real sandwiches with real ham and fresh lettuce and, eating them in the sun, I felt like writing a song myself.

On the other side of the road, a slender young woman in jeans and an embroidered denim jacket sat out the front, smoking and staring at the mountains. It could have been Linda Ronstadt as she appeared on her early record covers. The place was billed as an art gallery and café. She said she had been sitting out there wondering why she'd never gone riding in those mountains – the Magdalena Mountains. We went inside and she made coffee. She trained horses. Her husband last year ranked eighteenth in the world for roping steers. That was where he was: away at the rodeo, and he would be for another week or two. I ordered a second espresso.

She also had cannoli. I'd just eaten two sandwiches, but I said I'd have cannoli. She said I should, because I wouldn't get another cannoli between there and New York. As she filled them and talked, I formed the impression that she wasn't really happy with things. While her husband had done well enough roping steers last year, the good money was in riding bulls. Bull-riding is what they call the 'marquee' event at the rodeo; it's the one that people like to watch on television.

She reckoned it was a phoney sort of event compared to roping steers, because it's not something that cowboys do in their working lives. She thought the people who brought us bull-riding were probably sitting around getting drunk when they thought of it. She knew one man who had broken his neck twice, but he kept getting on bulls for the money and the glamour. Her husband wasn't making a lot of money, and the café and gallery were not making much either. It was hard, she said. And she said it again before I left.

I drove out of the town with *The Tracks of My Tears* playing in my head. If there had been a halfway decent motel, I might have checked in. I thought I could live happily in San Antonio for a week or two. The Rio Grande was just a little brown stream grown full of weeds: uninspiring, but a better look, apparently, than downstream at El Paso where it has been channelled into concrete to keep the border stable in times of flood. There was a sign a mile or two the other side of it as you got out on the plain: GUSTY WINDS MAY EXIST.

If you turn left and drive ten minutes to the north of this road between the Rio Grande and the Pecos, you come to Bosque Redondo, where once there had been a concentration camp for Indians. All the males of both tribes 'are to be slain whenever and wherever they can be found', General James Carleton said: unless, that is, they were willing to be herded into the camp. In 1863 Carleton's men killed more than 300 Apaches and locked up 700 survivors. Kit Carson took a contingent of men into Arizona and surprised the Navaho. He cut down their 3000 peach trees, burned their crops and drove 2500 of them, along with 3000 sheep and 400 horses, the 400 miles to Bosque Redondo and penned them up with the Apaches, their old enemies. Six thousand Navahos lived out their days in that camp.

The Navaho were adaptable and pragmatic people. The Apaches were less so: they contrived to slip away and, with the

Comanches, who were also still at large, waged a doomed and ever more vicious war. Yet, as anyone who has read Cormac McCarthy's *Blood Meridian* will know, this last chapter in the war was civilised compared to the Indian-hunting on the Mexican border around 1850.

'Virtues lose themselves in self-interest, as rivers lose themselves in the sea,' that other celebrated French courtier, La Rochefoucauld, said. But rivers of self-interest just as often lose themselves in seas of virtue. What is best for cattle and oil is worst for the heathen and infidel. What is best, therefore, for the private interest is best for the nation under God. What idea better suits a country founded by entrepreneurs and religious absolutists? Fighting the heathens – from the Pequods to the Apaches to the Vietcong to the Iraqis – has helped to cement the idea that in war, as in commerce, the most pragmatic means can produce the most providential end. In this way, they come honestly by their bias – to borrow a phrase of N. Scott Momaday's – and, having come to it, cannot always say with certainty if it is the pursuit of the good or their interests that motivates them.

The republic was itself created by a necessary violent act. It was reaffirmed by another one, four score and a few years later. 'All necessary force' has profound sanction in American history and America's greatest leaders have employed it, not only to defend the nation and the pursuit of national interests, but also to defend the pursuit of private interest. This is not difficult to comprehend, even if the definition of 'necessary' provokes dispute. Nor is it any surprise to see Christianity marching side by side with military might.

What startles sometimes is the disregard the people of the world's greatest military power have for their enemies. We expect soldiers to be ruthless to the extent that it is necessary to do their job; but we expect it less of media commentators. It's startling to hear them congratulate American troops on killing a certain number of the enemy. They sound like voices from an earlier civilisation, from the Crusades or Rome – or like al Qaeda. It's a shock to hear war debated without reference to the civilian dead and wounded, and to hear American leaders talk as if they bear no responsibility for the internecine fighting provoked by their invasion of another country.

One is more conscious of it in a country where the airwaves are jammed with people wanting to talk about their feelings, their pain, their sympathy, their love, their wish for 'closure'; and where the churches are packed every Sunday with people proclaiming the glory of the living Jesus. When George Bush Senior prayed with Billy Graham before Operation Desert Storm, he prayed only for the American troops and not for the benighted conscript army they were about to annihilate. No sympathy for the enemy their Lord advised them to love, no chance of forgiveness for the heathen, but any amount for the lustful husbands of Idaho. The United States is like a marshmallow: soft and downright gooey on the inside, toasted to titanium hardness on the outside.

Turn left towards the Pecos and the road takes you to Fort Sumner, from where the Indian campaign was conducted. Turn right and travel about the same distance and you come to the place where the first atomic bomb was exploded. It is all desperately forbidding country, and it's easy to see why, when they were driven away from the fertile land along the river, the Indians generally chose government rations over freedom. But the country to the north, though bad, is better than the country to the south. In the south is the White Sands Missile Base, and beyond that is Alamogordo.

On a long, flat, windy road, I stopped and looked over the fence and remembered Robert Oppenheimer. It is strange to look at a desert and think of a man in a grey suit and hat, but the father of the bomb left this Magritte-like mark on our minds. A new generation of physicists at Alamogordo now work on the construction of a space elevator, Jacob's ladder made real: a 100,000-kilometre carbon nanotube ribbon anchored to the earth so that people and goods may travel up and down it, in and out of space – all without rocketry and at a fraction of the current cost. The scientists say it could be up and running within fifteen years.

On the other side of the road were two forty-four-gallon drums for rubbish. It did for a picnic ground, but many picnickers had been unable to find the openings in the tops of the drums and litter and faeces were scattered through the scrub. A Winnebago went past. The driver waved. I'd seen them earlier, but his companion wasn't up the front now: I supposed she was dozing on the bed or making pancakes.

To reach Alamogordo you turn off at Carrizozo. Before you get there you pass a mile-wide stream of what looked to me like peat but turned out to be the Valley of Fires – a lava flow caused by an earthquake. 'They say we can expect another big earthquake in New Mexico within our lifetime,' said the lady at the information centre. New Mexico, it seems, is 'rending' a half-inch every year. California is rending two inches.

While I was thinking about this, a man built like a bison dismounted from his motorbike and came into the centre with a very short female companion. Everything from his waist up seemed to be of one piece, as if it had been fashioned from axe heads fused by intense heat. He wore jeans and a black T-shirt with JESUS LOVES BIKERS TOO embroidered on the front, and on the back: SUPPORT YOUR LOCAL SOLDIERS FOR JESUS MOTORCYCLE CLUB. He did not care for small talk. He just wanted to know how this happened – how this black shit got here. His devoted girlfriend watched with a sort of aggressive suspicion. The lady told him that the lava flow had been caused by an earthquake.

'When?' asked the Soldier for Jesus.

'They think about 1500 to 5000 years ago,' she replied.

'AD or BC?'

At that point history got a bit tangled. It was plain the biker had creation on his mind, and the lady could feel the ground shifting beneath her.

In Carrizozo, I turned right towards Alamogordo. A near-gale was blowing. The lady at the information centre had told me that if I went to Alamogordo I should wear very strong sunglasses to protect my eyes from flying sand. As for the car, she said it might get 'sand-blasted'. 'Remember, you're more than a mile up here,' she said. About three miles out of town, the sand was pinging off the car and I wondered what my standing with Alamo Car Rentals would be if I returned it with no paint. A coward, I turned back to Carrizozo.

Carrizozo is the seat of Lincoln County and, like many of these towns that sit out on the forbidding plains, it has charac-ter. All the wrecked cars of the county's history had been piled near a welcome sign, but everything else about it seemed to defy its location on the edge of what seemed like nothing. The centre of town was an intersection at which the roads went in four directions, and the motel on one was called the Four Winds. The other three corners were occupied by gas stations. There were other motels, the City Ranchers Bank, a Masonic Temple, a golf course, the Indian Summer Trailerhouse village, a market, a laundromat.

It was a town going places. In every direction the roads had been attended to by landscape gardeners. A long strip of land next to the golf course was being developed for housing. There was a Rotary Club and a Women's Club. On the wall of the Wells Fargo Bank a sign said: I WILL SAVE FOR MY FUTURE EACH TIME I RECEIVE MY PAYCHECK. It had everything. It had a

Union Pacific railroad. Two years earlier an eastbound freight train ran into a westbound at Carrizozo. The engineer and the conductor on the eastbound were killed. An investigation found that both men were asleep when the trains collided: they had been for some time, and the engineer was stoned. In his trousers they found a 1.88-gram stash, a hinged wooden pipe packed with marijuana, and a .22 pistol.

West of Carrizozo, the road climbs steadily to just shy of 7000 feet, but it doesn't feel that high. JESUS IS LORD IN CAPITAN, the sign said as I drove into town. Smokey Bear State Park is dry and forbiddingly elemental, but a lot of people seem to live here in cabins and trailers dotted through the coniferous scrub. The park was home to the original Smokey Bear, who as a cub was burned in a forest fire but survived and became a legend. Though he lived most of his life in Washington DC, Smokey was buried in the forest where he was born.

Robert Oppenheimer, Smokey Bear and Geronimo all on the same road, and a little further on there was Fort Stanton, which at various times was home to Kit Carson and General Jack Pershing. For the first thirty years of its life it was a base for fighting Apaches; later it became a hospital for tubercular marines and, during World War II, an internment camp for Germans and Japanese. Lew Wallace wrote much of *Ben Hur* at Fort Stanton. Billy the Kid was meant to be hanged there, but he escaped through a chimney.

And that's the next place – Lincoln, where Billy the Kid shot two men. Lincoln is the heart of Lincoln County, where the Lincoln County Wars were fought between a powerful shop owner in the town and a powerful rancher outside it. Both of them wanted to be *more* powerful and hired men for the purpose. The rancher hired Billy, a native of Manhattan. He killed a few men, though maybe not as many as he claimed. He killed two in Lincoln escaping from the gallows. Pat Garrett, a one-time buffalo hunter, was the sheriff at the time.

He chased Billy to Fort Sumner and shot him down in circumstances that vary with the passing of time and the fashions in films. The Lincoln Courthouse Museum is beautifully preserved, right down to the hole in the wall said to have been made by a shot the Kid fired. I asked the lady what she thought of Billy and she was clear about it: 'He shot two men in self-defence and two men trying to escape, and he was only twenty-one. He was a kid.'

From the room upstairs, which is set up as it used to be when it was a meeting place for the Masonic Lodge, you can see across the road to a little cottage with a fence. The lady told me that Douglas Fairbanks Junior stayed there when he was researching a film about Billy the Kid. He never opened the gate, she said; he always jumped it. The film was probably Howard Hughes's *The Outlaw*. Jane Russell's breasts made the film notorious. That it was not notorious for misogyny, plain perversity and its rendering of Billy and Doc Holliday as near-as-dammit gay is all that needs to be said about her breasts.

The Courthouse Museum also devotes a room to the Civil Construction Corps, which in the 1930s gave work and education to three million Americans, 50,000 of them in New Mexico. Among the subjects the unemployed studied were archaeology, the history of the Southwest and Spanish. I asked the lady what she thought of the Civil Construction Camps and the New Deal: she was solid in her support. She was pro Billy the Kid and pro Franklin D. Roosevelt.

It happens in America: you meet people and you want to settle in their town for a while. It might be the charisma that attaches to liberal convictions in an unkind climate. The harshness gives humanity the glow of grace. It encourages the idea of angels.

—

About fifteen miles west of Roswell, New Mexico, a man was singing on the radio:

I bin' thinkin' about this all day long –
Never felt a feelin' quite so strong.
I cain't believe how much it turns me on
Just to be your man

He went on to sing about turning 'the lights down low, and putting on some music that's soft and slow'; it was confounding to hear such preppy lyrics sung by a baritone. They'd been playing it everywhere for the past fortnight. I believe they played it once for every dead coyote I saw on the road. It burrowed into my head and pushed Bob Dylan clean out of it.

A lot goes on in Roswell. There are five museums and art galleries, a symphony orchestra, a university and a military college. The town has a racetrack, a dragway, a sports complex and a golf course; sports clubs and community organisations of many descriptions; numerous cultural festivals and fairs; the biggest mozzarella cheese factory in the world; and a mighty statue of the cattle baron John Chisum and his lead steer. But Roswell also has the 1947 flying saucer and the aliens that emerged, as it were, from the wreckage; and no responsible city could fail to grasp the competitive advantage inherent in these events. Roswell (population 50,000) has an annual UFO festival, and to mark the sixtieth anniversary of the 'crashed flying disk' that made the city famous they had decided on a four-day UFO festival for 2007. Believers and sceptics alike had been invited to participate and 50,000 visitors were expected. The city has a permanent museum dedicated to alien spaceships and declares it has plenty to offer visitors 'from this planet or from a distant galaxy'.

Somewhere between a fifth and a quarter of Americans

believe in alien abductions, a good proportion of those believe they have *seen* aliens, and it is averred by a sizeable cohort that they have been abducted by them. Some psychologists reckon these beliefs are the product of vivid dreams that the dreamers take for reality. If this is so, it seems likely that the dreams will be more common in places where the aliens are closer to the surface of human consciousness, as they must be in Roswell. Do people in Roswell dream aliens or the images of Georgia O'Keeffe? If they dream aliens, is it in the same part of the brain where their forebears dreamt Indians? And before the Indians, fiends and witches? Do the aliens appear from the same shadow as the serpent in the garden? Is it the same with monsters: that so many believe in them because they dream about them, and they dream about them because they have been there from the start?

Yet, from the outside at least, Roswell makes less of the great alien event of 1947 than one might expect. At first look, it is an archetype of towns so common you begin to wonder if they are not governed by a plan, or if there's some sort of American aesthetic that places the car yards, wreckers' yards, motels and eating houses together in the main streets. It must be the way they like it. I thought this all the more because I had come to like it too. It expressed a kind of hormonal freedom to be crass and ugly.

In the backstreets of Roswell, flags fly from the house fronts, religious homilies adorn letter boxes. One business boarded up, the other functioning; one motel open, another defunct; one car yard full of Toyotas, the one across the road with no cars, just the sign, NISSAN, and an acre of vacant concrete. Life's a gamble, a series of transitions; success, failure, bankruptcy, recovery; sin, forgiveness, repentance, rebirth – or being 'born again', as they say. The capitalist churn invested with the prospect of divine favour. Under the flag and under God, every American can choose everything. This is freedom.

I had the car washed in Roswell. Two teenage boys who looked like they should have been in school did it. They didn't say a word, not to me nor to each other. I tipped them five dollars and one of them said: 'Thank you, sir.' Driving past the acres of car yards and the huge billboards (and a sign saying $7 billion dollars would be spent on highway improvement), I listened to a preacher on the radio: 'Why must you be born again, you ask? Well, man has a problem and it's called sin.'

There were empty furniture shops, empty motels. 'Give us things that are alive and flexible, which won't last too long and become an obstruction and a weariness,' D. H. Lawrence pleaded. Roswell and a hundred thousand other American towns seem to have heeded him.

The preacher talked about God's tremendous forgiveness. 'Let's take a few,' he said. 'God says, "Thou shalt not murder." But if there are any murderers among us' – and here he spoke gently – 'God will forgive you. You got blood on yer hands and all that guilt down through the years – he'll forgive you.' He spoke over applause as he moved on to stealing.

East of Roswell, I drove over a low rise and it was as if the creator had taken up a different brush, or a different creator had wielded it. The land was sage and straw-coloured, and softer. Earlier there had been deer, with their white rumps shining, their heads down, their legs delicately bent. Now there were cattle. And oil pumps. Metal sculpture had become popular. There were cowboys, metal ships, horses, flying saucers and aliens. The little town of Tatum, which is just west of the Texas border and seemed to be clinging to life, had a metal sculpture of the marines raising the flag on Iwo Jima, and under it: SUPPORT OUR TROOPS. Way out here, under the huge lonely sky and among signs of decline, these clichés of American life have a sort of forlorn power, not for what they depict, but for the almost mechanical impulse that produces them, much as a guitarist produces chords when he's playing country music.

For metal art, nothing matches an oil pump. Standing before a dynamo at the 1900 Paris World Exhibition, Henry Adams began to pray to it: 'Inherited instinct taught the natural expression of man before silent and infinite force,' he said. In the dynamo he saw something occult: 'a revelation of mysterious energy', like that of the cross or the Virgin in pre-scientific times. He might have seen the same in an oil pump, had he stood before one as the sun sank and darkness flowed over the land. The pumps don't care about the night, or the weather, or wolves or spaceships, or the flag or sin. In that ridiculous, simple motion they just keep pumping the wealth out.

Across the border, in Plains, Texas (population fifty-three), one of those portable digital signals that are often used to indicate roadworks or traffic delays had been parked in the main street. It flashed away in the dark: SHOWER TEA. WEDDING SHOWER FOR SHAUNA BOX. The moon came up a deep red and it seemed to bring with it the smell of salt. On the radio, someone said that if Jimi Hendrix were alive today he'd realise that we had a lot of enemies and he'd support our troops.

A Mexican who had bludgeoned to death at least fifteen people along US railroad tracks said he had let Satan rule his life. Texas was preparing to execute him, despite protests from Mexico, which has abolished the death penalty. About twenty people a year are executed in Texas, far more than in any other state. While violent crime is marginally more common in the Lone Star State, it is nowhere near enough to explain the discrepancy. It can only be put down to the Texan way of doing things. Texas is Old South and Wild West, both of which were fond of summary justice – and Texans don't want for a sense of tradition, or for governors, wherever they hail from, wanting to live by it. The large number of evangelical Christians in Texas adds to the public clamour. The evangelicals believe the death penalty is a necessary weapon in the struggle with Satan, and that God demands it. And what God demands no governor of Texas is going to deny Him.

The ice machine and the Coke machine are the village wells of motel life. It is beside them that the managers stack the tourist promotions and religious tracts. At Big Spring in west Texas I took a brochure about Satan. It said that he was on his beat 24/7. As Mark Twain grew older, he took more of an interest in Satan. He wrote *Letters from the Earth* as if he *were* Satan. 'Satan hasn't a single salaried helper; the Opposition employ a million,' he said. But with enemies like the new fundamentalists, Satan might reckon he has little need of friends.

The Indian motel owner said he chose Big Spring because it is cheaper and quieter than New Jersey. There are three correctional facilities there; two state-run federal prisons and the Big Spring Correctional Center, which is run by Cornell, a listed company based in Houston with seventy-eight prisons nationwide. The Cornell company motto is 'People Changing People'. It's a good business to be in: nationwide, the number of prisoners has grown sevenfold in the past three decades, and now the United States has more prisoners and more prisons than any other country in the world. No-one ever seems to offer a good reason for this phenomenal increase. While zero tolerance and more prisons are widely believed to have reduced crime rates, especially in the big cities, they've not reduced it sevenfold, or even twofold.

I took off early. If they *will* put the lodging houses on the highway, they can't expect visitors to discover the pleasures of the town. The roadkill was fresh: turkeys, rabbits, skunks and many dead deer in that heartbreaking pose with their heads thrown back on their slender necks, their eyes burning in the sun. The road to San Antonio, Texas, is long and dull. The ranchers announce themselves with twenty-foot-high arches over their gates. Tammy Wynette sang on the radio:

I wrecked the car and I was sad
And so afraid that you'd be mad . . .

NPR was out of range. I listened for a moment to a man who quoted Corinthians in support of his argument for good eating and thanked the Lone Star Electric Company for sponsoring his show and 'unifying Christians in west Texas'.

Hardly a day passes without a new book about American politics, history, society, foreign policy; and not a week without several 'must-read' articles in the high-quality journals and magazines; several 'must-hear' broadcasts on NPR and even 'must-see' programs on C-Span. Every week there are another half-dozen conspiracy theories in hardback; a dozen political biographies or autobiographies; a few histories; another take on 9/11; another dozen takes on Iraq; another investigation of Washington or education or the prison system. From all this, conscientious citizens must choose. That's before they choose which elements of the mass culture – the newspapers, the major news networks, the major talk shows, the major soaps and satires – they must watch and hear and read to know what is going on minute to minute, day to day, week to week. And having done that, it is time to get on the net and read the blogs and watch YouTube and follow the links. No voters in the world know more about their democracy than informed American voters.

But not much gets to Big Spring, Texas. And even less, one suspects, to places twenty miles off the highway. Big stories come and go; the lights go on and off up and down the corridors; speculation, opinion and theorising pour forth without end; people write books containing evidence of events, associations, coincidences and motives which, if true, should see the mighty shot down from their perches and a week of prayer and reflection declared across the country. But great swathes of the country are passed by, or the inhabitants receive their information packaged into news and opinion by media that for all kinds of reasons – a few of them good – abridge, construe, dilute, traduce, *spin* it into a confection for what is presumed to be the popular taste.

This is not to say that the owners of the taste live in darkness, or that the information contained in, say, the *Report of the 9/11 Commission* should be delivered to every household. It is foolish to expect information to be distributed equally, or for it to be equally desired. Yet if we want to know why it was possible to persuade a majority of Americans that Iraq was responsible for the 2001 attacks, that weapons of mass destruction *were* found there and much else that is fanciful, we don't have to look much further than the confluence of American media and American politics, and its capacity for turning national debates and national events into something less challenging than the thoughts of Captain America.

This complaint about the corruption of American democracy and the stifling of American hope by concentrated wealth and media monopoly is an old one: as old as the hope and the corruption. Old, but still going strong: in the last twenty years, one per cent of the population gathered in more than half of the wealth, and twenty per cent gathered the rest. Far from complaining, the people voted a second term for the president who gave tax cuts to these super-rich.

The Marxist will say that the relentless concentration of wealth is in the nature of capitalism, and Mencken that it's in the nature of morons to confuse somebody else's interests with their own. And it's in the nature of democracy that everyone reckons he knows what the problem is. Solutions are harder to come by. Sometimes – when you're driving in the Southwest, for instance – it seems that with all its limitless possibilities, contradictions and dead ends, the only way to think about the United States is as a fabulist might: as a place governed by primitive and unalterable forces (including the Constitution) that yield little either to sociology or political analysis. But for the student of life, it reveals multitudes. It is the United States of *America*, after all – South America's 'blood relation', as Jorge Luis Borges once suggested: 'the deep continent that spanned so many mythologies, the continent of Sherman's march and Brigham Young's polygamous theocracy, of Western gold and bison beyond the sunsets, of Poe's anxious labyrinths and Walt Whitman's great voice'. Americans believe things that are not true and vote for their exploiters, because to do so is as consistent with their history as exercising pure reason. They are merely responding to reality.

—

Beautiful rain fell on the suburbs of San Antonio. A car flew off the freeway and rolled and rolled on the grassy bank and seemed sure to roll back into the traffic, but it stopped and lay on its side with wheels spinning. That morning two military jets had flown low over San Antonio to mark Martin Luther King Day. That they were flown by African American pilots did not satisfy some of the 100,000 people who marched in the rain: they believed it was a day for non-violence and there was nothing non-violent about military aircraft, whatever the colour of the pilot.

A host of things distinguish Texas from the other states of the union, but nothing more than history. Texan history, like Texan people, appears to follow an independent course; and more than other places, even as wealth, growth and modernity transform the place, the past comes along for the ride, hovering at elections and around barbecues. The themes are strung on a continuum going back to the conquistadors. Perhaps the most pervasive of them was epitomised by a character in John Sayles's film *Lone Star*: 'To run a successful civilization, you have got to have your lines of demarcation between right and wrong, between this'un and that'un. Your daddy understood . . . that most people don't want their salt and sugar in the same jar.'

In 1926 someone took a photograph of two dozen recruits to the new Immigration Border Patrol, lined up in front of their cars on the banks of the Rio Grande. They are all holding rifles, except for one who has a machine gun. They had been recruited to stop the flow of aliens and liquor across the border. A million Mexicans crossed into the United States in the first thirty years of the last century. The paradox was the same then as now. The United States, the sovereign republic, could not readily abide aliens coming and going as they pleased: the United States whose business is business could not do without them. The government had prohibited liquor as it now prohibits other drugs, but Americans wanted liquor as they now want other drugs – so the liquor came from Mexico, as the drugs do now. The United States was an English-speaking 'white' country, except the Mexicans were in the Southwest long before the whites, and in many counties there and elsewhere 'Hispanics' outnumber them – which does blur the definition of 'alien'. But these Immigration Border Patrol employees – forerunners of today's US Border Patrol – were not there to express the contradictions, but to resolve them.

Back in November 2005, the night before the train got into Jackson, Mississippi, I met a young Mexican man from Tampico. He said nothing during the meal except 'Thank you', and he never failed to bow his head when he said it. Later he told me that he and his wife and two daughters were living illegally in Oxford, Mississippi, and working in a Mexican restaurant.

He had been up to Chicago to see about a job in a Mexican restaurant. But it was not a good place, he said. Oxford was a nice place, although the people there were not nice to Mexicans. They were not nice to the Puerto Ricans, the Guatemalans or the one Cuban who lived there either. He found their rudeness to the Guatemalans the hardest to understand, because Guatemalans are 'noble people'.

'It is not easy to live in a town where the people do not want you,' he said. But in Mexico it was worse. Mexico was corrupt and 'the gangsters kill you if you break any of their rules and a man cannot make money to feed his family'.

Though it was not legal for him to do so, he worked in Oxford and so did his brother and mother. His mother worked in the house of a judge, whose whole family loved her. They hugged her when she had to leave because she did not have a work visa. He and his brother work in the same Mexican restaurant, one of several the owner has in Mississippi. 'The owner is not a good man,' he said.

I asked how much he paid them.

'Nothing. Only tips,' he said.

As nothing was only $2.13 less than the legal minimum rate for restaurant workers, the owner was indeed desperately mean.

'It is not legal, what he does,' he said. 'But we are not legal either.'

So why did he not go to California or somewhere in the Southwest where there are more Mexicans?

'Because they hate us there,' he said. 'The Chicanos don't talk to the new people. They speak Spanish to each other, but if I speak to them in Spanish they tell me they speak only English. And turn their backs.'

Primo Levi saw the same in Auschwitz: prisoners expressed their own humiliation by persecuting newcomers.

It was much worse to be hated by one's own people than by Americans in Mississippi, the young man said. He wanted only to work and make money for his family. He was a good Mexican and he resented the bad ones who came to the United States and made trouble with the police. They made it hard for all Mexicans, he said.

We shook hands, and he returned to his seat in the carriage full of all the sub-prime sorts of people who were stretching out under coats and blankets and laying their heads on whatever soft thing they had with them.

———

A friend in New York told me I shouldn't drive through the Southwest without calling on Ruben Solis. I took a taxi out to his once-grand Victorian house in a once-grand suburb of San Antonio that used to be home to wealthy Germans. Now it is home to the much less wealthy Mexican community – or 'Hispanics', as these days Mexican Americans are known. By language, culture, race and appearance, Ruben is Mexican. But he is also a Texan, and from an old family. His family was in Texas before Texas and Texans existed: before the Mexican Wars, before Sam Houston and the Texas Republic, before the Alamo, before oil and longhorn cattle – before all the history and tradition by which Texas is commonly defined.

'"Hispanic" is a joke,' Ruben says. 'As if we all came from Hispaniola.' 'Hispanic' is a convenient myth that obscures the truth of history and diminishes the status of millions. 'We did not cross the border; the border crossed us.' In this, he sees his situation, and that of his fellow 'Hispanics', as akin to that of the Palestinians.

Ruben runs the Southwest Workers Union. There's a bit of Trotsky about him, a formidable radical with the kind of deep historical perspective that feeds a sense of irony. Factory conditions and environmental hazards are among the big concerns of his union. When people in communities close to Kelly Air Force Base reported high rates of cancer, kidney failure and other diseases, the union ran a years-long grass-roots campaign to make the air force clean up the toxins left behind when the base closed. The union draws people into political and social action, and into 'social forums' constructed around specific interests such as the border and immigration. 'Philanthropists who don't wait to be asked', the friend in New York called them.

Ruben tells the history in sardonic shorthand. Mexico wins its independence from Spain in 1821, but fifteen years later this part of it is seized by Sam Houston and his gang. Here in San Antonio, at the Alamo, the Mexicans have their victory over the Americans: but soon after, the Americans drive them back across the Rio Grande and seize what will become Texas. And they turn the Alamo into a triumph of *American* courage and sacrifice. They make martyrs of Davy Crockett, Jim Bowie and Bill Travis. They deny the Mexicans their one victory. Ten years later, the Mexican War makes the conquest permanent.

A few weeks before I met him, Ruben had been stopped by the police as he drove three guests home. They were all made to get out of the car, produce identity papers and submit to questioning and frisking for drugs. White men in pick-up trucks are never harassed, Ruben says. Brown guys found with 'low-grade' crack cocaine get gaol sentences of up to ten years. White folks with high-grade cocaine get good behaviour bonds. Brown folk who drink and drive get thrown in gaol. White guys out on the ranches get nothing for the same offence. In San Antonio and in Texas generally, Mexican Americans experience racism every day. It is endemic, Ruben says: like corruption.

Americans have a problem. They need the Mexicans to do the dirty work (on both sides of the border), and they want it done for as little as possible and with as few workplace guarantees as possible. Nearly five million undocumented Mexican labourers presently do just this: the 1.6 million employed as farm-workers make up more than fifty per cent of the sector's labour supply. The absence of documentation is a matter of grave concern to authorities. It also creates hardship for the people who without it are denied services and have no bargaining power with employers. But of course, the absence of that power is what makes them an indispensable commodity. The North American Free Trade Agreement (NAFTA), which the Clinton administration sold to Mexico as great for business and jobs, in fact created industries in Mexico that pay even lower wages and impose worse conditions on workers than exist in the United States. NAFTA, Ruben Solis says, was a disaster for Mexico and Mexicans. Worse, it has done nothing but increase the number of Mexicans desperate to cross the border.

But, much as they want them and need them, and help to create the conditions which drive them to cross the border at any cost, Americans also *fear* Mexicans. Their presence in communities is widely associated with increases in crime, aggravated ethnic tensions, unfair competition for jobs, and lower property values. Substantiated or not, these are predictable and familiar responses to 'wetbacks' of all nationalities in American history. After 9/11, terrorism was added to the list. But 'Hispanics' create a more general, amorphous fear than other groups have. Legal and illegal, they have always been a very substantial part of the American population. Now they are the fastest-growing part as well. At forty million or so, they are more numerous than the black population, and if they keep coming and breeding at the present rate, pretty soon, it is believed, there will be more Hispanics than any other kind of American, and more Spanish spoken than English. Thus the country that appropriated the name *America* will more truly become America.

At each of the major border towns between San Diego and Brownsville, Texas, there are already walls extending well past the city limits. A bill to make the wall continuous passed the House late in 2005. It sharpened Ruben Solis's comparison between the Southwest and Palestine. The present border already separates families: the wall will separate them more completely.

Ruben Solis believes that an open border would be not only more just and less offensive to people who have as much right to live in the Southwest as anyone else, but more practical as well. It would cost less. At present the United States patrols the border with helicopters, planes, drones, men, horses, dogs, satellites and extraordinary electronic devices. It costs hundreds of millions of dollars for little practical result – unless you count the bottom lines of the manufacturers of the equipment and weapons and the contractors as a practical result.

After Ruben drove me back to the Crockett Hotel in his old American car, I walked over to the Alamo, prime site of my eight-year-old imagination. The Alamo Museum was founded by the Daughters of the Republic of Texas. It does for Texas history what oil and cattle do for the economy, and what big hats and those little string ties do for male identity. As the ultimate victors, Sam Houston's heirs and successors got Texas and all its wealth; as the vanquished of the Alamo, they also seized the franchise on sanctimony.

A glass case at the museum contained a variety of Bowie knives – or 'Arkansas toothpicks', as they were sometimes called in state legislation prohibiting them. They were of different sizes but around eighteen inches on average, with the first three to four inches sharpened on the top as well as the bottom. This is what made the upward jerk so effective when you were fighting Indians – the Bowie knife cut easily through bone. But there was a revisionist schoolbook on sale: it described Jim Bowie in unflattering terms and, with the same kind of fibre-sapping political correctness, revealed to modern students of the Alamo that, while Santa Anna had executed all survivors of the battle, he gave safe passage to the women, children and slaves within the fort.

I was the only patron in the bar of the Crockett Hotel. The barman wanted to talk. He had grown up in San Antonio, in a poor neighbourhood. Crime, violence and gang warfare were all part of daily life. While still a schoolboy, he was walking home with two friends one night when a man appeared from the shadows with a revolver and fired point-blank at the boy beside him. But the gun misfired. They stood and watched as the man cursed and fumbled with the gun – and then they ran for their lives. Ever since, he had wondered what it would be like to die.

He joined the marines. He just decided to one day, after working in an insurance company for nine months and realising he hated the job. He chose the marines over the other services because the boot camp was tougher. They promised him time to study but never gave him any.

He was sent to Okinawa and arrived just after three soldiers had raped and beaten a local girl and left her for dead. The Okinawans hated the American military. After the rape they banned them from a lot of clubs and bars. The barman didn't blame them. He never thought such stupid people existed until he joined the marines, especially those from small-town America. I found myself defending them. His buddies, he said, were ignorant, violent and bigoted. The military was all brainwashing; and the more ignorant you were when you started, the more easily you were brainwashed.

His parents chided him for not respecting his Mexican heritage. He told them that, as he'd been born in the United States, he was American. He had completed two years of an electrical engineering degree at Texas State. What he got on leaving the marines paid for that and some of the deposit he'd put on a $116,000 house. He was the only one in his high school class to get out of poverty.

Ignorance was the worst thing about the United States, he said. At school they were never taught about other countries, just everything that is great about America. You only learn some of the bad stuff if and when you go to college. He was surprised that Australians learned American history at school. The one good thing about the United States was freedom.

'There are other places that are free,' I said.

'Oh well,' he said, 'we never learned anything about them.'

The press reported that momentum was gathering in the campaign to build the 2000-mile fence. It was just eighteen years since Ronald Reagan had referred to 'a scar of a wall'. 'Mr Gorbachev, tear down that wall!' he had said. Now the United States was going to build one. No-one was calling it 'a question of freedom for all mankind', as Reagan had called the Berlin Wall.

The local San Antonio newspaper reported that Congressman Tom Tancredo, 'with an eye on the 2008 election', was touring the nation to alert people to the 'porous Southwest border'. 'America is at risk,' he told Republicans in Iowa. Terrorists could get through, he said. It would be the gated republic.

As I left the hotel the middle-aged woman at reception – a trainee, all homely warmth – said she hoped the ghosts had not kept me awake. I said I hadn't noticed them, and that this might have been because of the air-conditioning: 'You never see them where there's air-conditioning,' I said. She said she didn't know that. But they were over at the Alamo, for sure. She knew because her husband once took a job there as a security guard. He only worked one night. He heard the sounds of wagon wheels, chains rattling, men shouting and cannon loading, and he came home at half past three in the morning and never went back.

CHAPTER 11

*Among democratic nations men easily attain a certain
equality of condition, but they can never attain as much as
they desire. It perpetually retreats from before them, yet
without hiding itself from their sight, and in retiring
draws them on. At every moment they think they are
about to grasp it; it escapes at every moment from their
hold. They are near enough to see its charms, but too far
off to enjoy them; and before they have fully tasted its
delights, they die. That is the reason for the strange
melancholy that haunts inhabitants of democratic
countries in the midst of abundance.*

Alexis de Tocqueville, *Democracy in America*

AN HOUR AND A HALF FROM HOUSTON, THE ROAD BECAME A
monster. From a melee of trucks a hundred yards ahead, the
rim of a massive tyre came bounding, bouncing down the
highway at me. It flattened as it hit the tarmac, expanded as it
flew into the air, flattened and bounced again, and seemed to
gather speed. With a car behind me and a truck on my right,
there was no escape: time only to calculate that if it reached me
flat, it would flip me into the traffic; on the bounce, it would

263

come through the windscreen and kill me a second or two sooner. It landed ten yards ahead and disappeared from view beneath the hood. I think I ducked.

Nothing happened. No tearing metal or smashing glass, no smell of fumes and rubber; no oblivion. No death – unless, as a friend said, it was a Borgesian one. The thing had vanished. The side mirrors didn't reveal it. The rearview mirror revealed the same car still behind me. Beside me, the truck ploughed on. It was like the end of *African Queen*, when the German gunship hits the torpedoes just as Bogart and Hepburn are about to be hanged – except I had no-one to celebrate with. I drove on with all the people who had not been saved recently by a miracle.

A man sang on the radio:

She thinks my tractor's sexy,
It really turns her on;
She's always staring at me
While I'm chugging along.

And then two men were selling guns. 'We got a FN P90 shotgun, semi-automatic. Beautiful. Fifty-round mags. Also, we got a Century Arms Baal 308, comes with four mags . . . We've also got Armory USA AK-47s. Right, you need to make the call – 832237 GUNS.' The FN P90 is a submachine gun favoured by assault teams and tank crews, among others. The AK-47 is, of course, the legendary Russian machine gun that no terrorist, freedom fighter or psychopath should be without.

Just west of Houston, a car lay on its roof in a clump of bushes, the dust settling around it. It was four o'clock and a prodigious volume of cars swept along the road. Driving felt less like driving than manoeuvring a raft into the currents of a river – the *main* current, because that was Interstate 10 and anything else was likely an unwanted tributary leading to some backwater or impenetrable commercial maze. There was time to glance sideways at the city skyline and wonder if Houston should have been built. Not that the place is without accomplishments: its gentry and their clubs and high-tone neighbourhoods; its galleries and museums and sports stadiums. They turned oil into something serious. But is it worth the cost of the air-conditioning?

And, as I was wondering, a man on the radio said that as the oil capital of America, Houston had done its part, and so had Louisiana; but now it was for other states to pull their weight in the oil business. Drilling had to start in Alaska, he said, 'else we're just going to run out of oil – and you think our enemies aren't going to take advantage of that?' His colleague, not surprisingly, agreed. He liked caribou as much as anyone else – 'but hell! Get a grip, folks! Oil could go to $100 a barrel!'

On the radio that day, one of the Democrat presidential candidates, John Edwards, was taking questions from listeners. Since his failed run in 2004, Edwards has made poverty his business, and he talks with authority about the many millions of Americans who work every day but have nothing but hardship to show for it. For hardship, read living a hand-to-mouth existence with no cushion against misfortune or failure; being prey to illness, crime, drugs, ill-health and social predators of all kinds; working in the most unhealthy and dangerous conditions, with no security of tenure and minimal, if any, protections; and exploitation, harassment and indignity.

The top ten per cent of American society has a median net worth of not much less than a million dollars: for the bottom twenty per cent the figure is less than $8000. The gap is wider now than it was forty years ago, when Lyndon Johnson began the War on Poverty. Life-expectancy in the United States is now shorter and infant mortality higher than they are in – to name one of many places – Hong Kong.

The crime rate is a more cheering figure. Nationwide,

crime has been falling every year for a decade and a half. Cities like New York and Chicago now feel safer, and statistics show that they are. What's less encouraging is that the reason for the decline in crime is not to be found in programs which address its causes in impoverished, debt and drug-riddled communities, but in more prisons and tougher penalties. With five per cent of the world's population, the United States now has twenty-five per cent of its prisoners. Seven million Americans are in gaol or on probation or parole.

Every politician wishing to succeed must be tough on crime – *really* tough, tougher than anyone since Nebuchadnezzar – but as the prisoners return to their unreformed communities and resume their lives of crime and drugs (and as soldiers return from the war full of rage and PTSD), it seems reasonable to suppose that the arguments might have to get a little more sophisticated. It's even possible that one day, when some outrageous populist says the $400 billion spent on Iraq might have been better spent on poverty at home, he'll get a hearing in the media and won't be called a wimp.

Edwards wants a national health scheme that provides insurance for every American and an increase in the minimum wage. He wants a more effective safety net. 'No-one . . . should work full-time and live in poverty in this country,' he says. 'It is morally wrong.' He is not the most passionate advocate American politics has known: William Jennings Bryan would brush him off a like a fly. JFK or RFK, Edwards is not, but it's possible he knows more about poverty than they did. On that menacing road in Texas that morning, he was a shining light. Yet, it is the general belief, among even those who like Edwards, that he will not persuade the middle class to vote for the poor.

In her book *Nickel and Dimed*, Barbara Ehrenreich took the course George Orwell took to write *Down and Out in Paris and London* in the 1930s. She passed herself off as one of the working poor, living and working as they did, and then wrote a shocking book about it. In *The Working Poor*, David K. Shipler talked at length to menial workers (and the people who employ them) to build a portrait of their lives which reviewers described as 'heartrending'. Both books were published to general and thoroughly deserved acclaim. Of course, the country does not lack a conscience; it is the machinery for exercising it that is missing.

Shipler's book is subtitled 'Invisible in America'. This is common parlance on the rare occasions that the press talks about the working poor – or the non-working poor, for that matter. But 'invisible' seems an odd way to describe them. They are to be seen everywhere: in every eating-house, super-market and hotel. You see them on the street and in the parks of prosperous neighbourhoods looking after other people's children: at the doors of apartment blocks, behind the wheels of limousines, out the windows of Amtrak trains. Look a bit harder and you'll see the evidence of their existence in trailer parks, in the payday cheque-cashing facilities that take uncon-scionable rake-offs, in the pawn shops, the bail bond shops, and in the aggressive marketing of painkillers. The truth is that, for visitors from countries equally 'developed', the omnipresence of the working poor is one of the most obvious – and discomforting – qualities of American life, and one of the hardest to understand. The gaol population is genuinely invisible – although you can see where they are from the trains – but the poor are always easy enough to see.

To hear all the arguments for keeping the minimum wage so low, for not providing national universal health coverage, and for not protecting pensions or helping poor workers to save is rather like listening to the creationists – one is struck less by the quality of the argument than the fact that one is still hearing it. In other developed countries, while politicians still argue around the margins, there has been general agreement on the fundamentals for many years, and the people would not tolerate any radical regression.

But the United States is different. Though a straw poll would likely reveal that a majority across the nation think a living wage and universal health coverage should be among the rights of Americans, it seems they think a more important right exists. The United States is indeed developed, but 'developed' means nothing. Sending rocket ships to Pluto is not developed. Building Houston in the desert; turning the Chicago River south; making *The Sopranos* – take America's million greatest achievements, 'developed' has nothing to do with any of them. What animates the place is something 'undeveloped'. The day Americans think of themselves as 'developed' will be the day it's all over. Europe has societies that are developed; America has an inexhaustible frontier. In a frontier society, whatever the level of development, the imperishable value is liberty of the individual – the autonomy of the self – and no right is more basic or more exercised (or more contradictory) than the right of one person to employ or own another, for any task, however ugly or demeaning, and to pay little or nothing for it. And as providence would have it, in such a society there are always people to perform these tasks; and when they die or find something better to do, more people can be got from somewhere else.

On the other side of the freeway, two more cars were flipped on their backs. Two ambulances and several police cars were gathered at the scene and traffic had banked up for miles. Life suddenly seemed cheap. On the radio news, NASA announced that launching the space vehicle headed for Pluto was going to be put back a day. It seemed a small matter given that the vehicle was expected to take seven years to get there. A NASA spokesperson said that God had laid out the solar system in such a way that patience was demanded of those who chose to explore it.

God also figured in Mayor Nagin's Martin Luther King Day speech in New Orleans. He said God had meant New Orleans to be chocolate-coloured: 'I don't care what people are sayin' uptown or wherever they are, this city will be chocolate at the end of the day. This city will be a majority African American city – it's the way God wants it to be. You can't have New Orleans no other way.'

It did seem strange to introduce God, though no stranger than introducing Him to the Pluto probe. The mayor needed the black majority back in New Orleans to vote for him, and in the absence of any material inducement for them, such as an income or a house to live in, he had fashioned something spiritual. It seemed a little cynical, yet not beyond the reach of a charitable interpretation to imagine that he was as concerned for New Orleans as he was for his political fortune.

But charity was scarce that day. Riled white people phoned the radio stations, complaining that the mayor seemed to think they were lesser New Orleaneans for being white; that their presence in the city was not as valuable as the black presence, and not ordained by God as the black presence was. The radio hosts beat up on Nagin too. The next day he apologised.

Lafayette, on the Vermilion River in Louisiana, was settled by Acadians driven out of Canada by the British. It's a Cajun wellspring. So why was the car park at the motel full of the same gleaming pick-ups you see in car parks in Wyoming and Nevada? In 8000 miles, only once did I see anything in the back of a pick-up – a lawnmower and a bale of hay in Kansas. I did not see so much as a dog in any other pick-up. These ones in Lafayette were empty. Some had flags on their back windows, as if displaying the flag were the main function of a pick-up. A pick-up is a flag-carrier, in the main.

I hung around Lafayette until noon. I was recovering from Highway 10. Two days had passed since the exterminating tyre, but it was still bouncing at me, mysteriously vanishing.

The fiend from the shadows. The comic book death. I listened to the people talking in their soothing accents, and the soothing Zydeco music that wafted around. I went into a little shop and bought a copy of *Newsweek*. A 300-pound man served me while an older 300-pound man, whom I took to be his father, sat on a stool smoking a cigar stub.

He said: 'I see you got a book there.'

'Yes,' I said, looking at the copy of *Newsweek*. 'I have.'

I took the car to two gas stations and asked to check the tyre pressure. They both told me their gauges had been stolen. At the third, the young man looked like he had just injected something crazy. He stared at me as if I were holding an FN P90. At last, he handed me a gauge and said: 'Seventy-five cents.'

I said: 'I'll bring it back.'

'Seventy-five cents,' he said.

I gave him the money and went out to the car. The gauge was broken, useless.

I got out of Lafayette on the Evangeline SW Freeway, which must be named for the mythical Acadian heroine of Longfellow's epic poem – 'Faint was the air with the odorous breath of magnolia blossoms / And with the heat of noon . . .' – and turned onto the road that takes you through the bayous and the towns called Chacahoula, Des Allemands, Valier, Paradis, Boutte and Boeuf. Someone had hung a sign that said: GOD BLESS ST CHARLES PARISH, and the Assembly of God had hung another one saying: LOVE YOUR ENEMIES – IT WILL CONFUSE THEM. About sixty miles out of New Orleans, an Amtrak train ran parallel to the road: three double-decker carriages, but very few heads in the windows. Still, it was going to New Orleans and the sound of its horn was comforting.

All though the leafless bayous, over the old Huey P. Long Bridge across the Mississippi and through relatively well-heeled and all but unscathed suburbs of New Orleans, a man spoke with excitement on the radio about a new model for education in Louisiana. It was to be run by school boards comprised of parents and business: not educators, he said, because the people who love the children are the parents and the people who know how schools should work are business-people. Schools should work 'on the capitalist model': 'Principals will be judged every quarter on performance, and if they haven't got the outcomes that are demanded, they're gone.' And the same would apply to teachers. Under this comprehensive plan, Louisiana could have the pre-eminent education system in the United States, and 'our real estate values will go up and our lifestyle will follow suit'. He said this. Thus will the Enlightenment at last come to Louisiana – blown by a hurricane. As one think-tank said, what school reformers had forever failed to do, 'Katrina accomplished in a day'.

In the New Orleans menswear shop where I went to buy socks, the manager was aghast at Mayor Nagin. 'You don't talk to God that way,' he said. 'You don't presume to know His will.'

In this he was at one with Billy Graham, who believed no-one could say if the devil wrought Katrina, and that God's purpose in allowing it might not be known 'for years to come'. The manager asked me if I believed in God.

I said: 'No, though I was raised a Presbyterian.'

He laughed and told me that in Louisiana Presbyterians were called the 'frozen chosen'. He believed the Lord had left signs for us, and if we were alert enough to see them and chose to follow them, we would be saved. God, he said, loved freedom: this was why He made it optional to seek and follow Him. The manager thought hell might exist, and it might not.

It seemed not to worry him. Nothing did. He charged me twenty-six dollars a pair for the socks.

The menswear manager had no doubt that Nagin's remarks were made with a political purpose. It seemed a reasonable interpretation: and equally reasonable (and no less cynical) to imagine some connection between the manager's contentment and the prospect of a less chocolate-coloured New Orleans than had been the case before the hurricane. Moreover, it seemed possible that, no less than the mayor, the manager had seen signs of divine will at work in New Orleans.

Was it not possible, for instance, to interpret Katrina's selective devastation and the subsequent flight of homeless blacks as an opportunity dealt by providence to the hard-working white middle classes and entrepreneurial capital? There was now a chance to elect a white, pro-business mayor who might lead New Orleans to modernity and prosperity – with one of those business-directed education systems to match. Just enough of the black heritage might be retained to entertain tourists and keep the city's cultural distinction; but better all round if, in the familiar pattern of US history, the great majority of the black refugees were absorbed into the communities to which they had fled, or just as likely, allowed to wash into their fringes. For the manager and anyone else who believed that God left signs of His purpose and that salvation belonged to those who saw and followed them, it must have been hard *not* to see in the current situation evidence of divine favour – and just as hard for Ray Nagin to resist the temptation to try some spin of his own.

It was three months since I had been in New Orleans. The owner of the house in the Seventh Ward was still waiting for an insurance assessor. The tree was still across her fence in the backyard. Only three or four people had moved back into the neighbourhood. Trees still lay across houses, and satellite dishes still hung from powerlines. Thousands of rusted cars sat under the freeways and overpasses. Rubbish was still piled in the streets. The barge was still resting on the nose of the school bus down by the levees. The whole of the Ninth Ward still resembled the first pictures of Hiroshima. Two or three people were picking through the rubble.

'Under the thin glaze surface of conventionalities . . . a vast plummetless depth of democratic humanity is existing, thinking, acting, ebbing and flowing . . . that I would like, O so like to flatter myself I am giving or trying to give voice to.' Thus wrote old Walt Whitman to the Australian poet Bernard O'Dowd in 1890. But there's something about driving on the interstate, or parking in a mall, or watching the president on CNN News in a small-town motel, the president with his clownish Texan walk; performing these and many other conventional necessities of modern American life can make the surface feel plummetless and democratic humanity like the glaze. The mistake might be to draw a distinction between what seems to be superficial and what is purported to be deep.

Where the highway crosses it, the Pascagoula River appeared to be more of a bayou; a beautiful broad expanse of reeds cut through by deep, lazy streams. At the junction of two of these streams I saw a man sitting in a tiny boat that turned up at both ends. In the early dusk, perfectly still in this eccentric craft, he was fishing. On the radio, someone sang a blues song about the devil driving a long black train. It was like that moon over Lake Pontchartrain on the night I drove out of New Orleans to Biloxi: a scene to remind you that whatever objective assessments one makes about crime, drugs, mould, termites, the likelihood of more Katrinas and more Ritas, and all the failures of New Orleans compared to 'successful' modern cities, there are some places where people live for the light and the breezes. They are addicted to the sensations of the place. It's a physical, psychic or emotional attachment before it is anything that can be measured. New Orleans is one of these places. The man in the boat put me back on the mayor's side.

Biloxi's casinos were working again. They took $10.7 million in their first week, which meant $1.5 million in taxes for the state of Mississippi. The legislature of that state had just decided that Mississippians were too fat. To set an example for the people, one side of the House had accepted the challenge of the other to see who could lose the most weight – collectively – in a given period. It was to be called 'Weigh Down Mississippi'. It hadn't spread to Alabama, where the little huts from which they sell spare ribs were doing great business.

In one nation these things happened on the one day: scientists declared that a spacecraft which had landed in Utah a few days earlier had brought back first-class samples of star and comet dust from its 3.5-billion-mile journey; another spacecraft took off from Cape Kennedy bound for Pluto; and a radio pastor preached a spectacular sermon on the Four Horsemen of the Apocalypse – on *each* of them, in turn. It was also the day Wilson Pickett died.

———

Driving the highways by day is one thing; driving them at night is another. At night you feel less connection with the road – or with any reality, for that matter. There is nothing solid around you: just red, white and yellow light, shadows and reflections, green signs and brown signs, arrows at various angles and advertising hoardings that might tell you, in the space of two seconds, that Jesus saves or that you're passing an old battlefield, or there's a Mr Waffle if you take Exit 5B half a mile ahead.

You're in the fast lane trying to get past half a dozen trucks, and suddenly there *is* no fast lane. Or the lane that has been carrying you north in an instant threatens to take you east or west or even south, or down into the bowels of some place you don't want to go. Winds out of nowhere knock you sideways. Tailgating SUVs blind and menace you. A lost, sleepy, lovesick or stoned motorist appears before you, travelling at half your speed and obliging you to choose between braking and risking death beneath the wheels of the truck behind, or veering and risking it with whatever owns the lights looming in the lane adjacent. Somewhere near Charlotte, North Carolina, what looked like five floodlights mounted on a row of towering cantilevered poles only revealed themselves as planes lined up for landing when I drove beneath them.

You are an illuminated ant among millions of others: and as with ants, if you crash or flip, other ants will rush to pull you out of the road so the general progress is not delayed. But as frantic as they seem, ants travel at ant speed and in an ant element: you are driving an interstate at seventy miles an hour or more, which is not a human speed, and in an element that is not human but abstract, unfixed, unnatural. And while ants hear nothing unless it is the rustle of their feet, motorists hear that Satan lurks in abortion clinics; that He has used liberals for His demonic purposes, which include deceiving Americans about the nature of human life; or that Ted Kennedy is no better than a gob of spit.

In the United States, as in all societies, a good-sized part of the population can barely think their way out of bed in the morning, much less see through the most gormless politicians, the phoniest preachers and the direst celebrities. There are millions who believe that the earth was created in six literal days or that the World Trade Center was blown up from within by Jewish agents; that monsters stalk them and lots of fried chicken is really good for you. There are some who believe all these things at once. Yet they navigate these highways and their perils and confusions as if, like the paddle-fish, they have electro-receptors in their noses. Some part of the brain must have evolved to accommodate the demands of highway driving, perhaps at some expense to the parts that Whitman valued.

Cynthia Tucker is editor of the op-ed pages of *The Atlanta Journal-Constitution*. I had seen her columns about wages and working conditions syndicated in other newspapers across the country. She wrote about that unmentionable of journalism: class. I phoned her as I drove towards Georgia and she granted me half an hour. She is very striking and beautiful and her gaze is uncompromising, if not downright fierce. Because she is black, she gets racist mail every day.

I asked her why so little is written in the United States press about the social consequences of economic policy, including trade policy and globalisation. Why the aversion to stories dealing with the lives of the working poor? Why, in the great democracy where the desire of all citizens is to better their condition, are the big topics of the day not globalisation or education or health or wages or poverty, which impinge directly on their prospects of success, but abortion and gay marriage, which for the most part don't?

She said the first reason was that journalists are paid too much, or at least enough for them to forget what it is like to be poor and to have to shop at Wal-Mart, and to be so grateful for the low prices that they ignore the wages Wal-Mart pays its workers, or by any other moral failures. For the same reason, journalists are no longer hungry for stories. There is no worthwhile reward for digging deep into subjects where the material is often complex, the research unpleasant, if not squalid, and the stories hard to write. Articles about work and wages are not sexy, she said. That was her third reason: when journalists do write about the social consequences of economic policy, editors push them onto pages where journalists would rather not be.

The other reason is class. No-one talks about it, but class is the real story of modern America, including black America,

Cynthia Tucker said. Race distracts Americans from class divisions, perhaps because race taps into more basic fears. It's a very long time since anyone thought the working class might overrun the place: but the thought that blacks might overrun your neighbourhood, or that a new immigrant group might flood into your school or take your job, or that 'Hispanics' might overrun the whole country, readily takes hold. More people will talk about the threat posed by 'Hispanics' than, for instance, the consequences of unfettered markets. She was persuaded by Clinton and Gore that globalisation was good for American workers, but since then, she says, she has seen proof that it has made their lives much harder, as it has the lives of workers in developing countries. On the face of things this is not a popular opinion, but when opinions are hardly ever expressed on the subject we cannot say for sure.

There is, of course, another reason why the 'real story' of modern America is not the one that anyone hears: it is that the real 'real story' has long been the very opposite of class. Tocqueville was brutal about it: 'In democratic communities, each citizen is habitually engaged in the contemplation of a very puny object, namely himself.' Bettering one's condition in modern America is more than a question of economic mobility. It can mean improving your complexion or physique, your personal outlook, your television, your teeth, your sneakers, your cooking implements, your religion, your shopping in general. One can better one's condition with a personal makeover – and that is an enterprise with limitless commercial possibilities. Class, by contrast, was never much good for selling things. Status and its close relation, identity, sell heaps: but class is a marketing dud. Religion, patriotism, celebrity and ingenuity go equally towards being American and a hook on which a sales campaign will hang. Class is heretical on both scores. Worse, it's defeatist, which is also heretical. It's like abandoning the dream.

I left Interstate 85 and detoured into the woods of South Carolina. I came to towns called Seneca and Clemson, which were not as distinguished as their names suggested. Seneca, where it happened that John Edwards was born, was not named for the Stoic philosopher but for the Cherokee settlement, Esseneca; Clemson for the relatively undistinguished son-in-law of John C. Calhoun who was vice president between 1825 and 1832 and, at other times, secretary of state and secretary for war, and possibly the most fearsome-looking politician in all American history. He was also the most sophisticated and persuasive advocate that American slavery ever had, and perhaps the most fanatical enemy of an organised working class.

They were long thin streaks of towns along this road, shopping strips with every conceivable franchise represented, and long slow lines of traffic. Near a handsome old Baptist church with the familiar columns at the front, one sign said: JESUS LOVES YOU, and another said: NO PLACE FOR A NEW BORN? and gave the name of an institution that would care for the child. A 'gentlemen's club' declared: TIGERETTES WANTED. From Seneca, missionaries of the Crossgate Church go forth to places like Togo, Ethiopia and Honduras. Two members of the church are radiologists who hope that 'their faith is transparent in [their] daily practice of radiology'. They are raising funds to buy ultrasounds 'in order to enable more radiologists and sonographers to take their skills and, more importantly, their witness for Christ to the mission field'.

Between the uninspiring towns, the woods are filling with housing developments, but wild patches remain and these are beautiful. A hut on the roadside sold boiled peanuts, chicken and firewood. Another sold pecans and boiled peanuts. And another said: NOTARY, ICE, PICKLED PEPPERS. By a lake near the South Carolina state border, a couple of men in check shirts and hunting caps sat with their lines in the water looking down the length of the lake towards the forest in the twilight. And a woman sang on the radio:

> *Our little pony-tailed girl growed up to be a woman;*
> *Now she's gone in the blink of an eye.*
> *She left the suds in the bucket*
> *And the clothes hangin' out on the line.*

All morning I drove through a light drizzle, making for Washington DC and the end of a journey which at that moment felt epic. At a gas station an hour and a half outside Washington, a Mexican with no English tried to order a carwash for his battered van full of other Mexicans with no English. The granddaddy of all Winnebagos pulled in. It looked a good deal bigger than the house I was raised in. As the driver positioned it expertly under the awning with only an inch or two to spare, she in the passenger seat did not look up from her book. He stepped creakily down onto the tarmac and stretched his muscles and bones. On his door was written in large red copperplate: ALPHA.

The vastness of the United States – the combination of land mass and mass of population – is possibly the hardest thing for a visitor to grasp. It's hard for a lot of Americans to grasp. Yet when you drive through the countryside and see the new housing estates, each house nearer in size to the White House than a log cabin, you do wonder how much more hope-filled humanity the place can take. But one shouldn't wonder for too long about Americans' capacities. In a field on a hillside stood a skeleton of a boat and a sign that said: GOD'S ARK OF SAFETY. NOAH'S ARK BEING REBUILT HERE.

The unrelenting tide of cars bore down on Washington that Sunday like school fish obeying a preconscious urge. And suddenly everything that was dull, archetypal and familiar in the landscape gave way to the classical. It was dusk and we fish suddenly found ourselves in Constitution Avenue. The Capitol stood before us. It must be the best way to enter Washington DC. It must have felt like this to enter Rome on a cart.

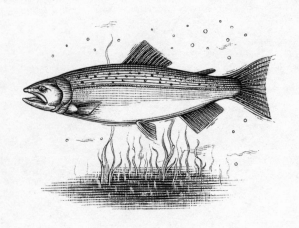

CHAPTER 12

'This is my claim. And yet everywhere upon it are pockets of autonomous life. Autonomous. In order for it to be mine nothing must be permitted to occur upon it save by my dispensation.'

Cormac McCarthy, *Blood Meridian*

CHECKING OUT OF THE CHANNEL INN IN WASHINGTON DC, the man on the desk, who looked very like Ricardo Montalban in his later years, looked at my credit card and said: 'You got big barracuda out there.'

'Not so big,' I said.

'Oh, yes they are,' he said.

'Well, not so big that they eat you,' I said.

'Oh, yes they do,' he said.

'It's the sharks that eat you,' I said.

'We got sharks in Florida, don't you worry,' he said.

'I know. And alligators,' I said, meaning to be polite.

'Yeah, we got them too,' he said.

'They say all life came out of the water, and in my case it was for good,' I ventured.

His expression changed. His face darkened.

'I never go into the water,' I explained.

283

'Who told you we came out of the water?' Ricardo Montalban became the wrathful Khan.

'The scientists,' I said.

'I came out of my mother and father,' he said. 'And they came from Adam and Eve. So did you and everyone else, and don't let anyone tell you different. Anyone tells you different, they're wrong. Don't listen to them.'

'Fair enough,' I said, and wandered off.

I went up to the mall to see the anti-abortion demonstration. The people had come from all over the eastern half of the country, and a few from further west. There must have been 30,000 or more and a great many were teenagers and children. They strolled up the mall towards the Capitol carrying banners saying DEFEND LIFE, THOU SHALT NOT KILL, CHILDREN ARE AN HERITAGE OF THE LORD and MICHIGAN LOVES OUR PRO-LIFE PRESIDENT. They chanted: 'Wade vee Roe has to go!' Some said Hail Marys as they walked.

One group had taken the chance to declare that Protestants would go to hell along with atheists and infidels. Others had photos of mangled foetuses, sometimes juxtaposed with pictures of Nazi death camps, and Jews and partisans lynched from trees and lamp posts. On the fringes, a burly black man playing a trumpet in the hope of raising a little money in his own cause gave the proceedings a taste of Mardi Gras.

It was cold. I crossed the mall where the speeches had been made and the march began. It was littered with leaflets, discarded banners and food wrappers. A handful of demonstrators stood around. Two priests were talking under a tree. A young man rode through on a bicycle and as he did he shouted: 'Blaaagh! Get back to the Midwest and take your trash with you! Blaaagh!'

I rang Julie. It had been a long time. There had been moments on the road when I'd wondered if she would make a good companion in a Winnebago. Now, as she put me through to an agent, she sounded like the same old Julie. The agent and I talked for half an hour or so. She liked Keith Urban. I was going to Chicago for one last journey westward and asked her to book me on the *Empire Builder* from Chicago to Portland, Oregon. But first I took the *Acela* up to Philadelphia.

To hang up from an Amtrak agent and dial Hotels.com is like being transported from an agreeable bar to a police lockup. To be employed at Hotels.com, you must have served ten years in the marines or have proof of an untreatable neurosis. Just as likely, six months working at Hotels.com will do it to you. They are never wrong and when they call you 'Sir' they mean 'Jerk'. If their screen tells them that your address is San Diego and you tell them that you have never been to San Diego, they will say they are only telling you what is on their screen, 'Sir'. And when you have persuaded them that you don't live in San Diego, they tell you that they will try to correct it, 'Sir' – but you know that they don't believe you and think you invented the San Diego address for some earlier criminal purpose. If they leave you holding on to a cell phone for twenty minutes, in which time your train begins to board, that is because of 'difficulties with the computer', but you are made to feel that those difficulties are consequent on your impossible request.

If for a moment you lapse into a description of your own difficulties and, for instance, tell them how hard it is to read your credit card number while boarding a train with two suitcases, or to write down a confirmation number while rescuing a child from the path of a railway station trolley, they will say: 'I am doing the best I can for you, Sir. Without this information I cannot proceed with the booking, Sir.' And if you are churlish enough to complain that you are only in this situation because you spent half an hour explaining that you don't live in San Diego, and it was not your choice to spend forty minutes of the day and two-thirds of your phone battery life on a hundred-dollar room in Philadelphia – don't even think about it.

As a boy, I heard *Philadelphia Lawyer* sung at a concert in a country hall. It was the first time I had heard of the place, or of the kind of lawyers they have there. Written by Woody Guthrie, the song concerns 'a gun totin' cowboy' who springs the smooth-talking lawyer 'makin' love to his Hollywood maid'. It thus comes straight out of the great geo-cultural divide and needs to be sung as Guthrie sang it back in the 1930s – as a coyote might sing it out in the desert, with the 'moon hangin' high overhead'. As the train arrived in Phila-delphia, 'We hold these truths to be self-evident . . .' were not the words that came to me but rather:

Now back in old Pennsylvania,
Among those beautiful pines,
There's one less Philadelphia lawyer
In old Philadelphia tonight.

A white American friend told me that if he were a younger man he'd move to Philadelphia: it is cheaper than New York, has antique charms and contemporary verve. It's on the rise again. A black American friend who grew up in the ghetto there says Philadelphia is a racist city and nothing could ever persuade him to return. As a child he slept in a basement next to a coal heater. He could smell the liquor on his father sleeping in the room above. He could hear him beating his mother. He doesn't know why some people he knows who did not sleep next to coal heaters have died of cancer but he hasn't. His life has other mysteries. When his friends could never pass exams, he could; and he sat police entry tests for several of them. When no-one else read books, he was derided for carrying a bagful of them. He liked classical music when no-one else did. He found a collection of 78 rpm records and, when his sister got a Victrola, he played them on it. He learned to whistle bits of Dvořák, Brahms and Beethoven, but his father forbade it because it was not the music of black Americans. One night his father came home drunk and smashed all the records.

He puts it all down to fear. His parents were frightened of stepping outside the safety of the black American archetype. But he wasn't. He doesn't know why. Fifty years ago he left Philadelphia to play professional basketball in Michigan, and for the forty years since he gave up basketball he's been a painter. The paintings in his Harlem studio are big, subtle, complex abstracts. Other black artists and white art dealers don't think his works are 'black' paintings. Black paintings are not about the Peloponnesian War. Black painters might paint Thelonius Monk, but not the music of Thelonius Monk. Black paintings, he says, are meant to be done in primary colours and contain sensual, brightly dressed human figures. He finds this funny, but depressing. He feels the same way when younger black men try to recruit him to old causes as if they were new; or when he sees black youths loaded with attitude and wearing the uniform of self-loathing and defeat: the jeans with the crutch below their knees, the caps turned backwards. He feels like he's fought the same fight all his life: against typecasting and fear, against being conscripted to both.

A lot of his generation escaped the ghetto through the military, but that was another thing he wasn't going to do. The war memorials by the river tell some of the story. Five hundred Philadelphians died in Vietnam – that is to say, as many from one American city as from all of Australia, its most enthusiastic ally in the Vietnam War. The names of the dead are inscribed on the memorial and so are these obscure, strangely reproving words: FOR THOSE WHO FOUGHT FOR IT, FREEDOM HAS A FLAVOR THE PROTECTED WILL NEVER KNOW.

—

Everyone who lives in a city experiences it in his own way, Gersh said. He picked me up at Chicago Airport and took me on another quick tour before I caught the train: the place that used to be the bowling alley where 'Machine Gun' Jack McGurn was mown down by fellow mobsters in 1936; the Puerto Rican school named after the great baseball player and humanitarian Roberto Clemente; the Russian Orthodox church designed by Louis Sullivan; and finally a little brick shed with cabs parked all around it. Inside, he said, were Pakistani men who tell their wives they're working but sit there all day and night, smoking and drinking coffee. He wondered if they might turn out to be the first group to live in Chicago without becoming part of the mosaic.

It was the day after the State of the Union address. The president said switchgrass could be used instead of oil. The people asked: 'What the hell is switchgrass?' *The New York Times* pointed out that since the administration had begun pursuing democracy in the Middle East three new fundamentalist governments had been elected there. It also reported that, on an average day, thirty US soldiers were flown into German hospitals with severe wounds. Perhaps that was why the president's rhetoric sounded hollow. The threats were clear enough: oppose the war and any of the measures taken by this administration, including illegal phone taps, and you were a defeatist, an isolationist, a person with a pre-9/11 mentality. But there was something rotten about the State of the Union.

It was not just what was said, but also the theatre surrounding it. It was the vice president's inscrutable, carbohydrate-charged mug riding shotgun behind the president. The way congressmen and women rose and clapped like a TV audience under instruction from the floor manager, or a

Kremlin full of hacks listening as Brezhnev tells them how well things are going in Afghanistan. But in Washington it's not compulsory: acclamation can be restrained or even withheld without life-threatening consequences. So why fake it?

Before the 'world-famous' *Empire Builder* pulled out of Chicago, the sleeping car conductor and another attendant stood on the platform and told stories of people caught smoking weed on their trains. There is only one ventilation system and it's all connected, so if you smoke weed in the last compartment, passengers in the first one will get a whiff of it.

It was too warm for early February. In Chicago people said: 'What a beautiful day!' but looked as if they meant: 'What gives with this weather?' North of Milwaukee: houses and lawns of meticulous neatness with well-placed conifers and maples, ochre-red barns, half-frozen ponds and streams, chocolate fallow fields – and not one snowflake. We stopped in a little town somewhere in Wisconsin and, as the evening grew dark, on the main street a string of coloured lights began to glow along the eaves. Then an electric American flag lit up and began to flash at two-second intervals. But still there was no snow.

At dinner, I sat next to a sturdy, blue-eyed salvage operator who had been down on the Gulf Coast repairing an oil rig. I didn't ask him, but he told me anyway: Michael Jackson was a 'freak' and it wasn't for the climate that he was living in Belize; tourists out looking for bears in Yellowstone Park were finding marijuana plantations; Angelina Jolie had adopted a 'little Somalian tyrant . . . flies and all', and the kid would grow up to be a crack-head or a junkie, for sure. He was never going down South again, he said, because they 'just won't get off their ass'.

'They sit around down there with their boat hangin' from a tree and nothin' will persuade 'em to get a ladder and a rope and get it down. They're still sittin' in rubbish that a half-day's work would've cleared up. You pay them ten bucks an hour and after two hours they say, "Man, this work is too hard for ten bucks, you got to pay me more."' And he would say to them: 'Then scoot! There's plenty more where you came from.' And they'd scoot.

A young Australian from Queensland and his white South African girlfriend were also at the table. The salvage man asked the Queenslander if it was true that 'the Japs had completely taken over' in Australia. Told that a lot came as tourists but most went home, he said: 'Not like our tourists – our Spanish-speaking tourists.' He told the South African he'd heard that in her country 'the natives will shoot you off your tractor, your cow, your horse, your toilet. Is it still like that?'

She nodded and said gravely: 'Yes, it is still the same.'

The salvage man said he moved around a lot because he could. That was the beauty of America: you could cross any border and take a job and set up most anywhere you liked. No government or police were going to stop you. Take this present trip: he'd left Gulfport, gone to DC and caught a train and now here he was on his way to Oregon to do some fishing in the Pacific Ocean; and later on he might look around and take a job: marine salvage, most likely, because that was usually pretty interesting. And the thing was – no-one was going to stop him.

There was nothing to be gained from passing on the information that these things were possible in many other parts of the world. It was of no interest.

Minneapolis-St Paul, the conductor told us, is halfway between the equator and the North Pole. St Paul's Cathedral in St Paul is modelled on St Peter's in Rome. The biggest shopping mall in the United States is just outside the twin cities. Minneapolis – a beautiful name for a city – comes from the Indian word *minnie*, for 'water'. He told us these things as we approached the twin cities in darkness and the salvage worker gave us his view of the world. Through the window beside him, among rows of houses glowing on a hillside, I could see one with an illuminated cross as tall as the house itself and nearly as wide. And I could see dimly the Mississippi and the barges, three or four hundred metres long, carrying soybeans, I imagined, to the Gulf of Mexico. And I wished I was on one – or, if not me, the salvage worker.

—

The couple at breakfast came from Minnesota. They travelled Amtrak a lot and took the *Empire Builder* every year. They travelled it enough to know that our breakfast waitress was a sixty-five-year-old grandmother who rode a Harley-Davidson and, tucked beneath her wig, had hair that stretched below her buttocks. They had been in the dining car one night when the head waiter had a nervous breakdown and began goose-stepping up and down and shouting orders in bad German. He had to be taken away.

The man's name was Jeff and for twenty-seven years he had been a crime scene investigator, specialising in the interpreta-tion of blood-spatterings. Retired now, he said he was letting his heart and mind recover from constant exposure to violent crime and death. Most times he presented evidence for the prosecution, and had always worried more about convicting an innocent person than failing to convict a guilty one. He was a slightly built man, I guessed in his fifties, with a small mous-tache and beard, and teeth that, because they were not up to the usual standard of American orthodontics, made me like him all the more.

He declared himself 'a sort of liberal' and she declared herself the same. They thought Americans had wanted Bush to go into Iraq and get out quickly. When I said I thought maybe he had fooled them into thinking Iraq was responsible for 9/11, I had a feeling for a moment that they had been among those he'd fooled. It was not the deception that made Jeff angry: rather it was when the president, who had 'basically dodged' military duty, said: 'Bring 'em on.' That made him sick. Now they both thought Bush was 'finished'. The country would swing back to the left within the next six years. It would correct itself. It always did. On the pocket of Jeff's much-worn pale-blue shirt there was a small American flag and embroidered under it was: 9.11.01 NEVER FORGET.

At Williston, North Dakota, there were cattle yards proving industry, and rusting car bodies and rusting yellow school buses suggesting decay. At the border of Montana at the junction of the Missouri and Yellowstone rivers, Williston has 12,000 people willing to endure winters in which the temperature can fall to forty below zero. Nearly eighty per cent of them are of Norwegian or German descent and, among other facilities, about eighty churches in the city and surrounds are there to serve them. Williston makes its living from oil, agriculture and tourists who come to hunt and fish and see the old US army forts nearby. The city advertises a 'low cost of living, hometown values – all in a technologically advanced community!'

The lack of snow seemed to make the country bleaker: brown grasses, grey skies, grey buildings, grey trees. The local North Dakota newspaper reported that January temperatures had been four degrees above average, the warmest January on record. The Minnesota couple said it had been the same in Minnesota, and there had been no good snow for several years. They had no doubts about global warming. There were a lot of very poor people in these bleak regions, they said. Well into Montana, the abandoned stockyards, collapsed huts and fences, the odd house or hut with half a dozen cattle – or in one case, bison – standing in a nearby yard spoke of destitution. An occasional grand house with commanding views and large herds of cattle only seemed to speak it more loudly.

The man in the next compartment had a portable television. He sat it on the seat opposite, with a bud in his ear for sound, and every time I passed he was staring at it with a belligerent look on his face. After meals he took the bud out to ring his wife and tell her what he had eaten, but even with the cell phone to his ear he watched the TV. Without music, the scenes outside the train window provoke questions and sensations, but with music on your MP3 player the world passes rather as it did in movies in the days of rear projection. If Wild Bill Hickok or a dinosaur should gallop past the window, it seemed likely that most passengers would think next to nothing of it. It is another blessing Americans have brought to the world: this blurring of distinctions between the notes of Neil Young's guitar and the sky over Montana. Those buds in our ears remove us from the many things in the world that needlessly demand attention.

Somewhere outside Havre, as we crossed a cocoa-coloured plain that had not only been cultivated but looked as though it had been combed, the conductor announced that 'a wine and cheese reception' for all sleeping-car passengers was to be held in the dining room. We were to go there as soon as we left Havre because it was 'a time-sensitive event'. The last carriage, the sleeper carriage, came to rest across the road. There was a Tire Rama, silos and a hoarding that said: DINOSAURS, HOMESTEADERS, OUTLAWS, INDIAN ARTIFACTS. A man in a red Chevy pick-up truck, immobile and expressionless, waited for the train to move. Way up in Montana, under an all but cloudless, pale, pale sky, still there was no snow.

In the dusk the low hills came closer; the grass revealed patterns, the blades themselves became distinct. Black cattle almost glowed. At the end of a mile-long track across the plain, there stood a single-storey house painted cream with a grey-brown roof and an attic; two outhouses in the same grey-brown thirty yards from the house; and thirty yards from the outhouses, four steel silos. Maybe five miles beyond the house there were two conical mountains in dark relief to the sand-coloured plain and the fading greenish-blue sky. Nothing stood between the house and God: it was fixed in the environment without shelter or adornment.

These houses looked as if they had been built to a model from a bare and honest region of the brain; or as if descended directly from the dwellings of the Old Testament. They are psychological houses, Edvard Munch houses, houses both forbidding and seductive. They draw you across the range to their doors. You want to enter and climb the stairs. A herd of deer came galloping down the rise towards the train. The plain faded into darkness as if a veil had been drawn across it. The lights went on in the houses and trailers, and the world became lonely. 'Where is the way where light dwelleth? And, as for darkness, where is the place thereof?' God asked Job, certain that he did not know.

———

Early next morning the train began cantering down the Columbia River Gorge. By nine am the river was a mile wide and looked like a loch in the Scottish highlands, or a set from a Wagnerian opera. Ribbons of water – 'burns in spate', as they would say in the highlands – cascaded hundreds of feet down the cliffs. Eagles circled. Flotillas of ducks and waterfowl sailed about in soft rainy light. From the plains of Montana to the Columbia Gorge in a single sleep; the mountains that Lewis and Clark and thousands of migrants laboured through on their way to the Pacific had passed by unseen. Now, in the observation lounge, the salvage man was going forth among the passengers with his unstoppable monologues. It was as if he must ventilate or explode. That morning, around dawn, I had heard his mono-maniacal ironic tones when I woke, and when I opened the curtains there on the platform in Spokane, Washington, I saw him in a red shirt, blowing cigarette smoke and his own steam into the air and sounding off to some innocent, unslept traveller.

It was the thirty-seventh consecutive day of rain in Portland. Lewis and Clark experienced much the same sort of weather when they got there in November 1805. Upstream they saw 'incredible' numbers of dead salmon on the banks and floating in the river. On the edge of the mighty Columbia on the fringes of Portland, 'incredible' piles of trash were being devoured by machines and spewed into containers as fine rubble. It wasn't pretty, but it was roughly in keeping with the savage nature through which we had passed. Freighters lay at anchor in the mist. The first malls appeared, the fast-food franchises came into view.

There's a sense of abundance about Portland, and it's not just the rain. In the midst of rich agriculture and raw nature, the city has all manner of sophisticated trappings: good cafés, pinot noir and boutique beers among them. Californians come for a liberal lifestyle that can be enjoyed at relatively bargain rates, a sort of cut-price Santa Monica with nature much closer at hand. In what other American city can you see from the business district a mountain as perfect as Mount Hood, or from an elevated position on a clear day an active volcano, Mount St Helens? It is a liberal enclave in Bush Republican territory, and the heart of the enclave might be the extra-ordinary Powell's Books – a sort of Uffizi of bookshops, the biggest independent bookshop in the world.

Portland has more planning regulations than most. It doesn't spread along the highways in the manner of most American cities, an aesthetic blessing that also keeps the city in touch with the agricultural and natural hinterland. Portland has farmers' markets, serious public transport – even trams – and extensive programs of urban renewal. By some accounts it's the most 'sustainable' city in the country. Among all America's urban renaissances, Portland's is probably the most mature – which is to say, it's the one that feels least like a corrective or an afterthought.

I drove from Portland to meet the writer Barry Lopez, who lives in an old-growth Douglas fir and cedar forest on the McKenzie River, about an hour out of Eugene. He lives among elk, deer, minks and coyotes and woodpeckers and ospreys, and every now and then, in the surrounding woods, bobcats and mountain lions. He has seen black bears in his backyard. But the real life force is in the river, which runs blue-green, a hundred metres wide and two metres deep across the road from his front door. Every year the Chinook salmon come up the McKenzie to spawn. He's watched them for thirty-six years; the female salmon shaping the gravel 'nests' that will create micro-currents and hold her eggs in place for the 'the blue-grey cloud of milt bursting from . . . male salmon'. Two weeks later the adults die. That's what Lewis and Clark saw in 1805: the bodies of the salmon that provide essential food for bears and otters and eagles and what Lopez calls the 'other carnivorous members of the salmon's community'. The corpses not eaten replenish the soil for the plants that grow on the bank and the water in which the salmon fry will grow.

Year by year Lopez saw fewer Chinook come to spawn. And fewer migratory birds: he heard less of their singing. Winters became warmer; snowfalls rarer. But in the last few years, for no apparent reason, the Chinook have increased. Pleasing as this is, the phenomenon is inconvenient for the theory that human activity and climate change are interfering with the Chinook's migratory habits. But marine biologists say that, for the time being, it is evidence of nothing except an anomaly; one that only close and continuous observation and sound reasoning will resolve.

And there, says Lopez, is the rub. The culture of self-interest and instant gratification is anathema to patient

observation and careful calculation. So is the religious funda-
mentalism which holds such remarkable sway. Now that nature
is so threatened that it threatens us in turn, how can remedies
be contrived by people who believe that God ordains its
exploitation and will destroy it when it suits Him? For Lopez,
there is an even more profound dilemma: modern Americans
are so out of touch with nature, so deficient in the skills and
senses that human beings once needed for survival, they cannot
hope to read the chapter in their own history at present being
written – a chapter in which, he says, the anomaly of the
Chinook outside his front door is but one short sentence.

Lopez writes essays, novels and short stories. His work is
sometimes placed in the tradition of Thoreau, but he says he
feels closer to Herman Melville. Like the young ranger in
Yellowstone, the first of his books I read was *Of Wolves and
Men*. It belongs to the major strand in his writing that deals
with the relationship between humanity and nature, and it
might also be the best book ever written about wolves. The
great novelist from the Southwest, Cormac McCarthy, whose
writing also owes something to Melville but is bleaker than
Lopez's and as close to the Book of Revelation as any modern
writer gets, came to Lopez for wolf knowledge when he
was writing *The Crossing*.

Lopez is an inveterate and seasoned observer of the natural
world and a master of describing what goes on in it. He is a
moralist, a teacher and a traveller; and, though he was born in
New York State, he is also a Westerner, or at least a Western
writer. Western writers, he says, are in general excluded from
the American pantheon; but, like a ripple from the frontier, the
best of them tend to be in advance of orthodox opinion and
awareness.

When he got back to St Louis in 1806, Meriwether Lewis
sank into depression and alcohol. Three years later he died of
gunshot wounds that most histories declare were self-inflicted.

There is something terrible in his decline: in the East I saw memorials to Lewis and Clark which portrayed them as mere boys, so lithe and light on their feet that they might have skipped across the continent. Barry Lopez thinks it is possible that Lewis grew depressed as he realised that the country he and Clark traversed would soon be conquered by European greed. A mission conceived in the name of Jeffersonian enlightenment, and carried out with exemplary courage and the loss of just two Indian lives, would bring only mayhem and depravity.

It's a theory about more than Meriwether Lewis, of course. It's a theory about the United States: that its trajectory is destructive – of life, of creation. Lopez's critics might say he is projecting his own sensibilities onto the depressive explorer: that he is a storyteller seeking poignant expression of his ideas, a radical humanist wanting a distinguished precedent. But like the prophesies in Revelation, this is one of those theories that depend less on revealed truth than on the force of the idea and the manner of its expression.

No-one can travel in the United States, or read about the United States, or watch the films and television that come from there, without noticing that 'creative destruction' requires emphasis on both words. Squalor co-exists with afflu-ence, the crass with the sublime, ruin with success. And no-one can fail to see the irreducible paradox of the liberated or autonomous self and the general supineness.

Lopez is one of those Americans who insist that through enlightened actions we can turn things around and save ourselves. Cormac McCarthy's novels are populated with people for whom these choices don't exist and enlightenment is mortal folly: 'We are our own journey. And therefore we are time as well. We are the same. Fugitive. Inscrutable. Ruthless.' If, unlike McCarthy or the wolf or the Chinook salmon, you cannot live with this assessment, you may well do what Lopez reckons Meriwether Lewis did. Or, more likely, you will do what millions of Americans do now and have always done: you will choose from the hundreds of churches of salvation that the country offers to those who, though believing in the values of the frontier and the unfettered individual, cannot face extinction without the comforts of religion.

What no-one can tell us is how to deal with the imitators of frontiersmen, the putative descendants of the Crocketts and the Boones who inhabit the media. Jefferson believed democracy depended on the salience of 'temperate minds'. What to do, then, when half the country lives in thrall to the professionally intemperate hard men in the radio studios? And when even the president, though a pale shadow of the mythical American, gets some purchase on the country's soul with his swagger? Driving back to Portland, I listened to the political commentator George Will talking to Sean Hannity on the radio. They agreed about pretty well everything: what was good and what was contemptible, what was American and what was fraying the nation's fibre. Probably because George Will is near enough to a conservative legend, Sean deferred when George saw some little thing to criticise about their side.

It was Saturday and the Super Bowl was Sunday, and at the end Sean asked George where he was going to watch it. George said he was going over to Irving Kristol's place and Charles Krauthammer was coming along too. Sean was impressed, and George said he was looking forward to it. 'You're a great American,' said Sean, and George seemed to say something very like this in return at about the same time, and for a second they sounded a bit like the Everly Brothers.

Rain was teeming down in Portland for the thirty-eighth consecutive day. In the hotel I watched an episode of *Deadwood*, set in the 1870s. Sixty years earlier, the St Louis of Meriwether Lewis must have had some of the same viciousness; or, if you prefer, the same creative destruction.

CHAPTER 13

They sure do love theirself, them actors.

James M. Cain, *Double Indemnity*

YOU DROP DOWN THROUGH THE HAZE ABOVE LOS ANGELES – the 'marine layer', scientists call it – and see the cars beginning to fill the streets in the early morning sun. Two decades ago the city had smog alerts a hundred times a year. Thanks mainly to the catalytic converter they have become very rare, but an expert at UCLA says new concentrations of ultrafine particles are killing or debilitating thousands of people. In some places, a piece of the air not much bigger than a pea contains a million or more of these things. You land anyway. Half an hour in a taxi will have you in Santa Monica – or 'the People's Republic of Santa Monica', as Republicans sometimes call it.

The signs in the back of LA cabs say that passengers are entitled to a 'driver that speaks and understands English . . . and is knowledgeable of major destinations'. But you don't get in for the entitlements. If you worried about your entitlements, you would worry that competence in driving and mental stability are not mentioned. You get in because in LA most often there's no other way to get where you want to go.

You might also get in because you could learn something about places which, though startlingly absent from the collective consciousness of America, remain home and alive for tens of millions of Americans.

'You know about Turkish massacre of Armenian people?' the driver asked.

'Yes,' I said.

'You think is true?' he asked.

'Yes,' I said.

'Only Turkish say not true,' he said.

'True,' I said.

'How many Armenian people die? One million, or one million and half?'

'I thought it was about a million,' I said.

'Okay,' he said, 'about a million.'

He told me there were 400,000 Armenians living in Glendale, which is twice as many as there are citizens in that suburb. Lost, he phoned one of them and asked for directions, but he sent us the wrong way.

———

It is early morning and, under the palm trees on Ocean Avenue, past the fun park on the pier where the old Route 66 ended and began, the homeless rise with the sun and pick up their beds. They put their belongings in plastic bags and drag them down the streets or push them in supermarket trolleys. Wrapped in garbage bags, on breezy days, before you see them emerging from the side streets you hear the susurrations in the plastic: grinding along the pavements with their heads bowed, rustling and whistling like sailing ships.

If it happens to be a Wednesday or the weekend, the streets between the ocean and the mall will be filling with the biodynamic abundance of the farmers' market. There is agribusiness with its phenomenal volumes of perfect – and perfectly tasteless – produce: and there are the farmers' markets, where chemical fertilisers, pesticides, preservatives, genetic modifications and cheap Mexican labour are fiends that have been banished from their gardens. If agribusiness satisfies the American desire to be big, to overcome all rivals, to achieve 'full-spectrum dominance', the farmers' markets and the burgeoning organic food movement go to the desire to be good. They might even go to the Puritan founders. People who eat the products of agribusiness *get* big: people who eat organic treat their bodies as the little temples that nature intended and get a feeling of virtue.

You can spend a lot of time thinking about your body in America. In a country where it is so easy to grow fat, it is also easy to be obsessive about staying relatively thin. Food is one of the great national divides, and Santa Monica falls emphatically on the thin side. There's less corn syrup in Santa Monica. The horrors of the American fast-food diet – fat, fructose and free radicals – have not been vanquished, but they don't have it all their own way. At an organic supermarket a few streets back from the beach, young people glowing with health patrol the shelves to help customers who can't decide which antioxidant is right for them. The sign says: LIFE ISN'T ABOUT FINDING YOURSELF. IT'S ABOUT CREATING YOURSELF. Perhaps Americans only *seem* to create themselves more than the people of other countries, but I don't think so. To me, they are the only people who are visibly evolving; always, like organisms watched through a microscope.

Should it be your misfortune to have evolved into a moderately shy person, now you can 're-create' yourself as a confident one. The first step is to not think of it as shyness – much less as an acceptable, or even attractive, human quality – but as 'social anxiety disorder'. Intensive political lobbying, the infiltration of health organisations and the expenditure of billions of dollars have enabled drug companies to persuade tens of millions of Americans that this is the case, and that the next step is to cure the disorder with a 'selective serotonin reuptake inhibitor' such as Zoloft.

In the 1980s, against the grain of Ronald Reagan's America, the City of Santa Monica came under the control of a coalition of liberals, Greens, Democrats and left-leaning Christians with a comprehensive plan for the city. Ceilings were put on development and controls on rent; and footpaths, bike paths and other amenities were built on the foreshore. *The Wall Street Journal* declared the whole enterprise a calamity and President Reagan kind of agreed. That's when someone called it the People's Republic. But the People's Republic became an international model of urban development, and far from fulfilling *The Wall Street Journal*'s prediction that the liberals would kill the place, it boomed. Property values streaked upward, the middle classes flocked and the good life blossomed in the soft southern Californian air.

They did not establish anything even vaguely socialist, of course. Free enterprise drives the place, albeit with some supervision. Santa Monica's saviours were middle-class American liberals who, in rescuing the city from the familiar beasts of development – the dehumanising malls, the ugly and unaffordable high-rise – were obeying communitarian instincts of long and honourable provenance. Think of the town squares of New England, think of Central Park. For that matter, think of the New Deal or the Great Society; but be careful who you tell, because there have always been Americans who believed the New Deal was a tumour on the vital organs of American freedom, and they are as zealous now as they were in Roosevelt's day.

Douglas built its DC-3s in Santa Monica during the war and a lot of the workers' houses are still there, most of them renovated and worth about a million each. In the same back-reaches of the city are the headquarters of HBO, the media company that brought you *The Sopranos*, *Six Feet Under*, *Sex and the City* and *Deadwood*. *The Simpsons* was invented in a hotel not far away. The place lays claim to an unusually large role in the invention of modern consciousness.

The commercial hub of Santa Monica is a model of modern enterprise. It is lined with all the usual brands and stores: all of them living by their business plans, their strategic goals aligned with their values and their mission statements; all of them evolved to the highest stage of modern management. It's strange that business so often resists the idea of planning, because nothing in the history of the world has been as thoroughly planned as modern businesses. In Santa Monica's main shopping strip, where half a dozen of them compete all day, it seems possible that even the street performers have business plans. It is orderly competition, but also intense – and intensely good, most of the time: so good that sometimes there will be more people around a pair of virtuoso guitarists than there are in any of the shops, and they will be selling as many of their CDs as the Apple store is selling iPods.

On the fringes of all this activity there are the beggars, whose own mission statements are scrawled on cardboard signs: 'Please help me – I have arthritis in both hands and elbows'; 'I am homeless'; 'I am trying to save'; 'I am trying to go back to school'. The social anomalies remain, but they are well-managed anomalies. They don't have speaking roles or any influence on the plot, but the indigent seem to have been recognised and given a part in the show.

Will Rogers lived in Santa Monica, and one can't help thinking the virtuosi of Santa Monica's mall are in some line of succession to him. The 'poet lariat', he called himself. His 1922 silent film *The Ropin' Fool* captured the man's rustic, laconic grace and used slow motion photography to display his astonishing ability to rope anything that moved or caught his attention: from galloping horses to hats, dogs, rats and cats.

He had learned his skills from a freed slave and cowboy on the family ranch, and the opening slide on *The Ropin' Fool* says the picture 'is a demonstration of what years of practice and application to one thing will accomplish'. This is a profoundly American homily, a piece of essential frontier wisdom, and one that has proved more durable than the one about a man being able to rise from a humble log cabin to the White House.

In Williamsburg, a restored mid-nineteenth-century lunatic asylum tells the story of Dr John Galt, who attended to his patients with more application than was the custom at the time. He administered laudanum in the usual quantities, but he also demanded that his staff observe their patients' behaviour and record every detail. In paying conscientious attention to small things, Dr Galt believed he was employing the great principle on which progress and success depend. To travel in the United States is to see a built landscape of prodigious scope, a multitude of fantastic monuments to human ambition, energy and invention. To look at Manhattan or Houston, to drive across Baltimore, to cross the High Sierra in a train with an iPod in your ear – the whole astonishing thing is built on the same principles of independent thought and intense application and attention to small things that guided Will Rogers and Dr Galt. The universal obsession with the 'puny' self creates immensity.

To guarantee the diversity of Santa Monica's population and to protect the elderly and others on fixed incomes, those progressives of the late 1970s came forth with the near-as-dammit un-American idea of rent controls – and the people voted for it. And despite modifications imposed by an outraged state government and several challenges in the California Supreme Court, they have survived, as has the only Rent Control Board in the United States.

Up on Wilshire and Eleventh, a company called Westside Rentals offers a free-enterprise version. It's a modest-looking place that could easily be mistaken for an internet café. But it is a highly successful business and a model of modern capitalism – even *enlightened* capitalism. At Westside they join prospective tenants to prospective landlords. In this sense, it's a real estate agency, but using the internet pushes the volume of its business into another dimension. In the nine years since its opening it signed up 178,000 rental agreements. The volume keeps the rents down and makes Mark Verge, the owner of Westside Rentals, very rich.

Everyone wanting to rent a property through Westside Rentals must pay a sixty-dollar joining fee, which the managers say saves the cost of the credit checks that landlords demand. Everyone who deals with Westside Rentals pays with a credit card. It's the most convenient filter: people without credit cards fall through to another level in the rental market: a level they are unlikely to find in Santa Monica or the adjacent suburbs.

Westside Rentals employs large numbers of students to run its operations. It pays them nine or ten dollars an hour to sit in front of computers with headsets on for eight hours a day. They are allowed a half-hour for lunch and are given a Red Bull energy drink after five hours. Bonuses are paid quarterly. The operators sit side by side in rows. An overseer sits to one side with a computer, on which he can monitor every call the employees make, and on his phone he can listen in. The computer constantly records each employee's activity, and at any time the overseer can call up this information, numerically or in a pie chart. Every word and reflex is observed and measured; every employee can at any moment be called to account for herself. And everything the operator can see, hear and recover, the owner can as well, without leaving home.

Westside Rentals has become something very close to a monopoly. According to one blog, you don't get an apartment in Santa Monica without them; and you don't get one in a lot of other places in Los Angeles. There's a good deal of loathing for Westside Rentals on the net. 'Douchebags,' one writer calls them. 'The business practices of Westside Rentals and its owner Mark Verge are worse then Enron's,' another one says. It could be that, as the critics say (and they include a Los Angeles business survey that damns them with a 'F' rating), it's the service, or the fee they charge, or the use they make of personal information. Or it could be that, in the modern management of Westside Rentals' operations, their employees feel something akin to the experience of earlier generations who worked in enterprises run on the principles of Frederick Winslow Taylor, Henry Ford and Joseph Stalin. 'Chuck' wrote on a website in August 2006 that 'half of the postings … . about Westside Rentals are posted by Westside Rentals employees'.

But this is California, and to remark that the company's cutting-edge micro-management of staff is really just new-fangled Taylorism is to sound a bit like an old-fashioned Fabian. Business generates ideas for more business, and more business means more jobs – and, yes, more ideas. Business also generates ideas that have less to do with business than with social improvement. The chief whiz at Westside was a young Democrat who figured that if he told the oil companies he wanted to buy five million gallons of gas for all the renters and landlords on the company's database, they might agree to cut the price: especially if he copied the correspondence to *The Wall Street Journal*, the governor of California and his old teachers at MIT Business School. If they didn't, he could expose them for price-fixing.

He had other big ideas. In particular, he wanted to use sport to change America – to 'change the discourse', he called it. He wanted governments to spend much less money on sports stadiums that are rarely used, and much more on public pools and gymnasiums, which are closed for half the year for lack of funds. He wanted schoolkids to have their teeth profes-sionally cleaned three times a year. They all seemed like good ideas to me. He believed the United States was desperate for an enlightened, charismatic leader – another JFK.

—

At the old Shangri La Hotel – where the breezes blow straight off the Pacific and into the rooms, and where Arkansas Governor Bill Clinton liked to spend his evenings and afternoons when he came to visit friends (and meet Hollywood stars) in the People's Republic – a man declared on television that when John Wayne died his body contained forty-four pounds of faecal matter. 'That's what doctors found!' he said. 'Look, we consume a hundred times the toxins our grandparents did.' His dual-action colon cleanser restored the 'natural undulating action of the colon' and removed these toxins.

On another channel, a man who manufactured seaweed capsules said that the Food and Drug Administration was trying to turn cancer into a 'chronic manageable disease'. The FDA was 'keeping the manhole on the sewer' of degenerative diseases 'running rampant' in America. Kelp, he said, had sixty times the nutrition of land plants. The Japanese eat kelp; that's why on average they live seven years longer than Americans.

'Our blood plasma,' he said, 'is essentially the same as sea water. The sea lives in us. God made us with the sea in our system.' God gave us the same pH value – if only we would see it.

On another channel, Stephany Schwarz, aged twenty-eight, talked about her life so far. She bought her first house at twenty-three, and what she wants most in life is her own successful business. Born in Wetmore, Colorado, as millions did before her she took herself to California to chase her fortune. Like all good parents, Mom and Dad are urging her on. Her mother is head of sales for her company. Her step-father, a Methodist and conservative Republican twice elected to the Colorado legislature and twice appointed to the state Parole Board, is a self-styled 'fiscal conservative' who will 'never abandon his Republican ideals of self-reliance, lower taxes and individual freedom'. He's backing Stephany as well.

Stephany looks just a bit like Monica Lewinsky. She's a follower of the Wiccan 'neo-pagan earth-centred' religion – it sounds like fun: 'And it hurt not, do as thou wilt,' they say. This is not such a long way from her stepfather's belief that he is closer to God when he is hunting and fishing than he is in a church. As the Wiccan website says: 'Wicca is full of metaphors which can co-exist with your current religious or scientific outlook.'

Stephany's professional name is Jewel De'Nyle. She is one of the big names in American pornography. Howard Stern was talking to her in the television studio. Howard Stern is the biggest barracuda in the millpond of respectable American life. He had Jewel's parents on the line from Wetmore. 'We're backing her all the way,' they said.

There is pretty well nothing that Jewel won't do on screen to repay their devotion. Stern played an audio tape from one of her porn flicks and asked her parents if they could recognise their daughter's voice screaming in real or feigned sexual ecstasy. Her parents listened, smiling: 'Well, that could be her,' they supposed.

In May 2005, when the *Southwest Chief* delivered us into the art-deco majesty of LA's Union Station, Fox News was hammering away at the breaking story of the real Deep Throat. It was emblazoned on all the billboards. For three days earnest men and women debated the questions: Was there only one Deep Throat? Was Deep Throat right or wrong? How important was Deep Throat in American history? Someone should ask how important fellatio is. How important is pornography? *Deep Throat*, as everyone over fifty knows, was the name of an early porn flick.

Today the US pornography industry is worth $12 billion: of this, $2.5 billion operates on the internet, where forty million American adults regularly visit porn websites, and where porn websites make up twelve per cent of *all* websites. In California, the porn industry employs 12,000 people and pays $36 million in taxes. The demand is so great that several Fortune 500 companies, like many conservative preachers and politicians, have been unable to resist temptation and now (within the bounds of their commitment to corporate social responsibility) help in modest ways to meet it. The great hotel chains, for instance, just cannot afford to pass up porn: fifty per cent of all their guests watch their pay-as-you-go 'adult' films, which deliver seventy per cent of in-room profits.

You could live in Santa Monica and, like everyone else in the world, know Los Angeles only through TV and the movies that are made just a taxi-ride away. A bus runs all the way downtown, but few residents of Santa Monica have ever taken it. There are plenty of films in the video store if they want to see the real LA. Or they can just watch TV. I went to see *A History of Violence*. I had not fully recovered when I took myself to see *Crash*. When *Crash* was over and I drifted out with the twenty other patrons, it was dark and the last and least able of the street performers were trying to extract a few more dollars from the day. Four white men were singing Jesus songs. A hugely fat man, who had been playing jazz at midday in the mall, was now making hard work of something classical and looked close to death. The place seemed to have turned itself inside out: the raw flesh was exposed. A man in an open-topped SUV shouted at two women in another car: 'Asians! Fuckin' Asians! Wouldn't you fuckin' know it?'

Before leaving elementary school, the average American child has seen 8000 murders on television. More than a quarter of citizens convicted of crimes of violence say they imitated something they saw on TV. In the last decade, 50,000

American children were killed with firearms. A child is murdered every two hours. Eleven times more murders are committed in the United States than in Japan, nine times more than in the United Kingdom. Every day four women die from domestic violence. Each year the number of rapes and attempted rapes is in the order of 132,000, and it is estimated that six times that number are not reported. There are 676 hate groups in the United States. Every state has at least one: Florida has thirty-eight, California thirty-six, Texas thirty-one and Pennsylvania twenty-seven. Of the 676 groups, 403 have internet sites.

The statistics almost defy belief, but not when you scan the local papers for a while. Everywhere, every day, violence is reported. In Jackson, Mississippi, five residents had been murdered in the five days previous to my visit; a local court was holding a hearing into the rape, torture and strangulation of a twelve-year-old girl by her parents. In Salt Lake City, a veteran of the Iraq War gunned down several people in a shopping mall. An obituary in New Orleans reported: 'November 15 was Joyce Frieler Rader's last day on earth. She was murdered and then she went into God's arms.'

So long as the Constitution guarantees the right to bear arms, a fair percentage of people will take that to mean the right to use them. And some of these will take it to mean that a man is not a man without them; and some others that true liberty depends on them; and others still that the rights of revenge and pre-emption are enshrined in the Constitution along with the guns.

Every day on American television an episode of *Law & Order* pits good against evil, order against chaos, the reasoned and objective law against subjective impulse and delusion. Evil is endemic and self-perpetuating in *Law & Order*: the battered child becomes the batterer, the abused the abuser. Just as the West made tough but honest citizens who civilised the frontier, the streets make cops and lawyers with the mettle to hold off the evil, deranged and weak who would otherwise scythe through everything.

But this is not the mythic violence of westerns or *film noir*. It's not the horror that myths transfigure and make bearable. It is common, everyday violence, as recorded in the newspapers from which the show draws all its stories. It is crime with specific causes, which can be identified by reasoned inquiry and dealt with by the law with specific, practised remedies. Though justice is not perfect every time, *Law & Order* unfailingly affirms the principle on which all hope for the republic rests: that the law is sufficiently good and sound and there are enough good, sound people to carry the day for free-enterprise democracy. It's the 'law' in *Law & Order* that requires a leap of faith: you have to believe in the probity of city hall, the integrity of the police force, the proper functioning of the bureaucracy, the disinterested and unstoppable operation of the legal system. In fact, every episode of *Law & Order* demands that we not believe in chronic social failure, corruption and dysfunction in America. And, somehow, that is what we want to do. 'In my opinion, human societies, like individuals, amount to something only in liberty,' Tocqueville wrote 150 years ago, and summed up the drama of American life.

Watching *Law & Order* almost every day for a month, I began to think I knew why so many Americans you meet are very sane, civil and kind. In the midst of every variety of weirdness, ignorance and brutality, it easily goes unnoticed that, in the day to day, America is the most civilised of places: how often you see in Americans and the way they deal with each other the graces you should like to see in yourself and your compatriots. They are more civilised, I thought, for the very reason that barbarism lurks on every corner, if not in every individual, and they must be above it, ready for it. Calm self-possession is all.

Oscar would say it is all relative. He has been driving cabs in LA since the day he came up from Honduras forty-six years ago. He has four grown-up daughters and many grandchildren in various parts of the United States, and all of them are doing well. His wife died a few years back. Now he has another four children under seven living with their mother, his second wife, in Honduras.

'Not bad for sixty-six years old,' he says. 'How old are you? You could do it too.'

He said he'd take me down to Honduras. He sends his family money from what he earns in his decrepit taxi, and every year he catches the bus for the five-day ride and spends a couple of months with them. He says LA is sometimes bad, but Honduras is bad all the time. 'You take a walk in the wrong place in Honduras, and if they want your shorts you better take them off or they'll shoot you. They'll shoot you for your shorts.'

He gave me his card, and the next time I saw him Oscar showed me photos of his new baby and all the other children standing in front of the security fence that surrounds their house and keeps out the gangs.

Seven million people in Los Angeles, more than seventy per cent of the population, are from 'minorities'. A lot of them are taxi drivers. A taxi driver said to me: 'A Jew is always a Jew and a Palestinian is always a Palestinian. As the Jews thrive wherever they go, so do the Palestinians. We are the cousins of the Jews.' He seemed perfectly free of prejudice, but he believed there would never be an end to the war because Israel would never leave the Palestinians' land.

He thought the invasion of Iraq had been a disaster for the United States. He held the US administration in contempt – both for its policies and for what he believed was its stupidity. That he and his fellow Palestinians were under permanent surveillance he neither resented nor feared. His compatriots' long experience made them very hard to infiltrate. He was curiously equable about it. Had the people who followed LA's Palestinians and tapped their phones been able to understand what they were hearing, they might have been less surprised when Hamas won the Palestinian elections, he said.

He had lived in LA for sixteen years, and for seventeen years before that in Kuwait. LA was better than anywhere in the Middle East. He would always be Palestinian, but nowhere in the Middle East could he be as free as he was in LA. In LA, he said, he could 'be himself'.

In the morning a friend left me at a bookshop where Ryan O'Neal was reputed to take his coffee. While browsing near a counter I heard a woman ask the bookseller about the rash on his face. What had caused it? Was he taking anything? Had he seen a dermatologist? The questions, which might have put some people in a very bad mood, seemed to put him in a good one. Yes, he had been to a dermatologist. So what did he say? Did he give him some cream? Did he say what had caused it? No, he didn't, the bookseller said.

'You mean he didn't know? What sort of dermatologist doesn't know what caused it?'

Was he a proper dermatologist? Was the bookseller 'eating something bad'? Then another customer asked if Viggo Mortensen was coming to give a reading on Saturday and they both forgot his rash; a pity, because I wanted to know more.

I first went to Venice Beach nearly thirty years ago. Rollerblades were the new essential item and people went gliding up and down watching the freak show of hulking men working out in cages like the ones that housed gorillas in unreformed zoos. The bodybuilders are still working out, but in an openair gym, and the effect is less startling. On the bat-tennis courts beside the gym, men and women applied themselves with McEnroe-like verve and fanaticism. Their rallies were long and gripping, the more because death seemed likely. No-one laughed. No-one gave an inch. No-one seemed willing to by any sign concede that this was not Wimbledon and not real tennis.

Those Santa Monica socialists have built a path along the beach from Venice. I walked back past people talking truth and eloquence to seagulls. A man who looked as normal as Garrison Keillor went past on a unicycle, which he rode on the inch-wide edge of the concrete kerbing. People were leaving the pier. Beneath the palm trees on the grassy strip between the beach and Ocean Avenue, the homeless were bedding down for the night. Those with homes were gathered by the railings, their jerseys swung over their polo shirts, watching the blood-orange sun sink into the Pacific.

AFTERWORD

I passed Slimgullion, Morgan Mine,
Camp Seco, and the rotting Lode.
  Dark walls of sugar pine – ,
  And where I left the road

I left myself behind;

Philip Levine, *Sierra Kid*

AROUND THANKSGIVING I TOOK A TRAIN SOUTH FROM OKLAHOMA City. I was aiming at El Paso but a death in the family obliged me to get off in Austin and go back to Australia for a fortnight. Oklahoma was in drought and the land and the lawns were dull brown. The creek beds were dry, silted and eroded.

We passed a few little towns with the familiar towers and church spires and the rest looked like it had been simply scattered on the ground. Horse farms seemed to be the main activity, and oil pumps. As always, the blue sky was shredded with vapour trails, and even the half-moon looked like something a plane had left behind.

Stopped in the middle of a refinery as the train filled with oil fumes, the young man beside me slept with his feet in cowboy boots jammed against the wall in front. Dirty jeans, cowboy shirt and his woollen hat pulled hard down on his head. Every now and then he woke and talked to me about his life. His life was something he was working on. Rich and poor, religious and secular, Americans work avidly at their lives. A 'work in progress', the young man called it.

He had been raised, he said, 'in a kinda cone' and never saw how other people lived. But he was learning. He spent a lot of time with homeless people in Fort Worth and Dallas and travelled with them on freight trains to Colorado and other places. 'They're cool,' he said. 'They don't starve. The charities look after them. You can't die of hunger in Texas, but you can die of the cold or someone might kill you for your shoes.' Then he went back to sleep: he faded in and out of consciousness, like someone who might be about to die.

We got going again, and when we were not far from Fort Worth the conductor, in a voice like Slim Pickens, called our attention to a huge structure on the left of the train: 'That there's the new Texas speedway. Next town comin' up's Hazlitt, Texas. Hazlitt, Texas, is next.'

Sure enough it came up, and we stopped on the site of a new housing estate. They were big plain houses with big charcoal-grey roofs and very big yards, fences with white rails as if the owners fancied keeping a few thoroughbreds as pets. Sprinklers were on and the grass was green but there were no trees, shrubs or flowers. Not a sign of a bird or a birdbath. For the hundredth time I wondered why Americans don't grow gardens. Adam was put into a garden 'to dress it and to keep it'. Heaven is often likened to a garden. 'In the place where He was crucified there was a garden.'

We sat there for half an hour and the young man beside me woke up again and told me he was a Christian. Most Sundays he went to one or other of the various non-denominational Christian churches outside the big cities. He was studying other religions, including Mormonism, and he wanted to 'understand' the Catholics as well, he said. He told me that many of the homeless men with whom he spent nights in parks and railway yards and under bridges were middle-aged and middle-class and, until they went bust or their marriages failed, successful in business. It could happen very easily and very suddenly, he said. Others, he maintained, simply chose to leave their conventional lives. They just gave up and walked into the other world.

A mile and a half outside Fort Worth we stopped again. After half an hour or so the lady from the snack bar told us that the driver of the freight train on the track in front had gone home. He had to, she said, because he'd completed his twelve-hour shift. There was a cemetery out the window. 'Right now, what we're doin' is watchin' a cemetery,' a man told his friend on the phone.

Slim Pickens came on the PA and said: 'I'm sorry, folks, but there ain't nothin' we can do about this freight train up ahead. We're at its mercy.' He recommended everyone phone USA RAIL 1800. Soon the carriage filled with the babble of people saying they'd been looking at a cemetery for two hours and wanted a refund.

We rolled into Fort Worth at four pm; the time the Austin train was due to leave. Amtrak was good enough to wait the few minutes it took to clamber from one train to the other and I found myself sitting next to an oversized Texan in a baseball cap who occupied, in addition to his own seat, a quarter of mine. Having heard me tell the conductor I was getting off in Austin, he asked me in a time-warping drawl if that was my home town.

I said: 'No. I live in Melbourne, in Australia.'

'Thought you might live in Drippin' Springs,' he said.

'No,' I said.

'Drippin' Springs,' he said. 'About twenty miles out of Austin. You take that road, whatsit . . .?'

He called over my head to a man in a check baseball cap on the other side of the aisle: 'What's that road takes you out to Drippin' Springs from Austin?'

'Three-ten, I think,' the man said.

'That's it, three-ten. Thought you might live out there.'

'I couldn't swear to it,' said the other man. 'But I think that's it.'

'It is. Three-ten. It's the three-ten takes you out there,' he told me. 'No doubt about it.'

We travelled down past Waco, site of the 1993 military rout of the Branch Davidian religious sect, birthplace of the Dr Pepper soft drink, and stopping-off point for the president on his way to the family ranch. It turned out this man next to me was a driver for the freight company that owns the line, and the other two were his brakeman and his conductor. He was not just any driver: he was the driver who had been called in to move the freight train that blocked our path outside Fort Worth. He'd been in a train behind us. He was a train driver, but in certain essential ways he could have been the president of the United States.

The young man who sought the meaning of his life among the poor and in religion, and the train driver who knew nothing of the world twenty miles either side of the tracks he drove, were both in their different ways expressions of American 'exceptionalism'. Tocqueville, who coined the term, would have found their like in 1831. That is to say, at some level both shared the assumption of Americans, from the Pilgrim Fathers to George W. Bush, that America is different from all other countries because America is a country – the *only* country – blessed by God.

The idea is essential to the doctrine behind the War on Terror, to the strength of religion, the weakness of the social security system, the pervasiveness of the flag and other symbols of the nation; to its violence, its self-deceits and hypocrisy, its inability to confront its own contradictions, its childish fears and paranoia, and its mind-numbing provincialism. It is also, very likely, the reason for its power, its creativity, its capacity for self-renewal, its numberless heroic examples and the desire of people everywhere to live in the United States.

In Savannah one evening, I was walking behind a man who seemed to me about fifty, moderately well dressed, clean and straight. But even with his back to me I could tell he was out of his element somehow, and when he stopped and looked across the street I could see the panic on his face. He looked around wildly. It happened in the space of just a few moments, and I was past him when I thought he might be someone who just that day had fallen through the cracks and into vagabondage. Night was falling and reality with it. He didn't look like him, but I thought of Edward G. Robinson – Hollywood has left us with a simulacrum for every occasion. There were a dozen possibilities. He'd lost his job? His wife had left with the children? His bank had foreclosed? Perhaps the hurricanes or capital's 'perennial gale of creative destruction' had blown him onto the street?

Just as it is easy in America to suddenly find yourself in an alien, hostile part of town, you see signs of how quickly the ground can give way beneath your feet. This man looked as if he had just walked into hell. Whatever else he'd lost – his wife and children, his money, his mind – what had most obviously gone was his dignity. He was as if stripped bare to the world.

In nature a thorn in your paw or a broken limb can mean death because you can no longer catch your prey or escape your predators. It means you're not competitive. That, it seemed to me, was why the man was panicking: he sensed his days were numbered. Life is uncertain and disaster is never far away – and sudden when it strikes. Who knows if it is because Americans believe this is the natural – or God-given – way of the world that their legislators seem so reluctant to ameliorate it: or if their prolonged inaction is why, to them, this world seems natural? 'Who provideth for the raven his food when his young ones cry unto God?' So often in the United States the answer is much as it was when God posed it to Job: God provides, if it pleases Him to do so.

It might be that the more 'natural' a society is, the more the need for religion; and the more religious, the more potent the symbols and rituals of the tribe. I may be churned in the economic mill, fall through the cracks, never get a chance, be of no useful account, but I cannot be cast out. Whatever befalls me will be according to the Lord's plan. I have that assurance, if nothing else. And I have the flag. The flag is mine as much as anyone else's. And freedom is mine. I am as free as every other American, and like every other American, I answer only to God.

Freedom is such an old chestnut of American rhetoric that it does not impress outsiders as perhaps it should. The more the president speaks of it, the less meaning it registers. When he says 'Our enemies hate us for our freedoms' we cringe, even though we know that, down the years, Americans have died in tens of thousands for the cause. In any case, we think, it's less for the freedoms that they hate you, and more for the influence you exercise. 'Our enemies hate us for our power, our hegemony' would be a truer statement, and little would be lost by stating it in these terms.

And yet, when one travels in America, the chestnut sheds at least some of its shell. You come to see that, to Americans, freedom means something that we incurable collectivists do not quite understand; and that they know freedom in ways that we do not. Freedom is the country's sacred state. Freedom is what must be protected. All over, they will tell you what is wrong with America, but freedom is the one thing they think right. And whatever the insults to my social democratic senses, that is what I find irresistible about the place – the almost guilty, adolescent feeling that in this place a person can do what he wants. He can grow absurdly rich; he can hunt a mountain lion; he can harbour the most fantastic ideas; he can shoot someone. He can commune with God or nature, buy anything he wants, pay anyone for any service and at any fee. He can be a social outcast or even a prisoner and yet, being American, believe that he is free.

If I am American, I am as free as a person can be. If I am free, I can do – or dream of doing – all the things that it is in my nature to do or to dream; no other place on earth need interest me. So long as I am guaranteed this freedom, I will forgive the things my country does that are not in my nature or my dreams. I will be 'spared all the care of thinking about them'. That is, of course, unless my country or some other place threatens freedom.

Sometimes in America, when you are watching television, or a scene on the street, or someone 'creating herself' in a café or train, you wonder if in their minds many Americans imagine they live just the wrong side of a kind of theatrical scrim, a thin floating membrane whose opening is almost impossible to find. *Almost* impossible: but it exists, and if you keep your hope alive and apply yourself hard enough, who can say if one day you won't walk through it and find yourself in the magical kingdom of celebrity – and soon after you will tell a television host how, like revealed religion, it was all meant to be.

It is just as the faithful think: you do not know when the moment will come and you'll wake on the other side. You do not know what you will see. The face of Jesus, or Dave Letterman? You do not know, and because you do not know you figure there must be a plan.

It may seem crass, juvenile and provincial. It has seemed that way to visitors since Tocqueville. But in the midst of this unworldliness, one also sees startling, unselfconscious acts of grace and generosity that might be possible only when something childlike and raw remains in the spirit of the place. Depending on the angle and the light, much that seems unworldly or unformed in America will, a moment later, manifest something older and better in our natures.

On a train between Winslow, Arizona, and Los Angeles, I sat beside a sublime black woman and her two nephews. They had been sitting up all night and were very tired. She asked the ten-year-old to thank God before he ate. When he mumbled, she said in a gentle voice: 'Please say it so that we can hear the words.' And the boy did.

ACKNOWLEDGEMENTS

For many things, thanks to Susie Carleton and Helen Smith, Sadie Chrestman, Meredith Curnow and Alice Truax; for expert editing at Random House, Julian Welch; and for encouraging this project in the first place, Jane Palfreyman.

Profound thanks also to the many people in the United States who were so generous with their time and advice. For hospitality as well as guidance, I thank Robert Henry, Francis and John O'Brien, Sue Toigo and especially Derek Shearer.

—

Permission to quote material from the following sources is gratefully acknowledged:

E. E. Cummings (edited by George J. Firmage), *Complete Poems 1904–1962*. New York: W. W. Norton & Company. Copyright © 1991 by the Trustees for the E. E. Cummings Trust and George James Firmage

Simone de Beauvoir (trans. Carol Cosman), *America Day By Day*. Berkeley: University of California Press, 1999

Rick Moody, *The Diviners*. New York: Little, Brown and Company, 2005

John Steinbeck, *Travels with Charley: In Search of America*. New York: Penguin, 1997. Copyright © John Steinbeck 1962

Richard Wright, *Black Boy*. New York: HarperCollins, 2005. Copyright © 1937, 1942, 1944, 1945 by Richard Wright; renewed © 1973 by Ellen Wright

———

Acknowledgement is also made of the following sources:

Henry Adams, *Democracy: An American Novel*. New York: Modern Library, 2003

James M. Cain, *Double Indemnity*. London: Pan, 1983

Jimmy Carter, *Our Endangered Values: America's Moral Crisis*. New York: Simon & Schuster, 2005

Bill Clinton, *My Life*. London: Hutchinson, 2004

Angie Debo, *A History of the Indians of the United States*. University of Oklahoma Press, 1983

Angie Debo, *Oklahoma, Footloose and Fancy Free*. University of Oklahoma Press, 1987

Andrew Delbanco, *The Real American Dream: A Meditation on Hope*. Cambridge, Massachusetts: Harvard University Press, 1999

Paul Laurence Dunbar, 'We Wear the Mask', in *The Norton Anthology of African American Literature*. New York: W. W. Norton & Company, 2004

Barbara Ehrenreich, *Nickel and Dimed: On (Not) Getting By In America*. New York: Henry Holt & Co., 2001

William Faulkner, *Go Down, Moses*. New York: Random House, 1942.

Richard Ford, 'Elegy for my city'. *The Observer*, 4 September 2005

Eric Hobsbawm, 'Only in America'. *The Chronicle Review*, vol. 49, no. 43, 4 July 2003

Lewis Lapham, *Waiting for the Barbarians*. London: Verso Books, 1997

François, Duc de La Rochefoucauld (trans. S. D. Warner and S. Douard), *Maxims*. South Bend: St Augustine's Press, 2001

David Lavender, *The Penguin Book of the American West*. Harmondsworth: Penguin, 1969

Philip Levine, 'Sierra Kid', in *On the Edge*. Iowa City: Stone Wall Press, 1963

Barry Lopez, *Of Wolves and Men*. New York: Scribner, 1978

Barry Lopez, 'Waiting for Salmon'. *Granta*, Summer 2005

Cormac McCarthy, *Blood Meridian: Or, the Evening Redness in the West*. New York: Random House, 1985

Frank McLynn, *Wagons West: The Epic Story of America's Overland Trails*. London: Jonathan Cape, 2002

N. Scott Momaday, *The Man Made of Words*. New York: St Martin's Press, 1997

William Least Heat Moon, *Blue Highways, A Journey into America*. London: Secker & Warburg, 1983

Joyce Carol Oates, *Them*. New York: Vanguard Press, 1969.

Anne Rice, 'Do you know what it means to lose New Orleans?'. *The New York Times*, 4 September 2005

Marilynne Robinson, *Gilead*. London: Virago, 2005

Richard Rodriguez, *Brown: The Last Discovery of America*. New York: Penguin, 2003

Theodore Roosevelt, *An American Mind: A Selection from his Writings*. New York: Penguin, 1995

William Tecumseh Sherman, *Memoirs*. New York: Penguin, 2000

David K. Shipler, *The Working Poor: Invisible in America*. New York: Vintage, 2004

Wallace Stegner, 'The Wilderness Letter', in *The Sound of Mountain Water: The Changing American West*. New York: Penguin, 1997

Jim Thompson, *Roughneck*. New York: Mysterious Press, 1989

Alexis de Tocqueville, *Democracy in America*. New York: Penguin, 1984; London: Penguin, 2003

Alexander Trocchi, *Cain's Book*. New York: Grove Press, 1992

Mark Twain, *A Connecticut Yankee in King Arthur's Court*. New York: Bantam, 1981

Mark Twain, *Life on the Mississippi*. New York: Penguin, 1986

Gore Vidal, *Collected Essays*. London: Heinemann, 1974

Booker T. Washington, *Up From Slavery: An Autobiography*. New York: Penguin, 1986

Thomas Wolfe, *Look Homeward Angel: A Story of the Buried Life*. New York: Scribner, 2006